Praise for *Fatal Mountaineer*

"A magnificent story . . . a drama worthy of Sophocles . . . Roper is interested in the big questions—fate, the ethics of risktaking, the flaws in character that lead inexorably to tragedy—it is strong medicine, and it makes for a strong book."
—Anthony Brandt, *National Geographic Adventure*

"A story that has all the riveting qualities of a novel and the added punch of truth . . . outdoor literature at its best. . . . Like the great flawed heroes of classic literature, Unsoeld's story ranges from awe-inspiring to tragic, producing strong contradictory feelings in the reader. It's a rich tapestry, a book for both the general reader and the climbing fanatic."
—Floyd Skloot, *San Francisco Chronicle*

"Engaging . . . a provocative look at the legendary climber who himself died in an avalanche in 1979."
—*Denver Post*

"[*Fatal Mountaineer*] is a cautionary tale of how pursuit of a mountain at any cost and in any weather can have deadly consequences. Unsoeld's philosophy—that life begins at ten thousand feet and above—must be challenged."
—Lynn Arave, *Deseret News*

"Riveting . . . you care intensely about what happens to the characters as they struggle for the summit of Nanda Devi. . . . Roper paints a complicated picture of Unsoeld, warts and all. The beloved teacher's passion for mountaineering and the outdoors inspired many, but his thirst for high-altitude risk cost him."
—Prentiss Findlay, *Charleston Post & Courier*

"Gripping . . . a provocative look at a still-legendary climber."
—*Publishers Weekly*

"Roper tells a story packed with adventure, suffering, scandal, heroism, and controversy . . . fascinating."
—*Kirkus Reviews*

"I longed . . . for the intellectual rigor of Robert Roper's marvelous *Fatal Mountaineer,* which I was reading concurrently with [another book under review] . . . I had to give myself ten-minute treat breaks [of it]."
—Carolyn See, *Washington Post*

"Like Anthony Bourdain's *Kitchen Confidential,* Robert Roper's *Fatal Mountaineer* is like a juicy absorbing magazine article that just keeps going and you want to stay with it for hundreds of pages . . . fascinating."
—*Our Town*

ALSO BY ROBERT ROPER

Cuervo Tales
The Trespassers
In Caverns of Blue Ice
Mexico Days
On Spider Creek
Royo County
Big Bets Gone Bad (coauthor with Phillipe Jorion)

FATAL MOUNTAINEER

FATAL MOUNTAINEER

THE HIGH-ALTITUDE LIFE AND DEATH OF WILLI
UNSOELD, AMERICAN HIMALAYAN LEGEND

ROBERT ROPER

ST. MARTIN'S GRIFFIN ✖ NEW YORK

For Mary Ryan,
mountaineer

www.stmartins.com

Photograph of Nanda Devi, Northwest Face,
on the frontispiece and p. xiii, by John Evans

Library of Congress Cataloging-in-Publication Data

Roper, Robert.
    Fatal Mountaineer : the high-altitude life and death of Willi Unsoeld,
American Himalayan legend / Robert Roper.—1st ed.
        p. cm.
    ISBN 0-312-26153-5 (hc)
    ISBN 0-312-30266-5 (pbk)
    1. Unsoeld, William Francis, 1926–1979. 2. Unsoeld, William Francis,
1926—Friends and associates. 3. Mountaineers—United States—
Biography. 4. Mountaineering—India—Nanda Devi. 5. Nanda Devi
(India)—Description and travel. I. Title.

GV199.92.U57 R67 2002
796.52'2'092—dc21
[B]   2001048865

First St. Martin's Griffin Edition: March 2003

10 9 8 7 6 5 4 3 2 1

On March 4, 1979, a man descending Washington's Mount Rainier was swept away in an avalanche. A young woman, coming behind him on a rope, also was carried down a steep slope beneath a pass called Cadaver Gap.

It was snowing hard. Visibility was low, and strong winds scoured the incline. In the last twenty-four hours three feet of new snow had accumulated on the mountain's southern side. The barometer reading was quite low. The weather did not look like improving.

In an avalanche, snow, no matter how powdery, turns into a substance that resembles wet cement. And as soon as movement ceases, it sets up hard. Thus the standard advice on how to behave in an avalanche—to swim with it, make a breathing space around your head—often comes to nothing. Everything happens with appalling force and someone buried just under the surface may be fatally entombed.

As it happened, the man descending first on the rope that day, a fifty-two-year-old college professor named Willi Unsoeld, was buried not too far under, but far enough so that his arms and legs were immobilized. His throat and nostrils filled with snow, and the pack on his back pinned him down. The slide that carried him and Janie Diepenbrock, the young woman, away did not crush their bones, but neither did it let them move. It simply held them and then it was all over.

Unsoeld was leading twenty-one people off the mountain, students of his at Evergreen, a state college in Washington. They had experienced Mount Rainier in some of its more elemental moods, huddling in snow caves for two nights and waiting out storms in nylon tents, which burst their seams from accumulated snow. After seven days it could be said that the group had shown a lot of spunk just getting up as high as it had, with some members climbing within fifteen hundred feet of the 14,411-foot summit. Most of them had had a good time. They were enrolled in an outdoor-education program at Evergreen, thus were self-selected for grit and adventure-hunger.

To climb Rainier in winter is always the real deal, but Willi Unsoeld was famous as a purveyor of the genuine article in the outdoors. "Throw in no line, catch no fish" was his philosophy, and his own life was a testament to the transfiguring influence of mortal risk. Fifteen years before, he had been America's strongest Himalayan climber. He would always be remembered for the 1963 first ascent of Everest's West Ridge, with Tom Hornbein, one of the most audacious high-altitude climbs in history. Usually the strongest, most forward-thinking member of any group going for a great summit, Unsoeld was also a plain wonderful guy, terrific company in a tent during a five-day blow. He was that modern rarity, a philosophy professor who had a philosophy. He was thoughtful and intuitive about other people. Among mountaineers he was legendary, and within his enormous circle of acquaintance deeply beloved.

At age fifty-two, with both hips recently replaced by orthopedic surgery, most of his toes missing due to frostbite suffered on that Everest climb, he was hardly a world-class specimen anymore. Still, you could do worse than to find yourself in a blizzard with Willi Unsoeld. He had climbed Rainier some two hundred times. After years as a professional guide there and in the Tetons, his mountain sense was highly developed, to say the least. At Cadaver Gap Unsoeld made a typically ballsy, yet calculated, move: with members of his party exhausted and borderline hypothermic, he chose the route of descent that, while marginally more dangerous, promised to bring them to safety quickest. (They were within a few hundred yards of a mountain hut.) He led off in the howling stinging whiteness, with Diepenbrock and two others behind him on a rope; but a snow slab, three feet thick and hundreds of yards square, sheared off under them and rudely decided the outcome of the day.

A death in the mountains by clean stroke may seem attractive, at a distance. Aside from the sad detail of a second fatality, Unsoeld's death came as if scripted by the mountain gods for a favored son of the heights. Indeed, Willi, who had a showman's instinct for entrances and exits, could not have asked for better. He was being spared further physical decay, and he might now ascend to climbers' Valhalla with a smile on his lips. The mythic resonances of the Northwest's greatest mountaineer dying on Mount Rainier were profound. The lines from Robert Louis Stevenson's poem "Requiem," which the author of *Dr. Jekyll and Mr. Hyde* arranged to be inscribed on his own tomb, on a mountaintop in Samoa, seemed appropriate:

> *Here he lies where he longed to be;*
> *Home is the sailor, home from sea,*
> *And the hunter home from the hill.*

Yet it was a tragic life. It was a big, noisy American life, full of extraordinary accomplishment and the bustle of heroic effort, touching thousands of others, but it was tragic at its core, tragic in ways deeply upsetting to those who knew him. The "funeral orgies," to borrow Mark Twain's phrase, that were celebrated in Unsoeld's honor in the days following the accident, before his body had even been brought down from Rainier, were tearstained but chipper, with lots of talk of Willi's great spirit now free to roam the peaks forever. In Olympia, the state capital, on the woodsy Evergreen campus, Unsoeld's widow, Jolene, and their three grown children staged a bumptious event under sunny skies, with speakers telling heartening tales out of the Willi-Bible, stories of his genesis (skinny Northwest kid discovers the mountains, becomes awesome hero), exodus (out of the Oregon flatlands, into the mystic snowy realm), leviticus (churchy Episcopalian becomes priest of the peaks), numbers (nine missing toes, two bionic hips), and deuteronomy (Moses dying in sight of the holy land). Because Willi had been so positive, so much a genuine encourager, there was a natural tendency to testify in a style like his own, with jokes and profane anecdotes, and with an attempted embrace of the mystic "meaning" of it all. But still—like a mocking, black-clad mourner at a garden party—a feeling of tragedy intruded. Not the tragedy of the end itself, the final avalanche moment, but something in the life as a whole. The more everyone sang a cheerful tune, the more a weird dirge sounded in the heart.

One of Willi's fellow teachers, a rangy outdoorswoman named Lynn Hammond, was rare among the mourners in saying something even a bit dark. She recalled that the weekend before the Rainier trip, she had accompanied Willi and several students up onto the lower slopes of the mountain, for practice on glaciers. Willi, despite his new hips, had been in a lot of pain, she said: "Some of the kids, without his knowing, lightened his pack, and then he could keep up better." In the tent that night, Willi confided to Hammond that when he couldn't come up into the mountains anymore, life wouldn't be worth living.

The mere suggestion that Willi had been at the end of his tether—that this muscular philosopher of the peaks, one of the founders of outdoor education in the United States, might have welcomed death—had a heretical sound. Hammond went on to say that the accident that day, coming in that favorite place and with such savage finality, might have been a blessing. This notion deeply offended Unsoeld's widow, who knew how hopeful Willi had remained, how fiercely he had fought through his recent hip surgeries. In a commemorative broadsheet released by Mrs. Unsoeld at the time, she pointed out that Willi had put off surgery for almost a year "while seeking more information on a new technique for resurfacing the hip ball. He opted for the newer operation because it lost less of the original bone structure . . . and because resurfacing could probably be repeated in later years if the first prosthesis were to wear out. Willi intended to wear it out!"

Willi's life and death—and the deaths of others who, over the years, had followed him into the mountains—raise blunt questions. What exactly *are* mountaineers after as they enter that realm of magnified risk? And what responsibilities, if any, does a man or woman of great charisma owe the rest of us? The quality that most inspires us—the boldness, the life lived in defiance of limits and fear—wins hearts while sometimes implicating the hero in the worst of human losses. Among the greatest climbers of the twentieth century, Unsoeld stands forth as someone who lived life much as he wanted, only to be undone by a series of catastrophes, fateful reversals out of some dark drama. The philosopher confounded by his own philosophy: this is not how exemplary lives are supposed to end, in woe so fierce that it cannot be borne.

At that memorial celebration, though—on that sunny spring day, with his tearstained friends raising a ruckus on his account—Willi would not have felt the doom. His spirit, if we can imagine it floating somewhere above, some shred of ectoplasm in the ether, would have sighed, winked, thumbed its nose, and offered a hug all at once. Like Walt Whitman, he contained multitudes, and his life had taught him something about pushing on regardless. Hip balls, indeed: his only regret, looking down from on high, was not to be there himself, in front of this rollicking crowd, *his* kind of crowd! Charming it, seducing it; *playing* it like a damned grand piano!

Summit
25,645'

Camp IV
24,000'

Camp III
22,800'

Camp II
19,900'

Camp I
19,100'

Advanced
Base Camp
17,100'

NORTHWEST FACE ROUTE, NANDA DEVI

....

July 14, 1976: Climbers and porters mill about outside a drenched village, Lata, in the Garhwal Himalaya of India. Only two and a half years before the accident on Rainier, everything is different for Willi.

For one thing, his hips haven't deteriorated completely. He gets along okay on his stumpy, toeless feet, in his funny foreshortened boots. A man of average dimensions—five feet ten inches, never more than 170 pounds—he has always harbored enormous power in his ordinary-looking limbs. And here he is at forty-nine, setting out without much preparation to climb Nanda Devi, at 25,645 feet the tallest peak in India. Not for Willi the punishing gym-rat regimes, the special diets and two hundred pull-ups in an hour of the hardbody climbers just then emerging on the scene; instead you shape up by going on a couple of hikes, maybe playing some handball during lunch hour, and you rely on the trek to the base of the peak to get the lard out of your ass.

On this unpromising, drizzly day, nine American and two Indian climbers are at last getting going, having traveled by truck to the end of the road. Beyond Lata is nothing but goat paths, steep forest tracks, rock ridges; the eleven, whom we might as well call sahibs, after the Indian fashion, are accompanied by eighty porters from the nearby villages, each with an ungainly sixty-pound bundle tied to his back.

There isn't a special moment, an on-your-mark, get-set, GO signaling the start of a mountain adventure; instead there's turmoil, last-minute uncertainty, out of which this or that portion of the group can at last be seen heading up the trail. Adding to the general harum-scarumness is the presence of 120 goats, each wearing a set of wool saddlebags containing food for the porters. Driven this way and that by the *bhakriwallahs*—the native goatherds—the animals move with sudden flurries of hooves, looking like a school of frightened fish.

Willi is the coleader of this impressive disorderly undertaking. He is surrounded by some of the people he loves best in the world. The offhandedness of the moment is much to his taste, too: in his beloved Himalaya, which he has been visiting most of his life, questionable caravans have been setting out for thousands of years in just this style, in rain and mud, to the bleating of goats, with the percussive sound of porters, many of whom look tubercular, hawking on the greasy stones.

Willi's coleader, H. Adams Carter, is editor of the *American Alpine Journal,* house organ of the distinguished American Alpine Club. Carter is as close as an American can get to incarnating the Victorian ideal of climbing's golden age, the era of the great British expeditions, Mallory and all that. There is a sweetness, a forthright decency, about Carter, a sort of *Goodbye, Mr. Chips* quality—which is exactly right, given that he *is* Mr. Chips, a legendary French and Spanish teacher at Milton Academy in Massachusetts. Carter has been a mentor and an admirer of Willi's for years. Carter and his wife, Ann, who at this moment is nursing a sore back in

Delhi, two hundred miles to the southwest, are close to Unsoeld's wife and four children.

One of those children—Willi's vital, splendidly blond, glowingly warm twenty-two year-old daughter, Devi—is another of the sahibs who at last have started moving up the trail. Her full name is Nanda Devi Unsoeld, and indeed, she's setting out today to climb *her* mountain, the mountain she's named for, after years of planning this trip and a lifetime of dreaming about it.

How an American girl comes to be named after an Indian mountain, which itself bears the name of the most awesome, most ecstatically worshiped goddess in the Hindu pantheon, is a story in itself. Willi has been telling it for years: how, as a green twenty-one-year-old, he went bumming around the world, traveled by tramp steamer, climbed in the Alps, got an iron-working job in Sweden, and when he reached India, tried to climb Nilkanta, another peak in the Garhwal—only to fail miserably. Sick, broke, and dressed like a beggar in rags, he was eventually rescued by a medical missionary. And then one day, as Willi likes to tell audiences, "I went wandering up on a windy ridge, and from afar off I saw this superb peak, and I was absolutely *smitten* by its symmetry and its mystery. And the thought occurred to me, twenty-one years old and a little retarded, 'You know, I need a wife,' a logical first step in the acquisition of a daughter. Because I suddenly wanted a daughter badly, I wanted her so that I could name her after that captivating mountain."

Devi, as she's called, is a good-looking, big-shouldered, pearly-toothed dreamboat very much in the countercultural style of the seventies. She's a feminist pioneer in a way, since women are still extremely rare on Himalayan climbs. She has a smile that breaks hearts and that heals them, too. She speaks pretty good Hindi, and the porters, spooked perhaps by her awesome name, and by her golden good looks (said to be a distinguishing mark of the goddess), by her Western female openness and naturalness, are already calling her *didi,* which means "older sister." As Lou Reichardt, another member of the team, will later write in an account for the *American Alpine Journal,* "Many may have suspected she was the Goddess Nanda returning to visit her mountain."

Three of the sahibs, with black umbrellas over their heads, suddenly break out of the mess of goats and porters and uncertainty. They sprint up the trail as if to put as much distance between themselves and the others as possible. Shreds of cloud obscure their going, and they soon disappear in the rhododendron forest.

All is not well with the Indo-American Nanda Devi Expedition of 1976.

Conceived of as an anniversary climb—to honor the first ascent of the peak, in 1936, by the Englishmen H. W. Tilman and N. E. Odell—already the expedition has an opéra bouffe quality, with hints of complete fiasco. The climbers have divided with shocking viciousness into two factions. Just the day before, the team's strongest technical climber, John Roskelley, a twenty-seven-year-old *enfant terrible* from Spokane, Washington, lit into the dignified, sweetly decent Ad Carter, accusing him of ineptitude. As Roskelley would later claim, in a self-serving and highly readable book, *Nanda Devi: The Tragic Expedition,* his beef with Carter was a matter of logistics and common sense: he wanted *either* Willi *or* Ad to step up, take the helm, no more of this coleader crap. Somebody has to give the orders and really mean it, assign tasks to the lazier team members, with the goal of everyone making it to the mountain in reasonably decent shape.

This outburst, not the first and not the last from Roskelley, and staged with maximal brutality, but in the name of "common sense," provoked Willi to an uncharacteristic rage. It also left Carter feeling deeply hurt. Carter *personifies* common sense, and he has been working hard for a year to see that they arrive at the base of the mountain with everything they need for a shot at the summit. To attack Carter and his mountaineering judgment is to . . . to attack mountaineering history itself! To impugn the essence of Himalayan climbing! Carter was on that first ascent of Nanda Devi way back in '36, a mere stripling of twenty-two who didn't get the summit but who carried well and earned a lot of merit, and his *bona fides* are not to be doubted.

The incredible snottiness of this Roskelley fellow, who was invited along only for his alpine skills (certainly not his charm), put Ad in a blue mood, and he confessed to Jim States, the team doctor, that he was thinking about not going to the mountain after all. That he didn't feel "needed." This is a little like General Eisenhower telling his men on the eve of D-day that he feels unloved and is thinking about sitting out the invasion of France.

In any case, a breach, a chasm, has opened up within the group. On the one side is Roskelley and his fellow Spokane climber, Dr. States, a recent med-school grad and director of Spokane's methadone program, a bearish, red-bearded fellow who has climbed all over with Roskelley, acting as his Sancho Panza. On the other side is everybody else: Willi; Devi; Carter; the expedition's only other woman, twenty-four-year-old Marty Hoey; Peter Lev, thirty-five, an experienced Tetons mountain guide; Andy Harvard, a law student and Himalayan veteran at twenty-seven; and Elliot Fisher, twenty-three, a Carter protégé on his way to Harvard Medical School.

Willi's faction wants an alpine-style ascent of the mountain: light, fast, aesthetic, leaving Nanda Devi roughly as found, with few signs of human presence. Roskelley and States want that summit by any means necessary, and they intend to get there by following the never-before-climbed North Ridge route. The Roskelley group considers it madness to think of scaling a peak as enormous, as deadly, as Nanda Devi in midmonsoon season without a ladder of camps at several elevations, plus lots of fixed rope for jugging along between the camps. There has already been a tremendous hassle over how much rope to haul in for fixing pitches on the mountain. Thousands of feet, shipped from Germany in six-hundred-foot spools, have been left behind in Delhi, despite Roskelley's loud protests. And before that, Lou Reichardt, joining Roskelley and States, secretly stuffed extra rope in what would become the porter loads, having despaired of convincing the others of the dire need for it.

But the rope problem is nothing compared to the toilet paper problem.

Devi, who spent several years as a child in Nepal—Willi had been director of the Peace Corps there, from 1962 to 1965—knows the folkways of the Himalaya much more intimately than does the average longhaired tourist. When she was a little blond kid, she was playing with Nepalese children her age, learning their languages, their games, sharing their outlook and their gastrointestinal infections. When Devi says something on the order of *People here have been shitting happily for five thousand years without using toilet paper, so why should we?* she may sound like a typical hippie diphead, rejecting all manifestations of bourgeois Western hygiene, the body-fearing obsession with being odor-free and squeaky-clean; but though she may sound that way, she's not just talking through her hat, and she's willing to put her privileged American bottom on the line. A year ago, at the planning session for the expedition, she was already taking a hard position on TP, mocking Roskelley for his wipe worries and making the environmental case against wasting trees. The general idea is that their trip to her sacred mountain be exemplary in as many ways as possible, the antithesis of the lumbering, siege-mountaineering extravaganzas of the past. They will not waste hundreds of thousands of dollars, and they will not leave behind a typical Western garbage-strew. (Roskelley, feeling he was in the presence of true madness, "made a mental note to add six rolls to my travel bag, just in case she won the argument.")

Peter Lev will later say about their expedition that "everyone acted out of character," meaning that the angry confrontations over every damned thing warped everyone's behavior. "Even Roskelley, who if he'd been on a trip only with his redneck pals, would never have caused the intense bad feeling that he did." Redneck vs. hippie, old school vs. new, the mainstream, oppressive, materialist American silent-majoritarian colossus vs. the airy-fairy, leave-no-trace, exquisitely sensitive youth-cult New Age. A quarter century after those strange days, it's difficult to recapture the state of mind that could lead educated adults to think that world history turned on how they wiped their behinds! Along with the toilet paper issue, there went a great debate over what food to take, Roskelley and his allies, who came to include Lou Reichardt, opting for ordinary freeze-dried fare up on the mountain, while the Willi-Devi-Lev-Harvard group argued for eating the local grub found along the way, in order to carry less but also to bring them closer to the native folk. The point is not that reasonable people might disagree about food, an important and vexed issue on any serious climb, but that they thought they were proving some larger point, that "the whole world is watching."

Ad Carter, prep school disciplinarian, might have been expected to put a stop to this nonsense. But Carter is strangely cowed (or maybe just dismayed) by the ferocious intensity of every debate. The thing about being a grand old man and a WASP blue blood is that it's fun only up to the point where people stop acknowledging your authority; when you have to really bang their heads, get them to behave, the point of the whole venture has already been lost. Carter keeps wanting to go off and photograph flowers. He's come this way before, up the torrential Rishi Ganga (*ganga* means "river," as in Ganges), and he wants to commune with his forty-year-old memories. His great climb with the immortal Tilman wasn't spent arguing about toilet paper!

That leaves Willi, but Willi is deeply implicated in the brouhaha. Cannot claim an impartial position at all. And truth be told, he kind of likes the turmoil. Why *not* invite a guy like Roskelley on your trip, a guy with a serious reputation as a hard-ass, a bigmouth, an in-your-face Iago. Aside from the fact that Roskelley's a brilliant climber—very much in Willi's own mold as a younger man—there's something promising about getting people of wildly different temperaments together and forcing them to deal with stark utter fear. They aren't proposing to climb Nanda Devi by the old milk-run route, but by a line on the mountain that nobody really knows anything about. There aren't even any decent photos of it. And they'll be climbing during the monsoon, when huge dumps of snow will create horrendous avalanche conditions. Somewhere in the back of everybody's mind is the thought *I could die here, I could really die,* along with the opposite thought, *Nowhere else I want to be. Too unspeakably beautiful and thrilling. Oh, Jesus . . .*

Now, *that's* a promising paradox. Willi thrives on impossible situations where you dig deep down and by some indescribable Promethean juju save your ass—and incidentally make your mark. Quite lovely to be acknowledged best in the world—*he climbed the West Ridge, yeah, that red-haired guy over there*—but that's not the point. On Everest thirteen years before, one of his fellow climbers, a sociologist trained at the University of Minnesota, conducted a study called "Communication Feedback in Small Groups Under Stress" while high on the peak, one of those ridiculous scientific-sounding excuses for getting more money from sponsors. Except that this guy, Richard Emerson, an old friend of Willi's and Tom Hornbein's, actually discovered something of note. Willi has been quoting it and elaborating on it in his lectures for years, and it somehow goes to the very heart of what dicey Himalayan expeditions are about for him, to wit: that intense desire and excitement vary inversely with certainty. When the outcome is shadowed by doubt and you may well be on a suicide mission, you feel most intensely alive.

Given a secure outcome, your average member of a small group will tend to go slack. Given a piece-of-cake proposition, a summit handily in reach, such as Everest's by the South Col, that insufficiently stressed member will even *manufacture* uncertainty to keep his head in the game, his feelings fresh. This current Nanda Devi venture, then, in line with Dick Emerson's insight, promises to be exceptionally on the alert, a hill scramble for the ages. Not only do they have the weather to worry about, and the unknown route, and the avalanches, and the porters and their bleating goats, plus who knows how many other objective obstacles to confront in the coming weeks—they also have each other. They will be attempting to climb this awesome peak while hating each other's guts.

TWO

The night before their departure, the local villagers sacrifice a goat on behalf of the expedition, to bring it luck. Willi goes along to observe at the funky local shrine to Nanda Devi, and he even eats a few pieces of the seared goat meat. His impressions, recorded in the notebook he always keeps on trips, are of decay and disorder, of a religion frankly debased, with half-naked village children running around and yelling, banging on the ritual drums and using the ceremonial sword as a toy. The headman of the village arrives after a while and lends the proceedings some purpose, if not much dignity. The local spirits appeased, everyone then straggles on home.

So much for getting right with God.

But the Garhwal region, the mountain zone that contains Nanda Devi, is said to be the holiest landscape in India. A former central-Himalayan kingdom, due west of Nepal, it is the actual abode of the gods. Thousands of pious believers make pilgrimage here each year, wending their way up from the lush lowlands toward the icy mountaintops, where the spirits are said to dwell. The season of pilgrimage coincides exactly with the period when the Americans will be climbing their mountain—the month of *bhado,* August/September.

Economically backward, out of step with modern, forward-thinking India, the Garhwal is a chronically underdeveloped area but also "a mythically charged geography," according to a scholar of Hindu practice. As parts of the Vatican are sacred to Catholics, as Jerusalem is precious to Jews and Christians and Muslims, so is the Garhwal consecrated to devotion, every peak, every river, practically every bend in every path connected to the goddess Nanda. "She permeates the whole area," Ad Carter will write in a sorrowful essay published after the expedition. "In the region drained by the Rishi Ganga . . . every nook and cranny seems in one way or other to be dedicated to her."

Willi and his daughter Devi, with other members of their group, are aware of the cult of the goddess. Willi was a kind of pioneer of spiritual awareness among American travelers to Asia, beginning with his shoestring trip back in '48, when he met a remarkable Hindu sage, Swami Jnanananda, from the Garhwali town of Badrinath. A grotto-dwelling holy man of impressive learning and good English, Jnanananda, the last two syllables of whose name suggest his devotion's focus, taught Willi about karma and other Hindu doctrines. The swami's great generosity toward Willi and his friends, which included walking with them all the way up to base camp, at fourteen thousand feet, made their half-assed climb of Nilkanta almost possible.

Laurence Leamer, author of a well-researched biography of Willi, *Ascent* (1982), wrote that an associate of the swami's donated all the rice and dal that the lads would need for their wild attempt, commenting that he "chose to consider [them] among the pilgrims whose welfare it was his duty to care for." Just like real pilgrims, they were heading up from the lowlands toward the snowy peaks—and their air of youthful enthusiasm gave their effort some of the feel of a quest. This confusion of a devout, often arduous, religious pilgrimage sanctioned by a thousand years of tradition with an ill-equipped hike in the hills was perhaps understandable, even charming in a poetic sort of way; and Willi, ever after, was likely to emphasize the similarity between the two kinds of effort.

On that first morning out of Lata, the climbers who outdistance the rest are Roskelley and States. They hike as if they never want to see the others again (which they half-don't). It feels good to be moving, to get these amazing, world-class legs of theirs, which only weeks before were carrying them up a peak in Bolivia, into gear again. Someone struggles to keep up: Roskelley slows down a little, and it turns out to be Marty Hoey, who's doing her best to catch them on the trail. Marty's a good-looking young woman, dark, warmly ambitious for the great summits. She works as a mountain guide on Rainier, and among male climbers she's a legendary object of longing. According to Lou Whittaker, the chief guide at Rainier and her boss, "every guide at Rainier Mountaineering fell in love with Marty. Each summer she would select a boyfriend and go with him for about a year. Then the next summer she would pick someone new."

Having been on a climb before with Roskelley, in the Soviet Pamirs, Marty knows how these things work. If you acclimatize fast, if you can carry more than the next guy, show yourself tireless and obsessed from the start, you may end up on the summit rope-team. From day one everybody is auditioning for one or two slots, at most. Willi and Devi may talk about *everybody going to the top this time, everybody,* achieving that impossible grail of expedition mountaineering; but Marty knows this to be only a pipe dream.

Marty never seems to eat, yet she has incredible energy. Roskelley warns her not to overdo it today: they have five thousand vertical feet to gain before Lata Kharak, the meadow where they'll make their first camp.

The thorny brush tears their umbrellas. They walk through terraced barley fields for a while, then dive into more of the lush green
stuff. The trek to Nanda Devi, which parallels the course of the
Rishi Ganga, is taking them through a horticultural omnibus of the
Himalaya, remnants of tropical rain forest in the lower reaches
yielding to stands of rhododendron and magnolia, with scatterings
of exotic trees completely foreign to American eyes, things with
names like *kharik* and *akhru*. The understory is thorny and complex, thickets of what look like wildrose mixed with Asian barberry
and mayapple. With each rise of a few hundred feet it all changes,
and now cypress and blue pine and spruce appear, real mountain
trees that look weird growing out of this soaked jungle. Above nine
thousand feet, yew trees and willows show up, then firs, then
honest-to-God white-trunked birches such as might be found growing alongside a trout stream in the Rockies.

Lata Kharak, when Roskelley arrives in the afternoon—he's long
since outdistanced Marty and States—is a classic alpine meadow
with primulas and other wildflowers growing in the abundant grass.
Birches, rhododendrons nearby. The rain comes down harder, and
the porters look sulky when they stagger up. Roskelley stacks the
loads they drop, making some order out of the mess. Soon the sahibs also wobble in, soaked and feeling the shock of the day's altitude gain. Despite being drenched and winded like the rest, Devi
impresses Roskelley with her sunny joshing and chattering to the
porters in Hindi: concerned for their comfort, she finds extra sleeping pads and a rainfly for them to huddle under.

It isn't that Roskelley dislikes women—not at all—but he has a
reputation as a dreadful chauvinist, mainly because he thinks that
they don't belong on expeditions. Consider Marty. On the Pamirs
trip in 1974, virtually every man made a play for her, it was just
unbelievable. Suppose that two guys had crossed hard-ons over

Marty high up on the mountain—suppose they both angled to sleep in the same tent with her, something ridiculous like that, and one refused to go down to a lower camp when he should have. It might have meant nothing, or it might have meant somebody dying. The beauty of being on a severe peak in that impossible brief moment when the summit can perhaps be taken—perhaps—is that everything else drops away, all of bullshit life, and the margins of error become *very* thin. At such moments elemental life—the opposite of bullshit—suddenly has your undivided attention, and if it does not, you or someone else may be in big trouble. Why else climb great mountains by extreme routes, if not for the way they force a thrilling narrowing of your focus to the few things that really matter, your rope, the weather, your partner, the ice and rock, your courage?

Further case in point: Peter Lev, who had been on the Pamirs trip in '74, also on Dhaulagiri with Roskelley in '73, has confessed to being in love with Marty. Peter looks like an ad for ski sweaters, like a Norwegian movie star, although in fact he's a part-Jewish guy from Fullerton, California, the thoughtful son of a lawyer. Sixteen years as a guide in the Tetons, an avalanche forecaster for the Forest Service, a veteran of climbs in Alaska as well as the Himalaya, and probably the only team member as skilled as Roskelley on ice and rock, Peter nevertheless has that whipped-puppy thing going where Marty's concerned, and this can only threaten the team's cohesion. What makes it even worse—insane! insane!—is that Marty casually mentioned to Roskelley in a phone conversation months ago that she was "trying to break up with [Peter] slowly . . . so as not to hurt him. I want to be back on my own."

Just great. And what else will they have to look forward to—Devi falling in love with Ad Carter? Or with one of the goatherds? Andy Harvard also has that misty-eyed look, though not necessarily because of Devi or Marty: as he confessed to Roskelley before they left the United States, he recently broke up with a girlfriend, someone he's "quite fond of," and he isn't really himself yet.

In their drenched meadow, the Indo-American Expedition beds down in two big tents. All night it rains. In the morning the porters don't want to move—something about their *atta* (wheat flour) getting ruined, the rain soaking through the woolen bags on the goats. They decide to stay put for the day.

In the 1930s, the approach to Nanda Devi via the Rishi Gorge was probably the most daunting trek in the world. British mountaineers had been trying to force a way up it for fifty years. Everest might be taller, but Nanda Devi fascinated by reason of its beauty, its mystic power, and the fact that no one had been able to get anywhere close.

Eric Shipton, a great British explorer of the thirties, described the problem this way: "[A]round the 25,660 foot mountain itself stretche[s] a huge ring of [subsidiary] peaks, more than thirty of them over 21,000 feet . . . unrelenting guardians of the great mountain." The only way in through this barrier ring was via the river, which drained the mountain's glaciers to the west, but when Shipton skirted above the gorge along the northern side of it, he looked "straight down a five-thousand-foot precipice into what must be one of the most fantastic gorges in the world . . . never yet . . . penetrated by any human being . . . believed by the locals to be the abode of demons."

Like the American team in '76, Shipton and his companions could only skirt above for a while; eventually they had to climb down into the gorge itself, cross the mad raging river several times, and climb along the three-thousand-foot sidewalls on slippery, downward-sloping slabs. This approach had killed men before, and it was in the nature of a last resort: British and German explorers, beginning in the 1830s with the well-named Englishman G. W. Traill, had tried to find a way in to Nanda Devi from the south, the east, and the north and had never come close.

Shipton's partner in '34, when the ring of guardian peaks was at last breached, was Harold William Tilman, possibly the century's most accomplished explorer/mountaineer. Like Shipton, Tilman was able to go forever on almost nothing; the two of them were life-hardened, pipe-smoking, tweed-wearing Brits, so chary of emotional gush that when Tilman climbed Nanda Devi two years later he wrote about the summit, "I believe we so forgot ourselves as to shake hands on it." The entire '34 expedition, which lasted five months, cost them 286 pounds, including all supplies plus ship's passage for two from England. They ate porter food and whatever else came to hand, and when little came to hand they ate little. ("Growing in vicinity of our new camp was a great quantity of wild rhubarb," Shipton wrote enthusiastically during one stage of the trip up the gorge.)

Tilman's own book, *The Ascent of Nanda Devi,* published in 1937, made clear the reasons for the English fascination with this mountain. In the first place, it was the highest peak in the British Empire; second, Nepal was closed at the time; third, there was a map, although it dated from 1868. More important, "Garhwal is the birthplace of the Hindu religion," Tilman wrote, "the traditional home of most of the gods . . . and the terrestrial scene of their exploits." Tilman was a "recluse," according to his friend Shipton, a truly rough character, someone who had "never even been inside a cinema," yet he was deeply stirred by the landscape, by its cultural and spiritual overlays. "[T]he Himalaya offer themselves to the more fanatical devotee," Tilman wrote, "and withal [are] to be approached through country of great loveliness, inhabited by peoples who are always interesting and sometimes charming."

His account of Nanda Devi—highest summit ever gained before Annapurna, in 1950—is full of religious notes. The Rishi is named for the Seven Rishis, he writes, the legendary Hindu sages who believed that "here if anywhere their meditations would be undisturbed." "[A]lmost every rock and pool [of the river] is associated in legend with the life of some god." About Traill, the English explorer of the previous century, Tilman notes that he became blind while attempting a pass on the southeast flank of Nanda Devi; the local people attributed this to the wrath of the goddess having been aroused, and Traill recovered only after making reverential offerings at the temple at Almora.

Another early explorer, Adolph Schlagintweit, tried the same high pass as Traill, and three of his strongest men suffered epileptic seizures. The porters understood this as the goddess taking possession of them, but because Schlagintweit had made offerings at temples beforehand, the men recovered.

On August 29, 1936, the day Tilman summited, a nearby river flooded following severe monsoonal rains. Forty people drowned in the village of Tharali, through which the expedition had recently passed. Tilman's feelings on gaining the top were joyous, then deeply remorseful: "It is the same sort of contrition that one feels at the shooting of an elephant," he wrote, "bought at the too high cost of sacrilege." He reports that a respected Indian newspaper said of the drownings that the anger of the goddess had certainly been provoked, and that she had avenged the violation of her sanctuary "blindly but terribly."

Tilman's tone throughout his book is mordant, amused, dry. For this reason, his unironic reports of what might be taken as instances of native superstition call attention to themselves. About the pilgrims who make their arduous journeys every year, he writes with sympathy and perceptive respect: they have a "downcast air" due to the "awe and terror most must feel in the presence of such strange and prodigious manifestations . . . of the gods [as] savage crags, roaring torrents, rock-bound valleys . . . and . . . the stern and implacable snows." Despite the malaria, dysentery, and cholera prevalent along the pilgrim route every summer, "they . . . attribute the faintness felt in the rarified air . . . to the influence of superhuman powers," and they believe that "the snow banner flying on Nanda Devi is [smoke] from the kitchen of the goddess herself."

Tilman struggles to overcome one of the basic beliefs of people of the West, the idea that there are sacred realms (of the spirit) and that they are entirely separate from the profane one (physical reality) in which we live. The pilgrims of the Garhwal demonstrate a different attitude, one that fascinates and attracts him. Particular places have spiritual qualities, mystic colorations; as it says in the *Mahabharata*, the classical Sanskrit epic of India, pilgrimage places are holy because of the very stuff they're made of, because of the *power of their earth* and the *efficacy of their water*. The molecules themselves have been altered by a godly presence, which never dissipates. Hence, to say that there are sacred vs. profane realms doesn't make much sense. It's all holy, and especially the *really* holy parts.

Tilman was a former artillery officer, earthy and frank. He wrote of the Garhwal, "If you eat only what the flies have not touched you go hungry," and about one of his climbing partners he noted, "We were startled to hear [his] familiar yodel, rather like the braying of an ass." All this talk of gods and spirits was bunkum, of course—and yet it was not. The emanations of the mountain got to him. Like other veterans of the Great War, Tilman abhorred blather, especially metaphysical blather, and he described the world in ways consistent with Hemingway's famous credo, from *A Farewell to Arms,* that there was "nothing sacred, and the things that were glorious had no glory and the sacrifices were like the stockyards at Chicago . . . Abstract words such as glory, honor, courage, or hallow were obscene." But something about Nanda Devi turned Tilman's head. As he pushed up the gorge with Shipton, and as he trod the summit snow-ridge two years later, he was conscious of a quality that could only be described using those terms ("sacred," "hallowed," "glorious"). Coming down from the top he trembled to imagine "the spirit of Nanda Devi . . . forsaking the fastness which was no longer her own."

Willi knows how to enjoy a rest day: if you have to lie about for thirty-six hours, as at Lata Kharak, listening to the rain pelting your tent, you may as well have a few laughs. He tells salty stories. He plays his harmonica, which he always brings along on climbs. He engages in comical talk with his tentmates about the struggle to come, and when the porters complain about their *atta* getting wet, he offers them plastic bags. Negotiations with the porters and the *bhakriwallahs* all go through Captain Kiran Kumar, the parachute commando attached to the expedition by the Indian Mountaineering Federation. Captain Kumar has a swaggering superior Il Duce way with the goat people—exactly what's called for—and is a thoroughly splendid fellow.

Come afternoon the porters kill an animal, butcher it and fry up a batch of fresh blood, a delicacy apparently. All the sahibs are offered a taste.

Nineteen thirty-six: the great Tilman was here, in this very spot. Willi was then a ten-year-old boy living in remotest one-horse Coquille, Oregon. He read Tilman's book soon thereafter—Tilman, the most remarkable explorer of that generation of great British mountaineers. Tilman and Shipton ate wild bamboo and fungus pried off trees when they ran out of *atta*. Of Lata Kharak Tilman commented, "A chill wind and mist are the rule at this camp." And so it is now.

Only Mallory compares to Tilman, for guts and romance. Willi read all about Mallory, too, and about Somervell, and Odell, and E. F. Norton—all the Everest pioneers in their puttees and Norfolk jackets, climbing to the top of the world while dressed as if for a stroll in the Lake District. The people who become climbers are unlike tennis players or football players or most any other kind of athlete in this one respect: they start out by reading stories. They have their noses deep in books when young, and after being thrilled by the great figures from the past they become mad to do the thing themselves. Willi was certainly that way, and an amazing number of the climbers he's known started out by reading expedition accounts. Charlie Houston, for instance, an American climber and all-round great fellow, member of the original '36 Nanda Devi team, who would've gone to the summit but for a few bites from a tin of spoiled meat, started out by reading *On High Hills*, G. W. Young's book about the Alps, at age twelve. Thereafter he became obsessed.

Willi plays campfire songs, and Devi joins him on pipe flute, while the others sometimes sing. Willi was famous in his years as a Tetons guide for greeting his clients in the morning playing the "Colonel Bogey March" on harmonica. Thereafter the day of peak-bagging would include generous doses of yodeling and whooping and harmonica, all kinds of lively noise. He has never taken a nobly reserved, tight-lipped, Mallory-esque approach to being in the mountains, although Mallory's great heart remains an inspiration. To be stoical and unyielding and undaunted, yet also warm and relaxed—this is the great ideal.

During their second night at Lata Kharak, the sahibs all start to regret those few tastes of fried goat's blood. They thrash about in their sleeping bags, getting cramps and breaking out in sweats. Some rush out of the tents to vomit. Roskelley has been lecturing them all along about not touching the local grub, about being vigilant in matters of personal hygiene, but the more hippyish among them have sampled the local fare, wanting to be at one with the people. Back in Srinigar, a little village they drove through in the truck, "Only Willi and Devi were able to down the cold greasy meal blanketed by green flies," according to Roskelley, who primly ate nothing but packaged sugar cookies. Now they must pay the piper. Elliot Fisher crawls out of the tent at 4 A.M., desperate to relieve himself. Jim States, who has been as hygienic as Roskelley, nevertheless has a fever and diarrhea, as does Marty Hoey, as do Peter Lev and Andy Harvard and Willi.

Suddenly, the tune they should all be playing is "St. James Infirmary." Marty and Harvard seem to be the worst off, with Dr. States a close third. He prescribes Lomotil and tetracycline with a free hand, advising Marty to drink a lot of fluids. Marty and Andy can barely walk when morning comes. Even so, the tents are taken down, everything packed up and given to the porters. To take another rest day so early in the trek would be a serious mistake.

The porters, who snagged an extra day's wages on account of the rain, now forge ahead with their cumbersome loads, coughing and hawking and smoking, trailed by the swirling herd of goats. In their wake come the feeble sahibs, some too weak even to carry their own packs. To the south a peak named Nanda Ghunti—"Nanda's Veil," "Veil of the Bliss-Giving Goddess"—shows a brilliant cap of fresh monsoonal snow. The rainy season, long delayed this year of 1976, has at last arrived, and if they ever make it to Nanda Devi itself, they will face miles and miles of the avalanching stuff.

THREE

....

In the Garhwal region of northern India, women do most of the work. The men of the villages are often gone, sometimes for years at a time; for a man to remain at home is to lose face. Travelers to the Garhwal often remark on how hard the women seem to work, both inside and outside the home. G. W. Traill, the first British commissioner, observed over 150 years ago that "suicide is very prevalent among females. . . . The hardships and neglect to which [they] are subjected, will . . . account for this distaste of life . . . the whole labor of the agricultural and domestic economy is left to them. . . . Suicide is never committed by males."

The men work now and then as porters; they plow small fields, tend animals, and that's about it. To see women bearing enormous loads, of firewood for example, while their men walk beside them completely unencumbered is common. Visitors to the Garhwal have noted, often with dismay, the aged appearance of village women who turn out to be in their late twenties or thirties. A woman of forty often looks like a crone.

To say that women of the Garhwal lack "equal rights" is to invoke a way of thinking that itself is foreign to the region. Elsewhere in village India women suffer oppression on account of their sex, but in Uttarakhand—another name for the Garhwal—the fix is really in. It has been this way forever, and the chronic underdevelopment of this region of exquisite mountain landscapes and ancient settlements perched high on steep hillsides, with tiny temples and terraced gardens somehow managing not to tumble down into the river bottoms, guarantees that it will go on this way for a long time.

As the members of the Indo-American Nanda Devi Expedition head in toward their mountain, they are thus walking through a geography of honest-to-God male chauvinism, one of the most unregenerate on the planet. John Roskelley has been griping from the start about how women don't belong on climbs, they aren't strong enough, they bring hassles that endanger everybody, and so on; and the two women, meanwhile, grow if anything more determined, since to their way of thinking it most certainly *is* time for women to be admitted as equals. Marty Hoey is a phenomenal climber, agile and daring, as she will show on expeditions in Asia and South America before her death, at age twenty-nine, on Everest. She has some of Roskelley's own unaccountable physical dynamism—"how can he/she climb so hard, at such heights, their muscles must not work the way normal people's do"—as well as a seductive female version of his emotional ruthlessness, whereby friendships become instrumental in the jockeying for the lead.

Devi Unsoeld, less gifted as a climber, is stronger. She can carry loads just like the brawniest men, and she has inherited, or learned, an attitude of stoical indomitability from her famous father. Devi has been butting heads with Roskelley for a year now, beginning with their first meeting back in Olympia, when the expedition was just being discussed. Roskelley came to visit them at the Unsoeld house; there he encountered Willi and Peter Lev, and immediately they were in a big thrash about the woman question, Lev chastising Roskelley for opposing Marty as a team member. Willi asked Roskelley what his problem was, why did he hate and fear women so much? Roskelley spluttered something, but as he later wrote, "Suddenly aware that I was standing in the way of a great American experiment, I grudgingly conceded." At this fraught moment, Devi entered the room, having ridden a bike eight miles after a strenuous pickup soccer game at Evergreen College. She was sweaty and glowing and buff, a big strapping Northwest gal in cutoffs and a tiny halter top.

"Why, you're Roskelley," she said, seeing his unfamiliar face. "I understand you've got a problem with women."

Without Devi, there would not have been an expedition, and so it was impossible to oppose her. She had convinced Ad Carter to undertake a climb in the U.S. bicentennial year; she'd convinced Willi—no problem there—and she still had hopes of convincing her brothers, Regon and Krag, thus to make it a real family outing. All her life she'd been intrigued by her namesake mountain. The extraordinary circumstances whereby she'd come to bear this name were like the elements in a fable, not quite believable but conferring a sense of legendary inevitability for that very reason. Willi sometimes joked about having made the whole thing up—seeing the distant magical mountain, vowing to have a daughter who could bear its name—but that was standard Willi tomfoolery, to claim such a thing after years of enthralling classrooms and lecture halls with the story. Swami Jnanananda wasn't made-up, nor was the inexplicable way the holy man had warmed to young Willi, so green and out of his depth in the Himalaya; nor was the botched climb of Nilkanta a fantasy or going hungry afterward or being rescued by Christian missionaries. If you looked at it all with an alertness to the possibility of fate taking a hand, as Devi was inclined to do—seeing the whole strange sequence of events as having been foreordained— you began to understand so much.

Even if it was made up, or partly made up, there was an intense message for Devi and for Willi's other young followers in the story, that we in some mysterious way are capable of shaping our lives as ongoing legends, that we stand on the stage of a drama we can write ourselves, if we only dare. Willi had done this with his own life. It wasn't just climbing Everest by the West Ridge, or any of his other down-in-the-permanent-record mountaineering feats—it was the way he self-invented every day, willed himself into being a powerful teacher and example, a Socratic inspirer, a charismatic. That sort of thing didn't happen on its own, without a great effort of will. And somewhere in this mix of fated events to which we are all passively subject, between self-assertion and self-creation, lay the thing itself, reality as we have it and it has us.

"It just doesn't work," Roskelley insisted in the face of this female titan, this avatar of seventies-style womanly dynamism. "Women on climbing trips just doesn't make it." But he was already defeated, and he knew that there would certainly be women on the trip, and that they would not be mere pushovers.

Out of Lata Kharak, at about twelve thousand feet, the path rises steeply again; there's mist but not much rain, with occasional gusts of chilling wind. The caravan clatters up the flagstones of a rocky ridge, following a dim sheep-track before crossing the ridge at Dharansi Pass (fourteen thousand feet). Roskelley, capable of great tenderness toward those he doesn't resent, walks alongside his pal Jim States, making fun of his frequent stops to relieve himself; he carries all of States's gear and supplies him with toilet paper. Somewhere back in the mist Devi is doing the same for Marty, supporting her along "a sensational traverse," as Tilman described it in '36, "across a mile of some of the steepest and most rugged cliffs imaginable." Rain comes in squalls. Marty weakens, and at the end of the traverse she can hardly walk. She speaks but doesn't make sense. She arrives at Dharansi, a barren plateau where the next camp will be, nearly delirious, wracked with chills. Devi climbs into a sleeping bag with her to warm her up.

Peter Lev is also sick, Andy's sick, Willi's sick; but Marty is *really* sick, scarily out of control. She can't keep down fluids or the Lomotil that States gives her, and eventually she passes entirely out of the conscious moment. Only the day before she was an intense, intoxicating presence, planning for the summit—already maneuvering to be on the summit team!—a woman about whom Peter Lev would recall that she had a "forever young quality . . . in a roomful of beautiful women, she would be the one with the longest string of suitors . . . effortlessly captivating"—and now she thrashes and mutters incoherently, too weak to get out of the tent to go squat somewhere. Devi tends her with sisterly sweetness, protective of her modesty. Elliot Fisher tends in the same way to Lev, who though sick is nothing like as far gone, and Jim States monitors both patients through the night.

The morning comes with more rain, cold and punishing at fourteen thousand feet. States examines Marty, and in the thoroughgoing way of a man with a new medical license he notes nausea, electrolyte depletion, dysentery, and hypothermia, and further notes to himself that they are several days from any backup medical personnel. He must judge this case correctly and make absolutely the right call. If he could only get her to take some fluids, but she throws everything right back up. In the early discussions about how much equipment to carry, the proponents of an alpine-style ascent leaned on him to leave the IV supplies behind, and he reluctantly

did so. Just conceivably this girl might die because of that decision—because somebody thought to save four or five pounds out
of the five thousand the porters are carrying.

States asks Roskelley to take a look at Marty's eyes. "I knew
Marty was in trouble the instant I saw [them]," Roskelley later
wrote, "[t]hey were opaque, dull, roaming. She tried to speak . . .
but her tongue seemed heavy and useless and her dry lips moved in
slow motion." Something very wrong in there—in her head. Roskelley hurries away to find Willi. He insists that they break camp
right now, carry Marty on down to the next stopping place, a
meadow called Dibrugheta, at about eleven thousand feet. If her
troubles are being caused by the fourteen-thousand-feet altitude,
this may help.

Something about the way Roskelley comes on—150 percent certain and with a built-in "fuck you" if you disagree—almost gets to
Willi. Willi never gets angry, or almost never: he believes that anger
in the mountains leads to accidents. "It can be used," he wrote for
a climbing magazine once, "with some effectiveness to counterbal-
ance fear, though usually a cold icy disregard is more effective
[against fear]. . . . Anger is very very seldom productive. . . . The
leader who really controls his anger in all situations has to be an
inspiration to those . . . under him." Anyway, that's the theory. But
Roskelley is a special sort of bully, someone who tromps all over
others in their most uncertain places, who gets his way by his willingness to say hateful things. He may be right about Marty, but it
hurts to have to agree with him. About anything.

Then Willi takes a look at Marty himself, and it doesn't matter
that it's Roskelley saying to move her—they *have* to move her, and
Willi rigs a rope-carry for transporting her down the grassy slope.
Sergeant Nirmal Singh, the second Indian officer attached to the
team, offers to carry her on his back, and they start out that way,

with Willi, Roskelley, and three porters offering support. The rain comes and goes, the slope steepens and gets muddy. Marty has to stop often to rest; she apologizes pathetically for being so much trouble, and Roskelley, as he described it in his book, turns away to hide his tears. Nirmal, exhausted, passes her on to one of the porters. Then it's impossible to piggyback her anymore, the terrain's too steep, and they down-climb with the barely conscious woman suspended between two porters. "I'm so tired," she says with her thick tongue, begging to be left behind. "Please forgive me. I don't want to be any trouble."

At Dibrugheta they put her in a tent, inside a sleeping bag, with her drenched clothes stripped off. When Peter Lev arrives later from the higher camp he looks in on her, discovering that his former lover "has that death smell . . . *Marty smelled of death* . . . it was a shock, and it broke your heart." Elliot Fisher, who as a future medical student is paying close attention to the crisis, writes in his diary that Dr. States now speaks of Marty's recovery as a question not of "when" but of "if." They try to make her drink fluids every few minutes, and States gives her a Marazine suppository to control vomiting. Still, there's nothing really to do now except wait. Willi sits with her. States sits with her. When Devi and the others arrive from the upper camp, they also come to be with her, they all can smell and see how it is with her now.

The camp at Dibrugheta—"an emerald gem," as Tilman described it, "a horizontal oasis in a vertical desert"—is oddly lovely as a place for this awfulness to be happening. A mountain brook runs nearby. The meadow is full of crimson potentillas and of anemones, the short-lived white flower supposedly created by Venus from the blood of Adonis. How odd that this should be happening to Marty, among all of them: to one of the vibrant younger ones, and one of the two women. It's as if Roskelley really knew something, after all. He's been saying women don't belong, but the actual dynamic is that by saying such a thing you create resentment and people begin to act out of character, to overdo it in small ways, thereby coming to fulfill your ignorant prophecy. The truth is that women *do* belong in the Himalaya and on the world's other highest mountains. There were pioneering Englishwomen as well as Englishmen, and just the year before, May '75, a fifteen-member Japanese Ladies Expedition put the first woman on top of Everest, Junko Tabei. In the same year a Polish Ladies Expedition climbed safely in Pakistan for four months, achieving honorable ascents of Gasherbrum II and III. These climbs, along with others involving women, were duly reported in the *American Alpine Journal,* which Willi of course reads religiously, as do most other serious climbers, including even roughnecks like Roskelley.

At a meeting in the early evening, Dr. States gives his diagnosis; the gravity of Marty's condition is borne in on all. They will sit with her through the night in two-hour shifts, two people per shift. Roskelley has something unfriendly and unwelcome to say—everybody can tell, you just have to look at his face to know. The unwelcome thing he now insists they recognize is that Marty is finished for the climb. She needs to be evacuated, pronto. No way she can come around and contribute after such an ordeal, on a mountain nearly eight thousand meters high.

No one says anything. It's not that Roskelley's wrong, necessarily; it's just appalling that he'd talk of this now, with Marty apparently dying in a nearby tent. The meeting breaks up.

Roskelley's faction—himself and Jim States—gains by a factor of 50 percent with the arrival that afternoon of Lou Reichardt, who left the United States later than the others and has been hurrying for some days to catch up. Lou steams into Dibrugheta with a single porter. Reichardt and Roskelley are not necessarily bosom buddies, but in mountaineering terms they're something even more formidable, a matched pair of summit-hungry, gifted climbers in their exalted prime. In 1973 they climbed Dhaulagiri together, one of the most deadly of the highest peaks, the first Americans to do so. Their pattern on that climb was to carry harder and longer than everybody else, simply walk the legs off the other team members, lead all the hardest pitches, get way out in front on the route to the top. Roskelley had never been above fourteen thousand feet before, never been in the Himalaya, yet he surprised everybody, possibly including himself, with his kick-ass energy and fabulous ability to acclimatize. According to Andy Harvard, also on Dhaulagiri in '73, Roskelley "fumed at inactivity" and seemed "spurred by anger" and would sometimes carry loads between high camps in less than half the time it took the others, many of them Himalayan veterans. The only one able to match him step for step was Lou Reichardt. Another scarily efficient acclimatizer, Lou resembled Roskelley neither physically nor temperamentally, yet there they were together at the end, sleeping in the same tent, planning a desperate final assault, and at last stumbling up onto the summit block of the world's sixth-highest mountain.

For Reichardt to arrive at Dibrugheta at just this moment, with this vexed, ill-starred effort on Nanda Devi looking less likely by the hour, is enormously cheering to Roskelley. "Lou was indefatigable," he wrote in his book, "a scientist in a strong athlete's body. I hadn't seen him in two years, but I knew from the look in his eyes and his firm handshake that he was as determined as I. . . . We had a chance at a new route now."

FOUR

···

Marty does not come around. She languishes, she fades. Willi sits with her in the tent that smells of death, talking the options over with Dr. States, who injects her with Compazine. There are no options, actually; they can only wait and, if she somehow survives the night, do something like what Roskelley suggested, send a runner out to summon help. The military base in Joshimath is one or two days away, then there'll be several more hours, or days, while the Indian air force scrambles a chopper. For Marty to survive such a prolonged wait in her present condition is unthinkable.

Willi has seen little of death in the mountains, a remarkable record considering his thirty years of climbing high peaks. On Everest in '63, a close friend of his from the Tetons, Jake Breitenbach, died in the infamous Khumbu Icefall, crushed beneath a shifting block of ice about as big as two railroad cars. Willi led the rescue effort, allowing himself to be lowered into crevasses around the gargantuan unstable blocks, which could be heard to groan and pop. He called and yodeled for Jake until there was no more hope. But that was an instantaneous, brutal-stroke type of death, the kind about which other climbers are likely to say, "Well, at least he died in the mountains, doing what he loved." Of the present sort of tragic, foul mess, the grim stuff of nightmares, of third world indigents' wards, Willi has seen little. He and Dr. States get to talking about Marty's neurological symptoms. The coma and so forth are related to her extreme dehydration, but it's odd how closely they resemble the symptoms of high-altitude cerebral edema, a dangerous swelling of the brain with associated release of intracranial fluids. Cerebral edema comes from hypoxia (oxygen starvation); the best thing to do is to take the patient down to a lower altitude, with a richer oxygen saturation. But they've already done that for Marty. Or, give her some bottled oxygen. At that moment, Roskelley sticks his head inside the tent and says quietly, so as not to wake Marty—as if anything could wake her—"I think she has some symptoms of cerebral edema. I think we should put her on oxygen."

Hardly daring to hope, they find the few bottles they've brought, stored deep in one of the porter loads. They rig up a delivery system (mask, regulator) and in a remarkably short time Marty opens her eyes, seems to become aware of her surroundings. They keep her on oxygen through the night, and by early morning she's answering questions, drinking Tang, urinating. She has returned from the dead. The other climbers, as if in the presence of a miracle, embrace, shed tears. After nearly forty hours Marty has come back from the other side, reasonably intact though still not quite right, showing lingering effects of her ordeal.

States examines her at about 6:00 A.M., and sometime on this day, July 18, he also examines Devi, who has a bulge in her abdomen she wants him to look at. It's a small hernia, not a cause for alarm but something to keep an eye on. At 7:00 A.M. the team members get together, and States says that while Marty looks better, she may still have to be evacuated; he'll watch her closely and make a final decision by noon.

As a team they've conducted themselves well. In a mortal crisis, they've been resourceful, caring, dedicated; Devi especially has made a powerful impression on Roskelley, with the sweet protectiveness she's shown Marty and others. "Devi worked feverishly around camp," he wrote, "and later cooked a cheese sauce for our potatoes, which became our favorite meal. I had been listening to her contribute good judgment and compassion to the group. . . . Although she was young and idealistic, she would defer to experience. . . . I was amazed at her energy and willingness to help." Perhaps there's hope for all of them, then—hope they can put their differences behind them. This hope goes missing almost immediately. At the noon meeting, States announces that Marty's lingering symptoms require that she be evacuated; yes, she's walking and talking pretty well now, able to go down to the stream and take a bath, but she's still uncoordinated, doesn't look or sound exactly right. She can't remember what happened. If she were a football player who got knocked on the head on the field, then started exhibiting such symptoms, as a physician he'd have to insist on "a brain scan or EEG to find out if additional damage had occurred that could not be seen."

Roskelley supports States 100 percent. Lou Reichardt thinks evacuation's the way to go, too. But the rest of them are shocked—Marty's back, she's on the mend, why ship her out now, kick her off the whole climb? It doesn't make sense. States explains that cerebral edema is insidious and can result in permanent brain damage, not to mention that if Marty climbs higher and has a recurrence, she could suddenly drop dead. He wants her on the team as much as anybody. But she has to have a thorough clinical workup, he can't allow her to continue without one.

"I think the patient should have some say about her treatment," Willi puts in. He's not quite persuaded by all this dire medical talk.

"I'm willing to take that advice of Jim's and sort of crank it into the general scheme of things. As a doctor, Jim's bound to consider the worst possible results and not necessarily the most likely ones. Nothing can be sure from the diagnosis and we're all here to take our chances." And then he adds pointedly, "I think we should lift this responsibility from Jim's shoulders."

This is also a shocking thing to hear, in its way. Young Dr. States has been making a great effort to be conscientious, fully realizing how much is riding on his judgment, that further delays—waiting for a copter and so on—will work mischief with their careful calculations about how much porter food they have and how long it will take to get to the base of the mountain. Also, if Marty is forced off the climb now, will Peter Lev want to abandon it, too?

States is stung, and Roskelley, insulted on behalf of his friend, explodes. "That's a *medical* judgment, Willi," he cries. "You don't seem to understand—it's a *medical* judgment."

"I know," Willi replies in his mostly kindly way. "And I recognize it as such. But Jim has very little data to be judging from. It's Jim deciding for Marty when she's capable of deciding for herself. I mean—she's perfectly conscious now."

Thus begins a five-hour argument. Roskelley fumes, States gets upset, and Willi makes their disagreement a question of philosophical differences, their recent rows over women and how to climb the mountain and what equipment to take and whether to use toilet paper and all of it somehow involved. For Willi the situation only starts to get interesting when a decision of this kind has to be made, whether you're willing to risk all, including your precious brain, to do that most useless of things, climb a mountain. You can't be intervening every time a terrible cost is to be exacted. In particular, you can't intervene for somebody else. Great mountaineers have often pushed on in the face of terrible, impossible odds, sometimes achieving momentous things. And sometimes being destroyed. But this isn't a game of Ping-Pong, after all.

Willi in debate is *very* impressive. He teaches now at that touchy-feely college, Evergreen, where the longhaired students are off in the woods half the time, and academic standards have grown relaxed in the potheaded seventies. But before Evergreen there were more standard academic appointments and a long preparation for intellectual effort of a high order. He majored in physics in college. Then he went on to graduate school in theology at Oberlin, in the 1950s one of the most distinguished American programs. He got his doctorate in philosophy at the University of Washington, in a high-powered department dominated by analytic philosophers. Somewhere along the line he learned how to win with words. His ordinary method is to listen closely to debate opponents, remaining self-possessed at all times as he picks up their logical flaws and then with an air of benevolent let-us-reason-together nails them to the floor. All this accomplished without preening, without superiority, without meanness of spirit.

And there *is* a philosophical difference, there's no mistaking that. They've been arguing about Marty, but Marty only insofar as she raises the question of whether a Himalayan climb needs to be some sort of Darwinian process, the weaker and less aggressive ending up shattered and discarded along the way. Everyone knows Roskelley's game, that everyone not a summit climber (as he is sure to be) becomes a pack mule, a drone, serving the two or three summiteers by carrying loads to the higher camps. As Peter Lev said of Roskelley after the expedition, "You could either be his slave or you could be his enemy." A new approach to mountaineering has emerged in the seventies, with a new professionalism. Roskelley senses, correctly, that he has a chance to make a world-class career for himself, just like Christian Bonington in Britain and the Austrian Reinhold Messner. At this moment he's almost certainly the strongest American high-altitude climber, just as Willi was for a period in the fifties and sixties. To be invited on more climbs, to attract sponsors, press coverage, book contracts, all the goods and services of such a career, he needs to get the great summits. He needs to get them by diabolical new routes, to prove to the world how good he is and meanwhile to fulfill his undeniable talent.

At the moment, though—considering Marty—Roskelley may well be less selfish than merely right. No denying the girl was all screwed up in the head. He doesn't want her to die, it's as simple as that. With cerebral edema there can be blood clots, and climbing to great altitude thickens the blood anyhow. Lou Reichardt, who as it happens is a research neurophysiologist at Harvard, had a problem himself of this kind on Dhaulagiri, suddenly couldn't distinguish his left side from his right, couldn't keep his balance. No doubt the cause was a mini-stroke on the left side of the cerebellum (Reichardt diagnosed this himself at the time). Now Reichardt argues for getting Marty out of there immediately, and Ad Carter asks over and over for his "expert" opinion, needing to hear the Official Harvard Neurology take on things. But Willi isn't convinced, or intimidated, either, to hear the orthodoxy out of Harvard or wherever; this is one of those situations where people make or break themselves by refusing to genuflect in the direction of any anointed authority and instead simply step up and *do it themselves*. They have to ask Marty about it, he insists. It's Marty's brain, it's her life, let the brain of Marty decide.

Twenty-five years after this day in the meadow, after the whole expedition was over, when this afternoon of red-faced spluttering argument in a wet tent was long past, Jim States was still mad about it.

"I'd thought of Willi as this extraordinary man," he recalled. "But in that situation, I saw that he was merely arrogant. He was disrespectful of the mountains and their power to harm. I'd say that as a man he was more philosophy than reality, on the basis of that. The Marty question was a no-brainer, if you'll excuse the expression. . . . Willi made a great argument out of it, though, a kind of object lesson. I said to myself, 'He's gonna win this debate, and this girl's gonna die as a result.' In the end I had to start crying to get their attention."

States does just that, breaking down sobbing, practically tearing his hair. This is a life-and-death issue, he insists, yet they're sitting around scoring debater's points. Roskelley stomps out of the tent, States stomps out. Marty has let it be known that she wants to stay on in Dibrugheta a few more days, to recover, and after that she'll hike on in to Base Camp and catch up with the rest of them. And then, of course, climb the mountain. States has examined her and found residual problems, ataxia, some visual impairment, mumbled speech. Clearly she's much better now—she isn't dying—but he remains adamant on what has to be done.

Devi soothes her father when he gets overbearing in the argument. She basically takes his line on Marty, thinking Marty should have the final word, as does Andy Harvard, who in lawyerly fashion points out that a doctor can recommend a course of treatment, but he cannot *command* that it be followed. Peter Lev worries about the emotional harm to Marty if she has to give up, abandon the mountain she's been so eager to climb. Remembering the funny-farm quality of the discussion many years later—it seemed truly mad to him at the time—States felt that the feminist motive wasn't really important, it was just that Willi and these other people "wanted to have this nice woman be allowed to stay on their climb, because she was nice and they liked her and it would be more fun that way."

In the end, Marty does have the final word. She hears all the arguing and can't stand it anymore. "If there's any trouble because of me, I want to go back," she says. "I don't want any more arguing."

Willi forces Roskelley to say to her, point-blank, whether he wants her on the climb. "I don't want Marty on a rope with me when her problem may return at high altitude," Roskelley freely admits, and then, looking directly at the young woman, he says, "In my opinion you were as good as dead [last night]. I don't feel you're [mentally] able to make a proper decision on this issue."

With that, Marty, whether *compos mentis* or not, is too heartsick to go on. She retreats to her tent and announces through Peter Lev that she won't be continuing. And for the next twelve hours or so, it's not clear that any of them will be going much farther on this mountain. There's just too much bad blood. Too deep a split. Bad faith and disdain and disharmony settle over the camp like the monsoon overcast, which also returns. Willi accuses Roskelley of trying to take control of the expedition, and Roskelley insists that his motives are as pure as the driven snow. (In his book about the expedition, published eleven years later, Roskelley will continue to show a remarkably tin ear for the finer music of emotional interchange, failing to register the possibility that his harshness created resentments that became problems in their own right.) Devi writes a letter home from Dibrugheta. To her mother, brothers, and little sister she puts a good face on the near catastrophe, saying, "In the ten days we have been together we have become a group, so that the absence of one member leaves a hole that is quite large. We have not strayed into cliques and there is only one focus." The startling untruth of this statement suggests someone completely out of touch with reality, although a more likely explanation is that the mountain has begun to draw her on, that finally being this close to it, after a lifetime of yearning, makes her determined not to *let* them stray into cliques. With Marty gone, Devi more and more assumes a multiple burden, that of being the sole womanly presence, peacemaker and wound-binder, as well as climber and load-carrier and all the rest. Outwardly her spirit remains strong, while inwardly her dedication becomes if anything more absolute. Her joy to be near her mountain at last, at this moment in her life, in this company, communicates itself to the others, impressing even the most hardened among them.

FIVE

....

Willi comes to regret his behavior at Dibrugheta, his browbeating of the young doctor. In a letter home he admits that he "performed poorly during the Marty discussions . . . lunged cuttingly at Jim States' naivete and sliced so shrewdly with words that Roskelley had to leap up and leave the tent." Marty remains at the camp, tended by Ad Carter, Peter Lev, and others, while a porter hurries out to fetch a copter. The rest of the team limps on up the Rishi Gorge, in squalls of rain.

Willi is feeling his age. In the many public addresses he will give after the expedition, he'll explain his eagerness to go to Nanda Devi in terms familiar to any aging athlete: "I woke up one morning and it had been eleven years since Everest, and what had I been doing? I had no answer. . . . The doctors told me I had *arthrosis deformans,* a degenerating hip, with very little articulation left . . . not to mention a deteriorating fifth lumbar vertebra, *spondylolis thesis,* as they call it. Well, with maladies like that, there's only one remedy: *frantic activity.*"

Willi onstage, in front of a class, in any public forum, is unmistakably a performer. His voice is measured and penetrating, aware of its effects. He neither hems nor haws. For years now he's been honing a presentation that recalls Will Rogers, the rope-twirling cowboy vaudevillian of the twenties and thirties. Like Rogers, and like Mark Twain, too, another prolific after-dinner speaker, Willi has a down-home American tartness and sweetness. He's ironic and there's a twinkle in his eye, yet his intelligence isn't threatening. He has a talent to amuse and he says things sometimes that veer perilously close to real wisdom, although he makes no claims for such. Again like Rogers, also like Twain, Willi has developed a costume that he wears when in public. Over the years he's been shaping a persona called the Old Guide, a wisecracking, broke-down mountaineer who's seen it all and then some, and this character—Willi as the multitudes know him—always wears Levis, clunky hiking boots, a flannel shirt with the sleeves rolled up, and (optional) a red bandanna and a floppy Gabby Hayes–type hat. He appears as the Old Guide while leading people into the mountains, or fulfilling his professorial duties at Evergreen, or sharing a stage with Herbert Marcuse, the famous radical intellectual, at an academic conference called "Wilderness and Human Values."

Willi began climbing early, with the Boy Scouts. An all-star football player despite his modest size, he could do phenomenal things on rockfaces and snow-slopes almost from the start, and he chose as his credo the phrase "Life begins at ten thousand feet." His family was churchgoing in a relaxed way, following the lead of his adored, hardworking Episcopal mother, Isabel Trahearne, an Englishwoman who managed to be both ladylike and unstuffy while raising five children. When Willi's father, George, an immigrant from Germany, declined in status through a series of jobs in dry-goods stores, Isabel took in boarders; to help her with the children she hired Miss Edith J. Scott, a retired schoolteacher, who became profoundly attached to Willi, the baby of the family. (The name

Willi is part of the public performance, an early step in the Old Guide business; in his family he was called plain Bill.) Miss Scott, a woman of great moral force and the highest standards, was highly "respectable" but not a churchgoer. Willi's hard-drinking, tyrannical, economically at-loose-ends German father, a cultured man out of place and out of time in the lumber towns of the Depression Northwest, actively ridiculed churches and religion. Willi went to church nevertheless, and while it may be going too far to say that he was "rebelling" by doing so, he went because he found something there, because the realm of spiritual questions made sense to him.

In a lecture he gave many times in his life—usually under the title "Wilderness and Spiritual Values"—he talked about a sense he had as a boy of a sacred force, something that drew him and that he wanted to know more directly. "I looked in church for a *long* time," he told audiences. "I really concentrated at the altar rail, staring up at the cross . . . nothing, just nothing. I found I couldn't summon it no matter what I did. I think it *can* be found in church . . . for Catholics sometimes something happens at the moment of transubstantiation, they say, when the bread and wine become the body and blood. That's an injection of a mysterious sacredness into the profane. . . . But for me after a certain age it only happened outdoors."

In his early twenties, applying to divinity school, Willi wrote a frank essay about his spiritual background. "As to previous church participation and religious experience," he confessed, "they have been spotty. I was baptized and confirmed in St. James Episcopal Church in Coquille, Oregon . . . subsequently being trained as an acolyte and acquiring a 5 year perfect attendance record [!]. Upon moving to Eugene, Oregon, I was again active in the High School Young People's Group . . . taking my turn at helping the rector, Father Bartlam, with the service of morning prayer. . . . I was assailed by the doubts customary to my age. . . . Communion proved an especially tough question to reconcile, and in the end, the feeling of being a hypocrite drove me to abstain from it completely."

Willi goes on to describe his seven months of travel in India and Pakistan, during which "I was greatly impressed by the work undertaken by the various missionaries with whom I came in contact. . . . I determined at the time to . . . return to India as a science teacher in a Mission school. . . . My main reasons for wishing entrance to your School of Divinity, then, are: 1) My profound admiration for the example provided by the individual missionaries . . . and: 2) My conclusion . . . that a career . . . somewhere within the Life of the Church is the only type in which I can ever hope to find the kind of 'life's fulfillment' [that] I seek."

Oberlin snapped him up: someone struggling with disbelief, anxious about being a hypocrite, who yet feels he can find fulfillment only within the "Life of the Church" is just what they were after. Or maybe it was that five-year perfect attendance record. In his time at Oberlin, and later at the Pacific School of Religion, Berkeley, California, where he took a BD degree (equivalent to a master's in theology), he dove deep in the respectable pond of American liberal Protestantism. His professors at Oberlin were honored scholars; one of them, Walter Marshall Horton, was the most popular religious writer of the day. Oberlin in the early fifties was ecumenical and internationalist, intellectually open to other fields of study, such as archaeology and linguistics. One of the century's greatest Christian scholars of the Old Testament, Kemper Fullerton, had retired by the time Willi arrived, yet his rigorous approach to the study of ancient texts defined Oberlin's ethos for decades after.

Not that Willi was won over. He was terribly homesick for the West: Ohio's pathetic little hills made him long for something high to climb, and when his first child was born, Willi and his new wife, Jolene Bishoprick, named the boy Regon—*Oregon* minus the *O*. While at Oberlin Willi studied Philosophy of Christianity and Homiletics, and he read religious philosophers such as Rudolph Otto, the German Lutheran idealist, author of *The Idea of the Holy,* one of the great religious books of the twentieth century. Otto was an influential European interpreter of Hinduism—like Willi, he'd traveled in India and been transformed. At the heart of everything Otto wrote is a sense of the profound mystery and terrifying "otherness" of God, an idea that liberal Protestantism had lost sight of, he believed.

For the rest of his life, Willi loved to quote Otto's spooky-sounding Latin catchphrase about the holy: that it rests on a *mysterium tremendum et fascinans,* a mystery both enormous and beyond our capacity to comprehend. "The *mysterium* means raw power," Willi told his audiences, "and allied with this in the old days was the *fear* of God. There's a ringing tradition in the Bible . . . the ark of the covenant would be carried into battle, and the Hebrews would dance around it . . . when one touched it accidentally with his elbow, he was *instantly obliterated.* . . .

"I'm talking about genuine *fear,*" Willie would tell his Outward Bounders or his Sierra Clubbers or the Spring Planning Conference of the Washington State Office of Community Development (to name but several of the organizations that invited him to speak). "Angst, existential fear, fear of radical dissolution . . . to be nullified by sheer overpoweringness. How many people ever feel this today? It's gone out of life today and also out of the churches [because] the sacred has something forbidding about it, something of the ghastly. It isn't very fun, you know . . . and it comes dangerously close to the graveyard.

"You don't measure yourself against the sacred. You don't be-cause there are *just no calibrations small enough to notice you* . . . against it we're completely insignificant. And I found this quality . . . only in the mountains . . . keyed to the presence of physical risk. In the Outward Bound programs parents would ask us, 'Can you guarantee the safety of our Johnny?' And our response would usu-ally be, 'No, we certainly *can't,* ma'am. Fact is, we go the other way and guarantee you the *genuine possibility of his death.* And if we *could* guarantee his safety, the program wouldn't be worth run-ning—d'you see?' "

Oberlin paid less attention to Henri Bergson, the famous French philosopher, than it did to Rudolph Otto. But almost certainly Willi heard Bergson mentioned there, and he may have first encountered Bergson's ideas in his Christian Philosophy course. Bergson at the dawn of the twenty-first century is mainly missing from academic philosophy, and the writer of the book you're reading contacted a number of universities and found no courses on Bergson being of-fered, and a general head-scratching response to questions about his influence. But at the turn of the twentieth century Bergson was the most controversial philosopher in the world, an international celebrity and the most charismatic intellectual in Europe. People made mystical pilgrimages to his lecture hall, Salle 8, at the Collège de France in Paris, or bribed his barber for a lock of his hair. Like Willi, Bergson started out studying physics; his first published paper was a solution to a math problem posed by Pascal to Fermat in a letter. A subtle and poetic thinker, Bergson had scientific rigor but made his mark by attacking the extreme scientism of his day, the positivism and mechanistic determinism that by the end of the nine-teenth century was enshrined in many fields of study. Bergson loved science and throughout his life followed it closely; but he also felt keenly the moral discouragement of modern people, who were being told that their intuitive sense of reality and their inner feelings of freedom and personal uniqueness were illusions.

Bergson tried to bring life as most of us know it, in the privacy of our head, back into serious discussion. He pointed out what was imprecise about rationalism. Human reason has evolved to make us successful in the physical world, he said; its method is to break matter down into smaller elements, to analyze, to weigh and compare. A mechanistic approach has undeniable benefits, such as allowing us to build skyscrapers, but problems arise when we try to segment the flow of time and sensation as we know them into constituent parts, as if they were separable objects in space; then the soul and truth of our inner lives are inevitably lost. Bergson gave a central role to intuition, a much dishonored faculty among rationalists. Intuition allows us to understand reality "from the inside," he said; his famous example was to ask a student to raise an arm, then to compare the way he experienced and understood this to the way a scientist, observing him, might deal with it. The scientist would describe the psychomotor reality in all its complexity, making reference to mechanical stages and muscular adjustments, but the flowing wholeness and essence of the thing would remain hidden.

Intuition yields an unmediated, undivided awareness of the processes of life, and who's to say that this "ordinary" sense of things is without value? In a long career of lecturing and writing, Bergson sought intellectually respectable ways to honor his own intuitions about the flow of time and the existence of spirit. Probably his best-known idea, and the shorthand most scholars use to identify him, is the concept of the élan vital, a life force that surges through material reality. Bergson hit on this idea of a vital force always struggling against and incarnating itself through raw matter while studying Darwinian evolution, which posits an absence of design in nature, explaining the complexity of life in terms of accidental variations selected for survival. Bergson found this idea unpersuasive, or incomplete. The development in the direction of ever greater complexity—complexity in types of organism, and in the organs within those organisms—seemed to him wonderfully mysterious and in no way "inevitable" given natural selection. There was something bizarrely creative about the way life kept ramifying, going beyond itself.

Bergson had a profound effect on Willi. After coming within a hair of ordination as a minister, Willi wrote a complex, original dissertation on Bergson's metaphysics for the University of Washington; his thesis, accepted in 1959, the centennial of Bergson's birth, is one of the most illuminating general discussions of Bergson in English. The professors on Willi's thesis committee commented, "Mr. Unsoeld's critical evaluation is . . . of such a quality that we definitely consider his work acceptable" for the Ph.D.—in the dry manner of the academy, that "definitely" was uncommon praise. By the late fifties, Bergson was out of favor among American philosophers, considered old hat and imprecise; even those who continued to admire him, such as the historian Thomas Hanna, noted the "tantalizing" nature of his writings and commented that readers "reach out to grasp his body of thought [but] it seems to disappear with a teasing ambiguity." Willi found Bergson's writings vague, even incoherent at times. "It seems that the only . . . way of ever getting clear," he wrote, "about his favorite concepts . . . is by watching Bergson at work with them. The initial obscurity . . . is slowly mitigated as we watch Bergson applying them to such all-time conundrums as the problem of free-will or the reason for there being anything at all."

Willi refused to throw the baby out with the bathwater. The

reason for his great persistence with Bergson is that Bergson was simply too valuable to him as philosopher—too important as a powerful, original mind engaged with problems that really mattered. In his later years, Bergson wrote mainly about religion and mysticism, building on his core concepts of creative evolution and the élan vital to suggest a kind of Unified Field Theory of life and consciousness. Willi is most attracted to—and critical of—later Bergson, the writings on religion. In particular, Willi wants to know what Bergson has to say about the question of whether there is any connection between having mystical insights and living a moral life. In 1954, on an ascent of Makalu, an eight-thousand-meter peak in Nepal, Willi had a full-bore mystical illumination that he later poked fun at—but continued to speak about—for the rest of his life. It was a continuation, or an intensification, of other mystic moments he'd had, in other high places, and Willi knew enough about such phenomena to recognize all the symptoms in himself, the oceanic feelings, the rapturous certainty, the way "it gives you your basis for proceeding," as he later told audiences.

The problem was, how to keep hold of such feelings, since ordinary ways of thinking reassert themselves so soon; and how to tie this subjective, almost solipsistic, experience to what he felt was his inescapable role in life, to live responsibly among other people. Having tried life as a mountain recluse, Willi "got bored stiff after three months. I decided I needed people even more than I needed mountains," he told an interviewer. "I'm here on earth to work with people, for people and around people. It's people that are the eventual and continual fascination of my life." Bergson's way of connecting the two modes was to say that the highest degree of mysticism always found a "consummation in action," that the greatest mystic insights were inseparable from "action, creation, love." He downgraded any traditions that he felt were quietistic, such as Buddhism, with its idea of nonattachment. Willi wasn't quite so sure about that: "[I]t is surely a legitimate question to ask," he wrote, "if Bergson does justice to the whole sweep of mystical history when he arbitrarily relegates such men as Gautama [Buddha] and Plotinus to the ranks of the second-raters."

At any rate, Willi made a careful study of Bergson's ideas on morality. In *The Two Sources of Morality and Religion*, the main book of his later years, Bergson spoke of an "absolute" morality, by which he meant something far more important than simple ethics or common decency toward others. True moral heroes—what Bergson called "geniuses of the will"—perform free acts that "have made mankind divine. . . . Sure of themselves, because they feel within them something better than themselves, they prove to be great men [and women] of action." Bergson was thinking of people like Saint Joan, who, possessed of holy insights, become capable of extraordinary undertakings, efforts that extend the area of moral concern radically. These undertakings, motivated by and expressing a radical love, are the "freest" acts of which humans are capable— free because not predictable nor explainable in terms of self-interest, or in any other way. "[I]t is the whole soul," Bergson writes, "which gives rise to the free decision. . . . [T]o the surprise of those to whom mysticism is nothing but visions," these acts can have enormous effects in the real world.

Willi didn't necessarily disagree. But he noted, "It is [the] *personal* quality of absolute morality which Bergson emphasizes over and over again." Absolute morality rests on a human appeal—on the attractiveness of a specific personality, an exemplary individual. "[O]nce . . . an emotional atmosphere has been established by the moral hero," Willi wrote, "followers . . . spring up to absorb it . . . they enter into that emotion that characterizes his particular genius [and are] carried along toward . . . suitable action."

No doubt mindful of his own charisma, Willi both responded to this formulation and recoiled from it. "There is no particular morality at all involved in Bergson's . . . version of absolute morality," he wrote, and went on to observe, "While freedom may be a necessary condition for moral action, it is far from being a sufficient one. Its insufficiency is demonstrated by the fact that freedom is a necessary condition for immoral action as well." Bergson tries to rope all his concepts in at once and to make the "freedom" of free acts an instance of the moral hero incarnating the élan vital, since the creativity of the life force supposedly consists in its always taking unpredictable, entirely "free" forms; but Willi remained unconvinced. "Insofar as the mystic immerses himself in the drive toward the production of eternal novelty," he wrote, "there is nothing in Bergson's description to prevent that novelty from being purely immoral. . . . It is only by identifying the vital impulse with the mystic vision of universal love that Bergson succeeds at all in introducing a moral element" into his system.

The short answer for Willi, then: there *is* no necessary connection between mysticism and morality. Bergson's solution is to say that the highest form of revelation, the one we ought to admire most, is concerned with universal love, and specifically a Christian love; but Willi thinks Bergson arrives at this conclusion by something like a sleight of hand. Willi *wanted* the content of his own revelations to be about love, to imply a great connectivity, but the truth was that they felt personal, even selfish. They were undeniably "real" for him in some brilliant, transfiguring way, but they didn't necessarily point the right way to live.

Willi's attraction to Bergson rested not on final answers, but on an intellectual style. The rude American mountaineer simply *enjoyed* what the Frenchman was about. The attack on rationalism, on the puffed-up certainty of scientists and technology types: this was surely welcome, although, like Bergson, Willi remained powerfully logical and refrained all his life from a full-on embrace of any mystical system.

Willi also responded to Bergson's vitalism. "There is a genius of the will," Bergson wrote in *The Two Sources,* "[just] as there is a genius of the mind." His work is full of amazement at the creative transformations that can be worked by strong individuals. This idea made profound sense to Willi. He liked to tell people that the only reason he became a mountain climber was because he couldn't make it as a hiker: as a freckle-faced, redheaded kid, he was terribly allergic to poison oak, which infests much of lowland Oregon. But the *real* reason he went high over and over, safely above the poison oak zone, was because he found to his intense pleasure that the terrifying and seemingly impossible physical challenges of climbing awoke something in him, gave exercise to his formidable will. He could say, in the face of a previously unclimbed route or bad patch of rotten ice, "I will do this, even though it scares the hell out of me and out of any sane person who contemplates it even for a second," and then go ahead and do it. Do it in fair style, too, not gripped by terror but rather with a kind of blooming infectious joy.

Was this the élan vital that he felt in himself? For want of a better way of describing it—yes, it might be, it might very well be. All of Bergson's books and public disputes boiled down, more or less, to an effort to restore to people their conscious lives, their ordinary subjective understandings, and Willi's interior life was awash with a sense of transforming vitality. As he said in one of his critiques of Bergson, "The work of the moral creator is . . . to burst the bonds of physical necessity." As a thesis subject, Bergson attracted him because the main intuition of his young life found a serious and ingenious development in this philosopher's work. The idea of an intractable physical reality—let's say, high mountains—yielding to the will of an individual—yielding but also half-capturing, always threatening to crush—made exciting sense to him.

The other way that Bergson appealed was by his discussion of the moral hero, the "genius" of will whose work is to influence "the wills of his followers through the inspiration of his own life and personality," as Willi summarized it. In the early fifties, in the wake of a grotesque world conflict brought about, at least in part, by the demented inspirational power of a few unspeakable geniuses of will, Willi might have had a less sanguine view of this ability than did Bergson, who died in 1941; but one thing Willi knew about himself, and knew absolutely, was that he inspired others, that groups always formed around him. For some reason he was an *instinctive* leader; people gained confidence and direction just by being in his presence. Laurence Leamer, Willi's biographer, would observe many years after Willi's death—and after a long career of writing about influential and celebrated Americans—that Willi "was one of the two or three people I've known who could come quietly into a room of whatever size and simply *dominate* with their presence . . . it was a certain moral force . . . electrifying. He hardly had to say anything, but he shifted the level of discourse [and] made people confront themselves, ask what they were about."

Willi was surely aware of this power. He was comfortable with it, and at pains to use it well. For him it was tied up with love of others—with a kind of Whitmanesque embrace of all his brothers (and sisters), what he learned at Oberlin to refer to as *agapeic* connectiveness, from the Greek word *agape,* meaning openhearted love. In the Christian tradition *agape* refers to Christ's love for all mankind, and on a mundane level to the spiritual (nonsexual) love of one Christian for another, inspired by the love of God for man.

Again like Will Rogers, who famously declared that he "never met one I didn't like," Willi embraced all kinds of men, relished encounters with people from many backgrounds and traditions, effortlessly transforming these encounters with infusions of that homegrown charisma that was his from very early on.

....

SIX

Despite his personal magnetism, Willi isn't inspiring much devotion in John Roskelley: the outcome of the incident at Dibrugheta is that Roskelley comes to see Willi as a dangerous quantity, a "mountain-man" "guru" prone to making bad judgments. Willi's talk of cranking a scientific medical diagnosis into the general scheme of things, or in other words, plain flat-out ignoring it, offends Roskelley's sense of the proprieties. Fortunately, Willi doesn't get his way at Dibrugheta. Fortunately, Marty gets coptered out and the other potential weak sisters—Peter Lev, Ad Carter, whoever—can just sort themselves out, either decide to give the mountain a 100 percent effort or forget about it.

After Dibrugheta, "the team never was the same" again, Roskelley would write in his book; this implies that there was an earlier period of blissful agreement, but the team was in confusion even about the route to be taken on the mountain. Peter Lev, who stayed behind with Marty waiting for the copter, then, despite his still-strong feelings for her, caught up with the rest of the team, was under the impression that he'd signed on for an ascent of Nanda Devi by the original route, the one pioneered by Tilman in '36. This, in his opinion, was feasible for the sort of group they'd put together, with "the women and a couple of older climbers and some members strong enough but not really skilled on high-altitude ice."

"When the trip left for Asia," Lev says, "our goals were dual: the old route plus maybe an attempt on the Northwest Ridge, which Roskelley wanted badly. That was my understanding, anyway. I personally had no interest in doing the Northwest Ridge. Ad got overwhelmed by Roskelley's ugliness about the new route, and I kept nagging them to remember the original route as an option . . . they needed a large contingent of slave labor for their plans, a whole pyramid of labor, and I wasn't into that. I wasn't a team player, to their way of thinking."

The Northwest route was only a dream, in any case. No one had ever attempted it. Shipton and Tilman were the first humans to get a good look at the northern ramparts of the mountain, in 1934, and they quickly concentrated all their hopes for an ascent on the southern side. It looked less suicidal. In 1976, the northern approach was still so unknown that the best photo had been taken from several miles away, on Changabang (22,520 feet), one of the ring of great peaks that surrounds Nanda Devi; it showed the upper three thousand feet of the climb but was fuzzy and almost useless for route-finding purposes.

The photo had been taken by Chris Bonington, one of Roskelley's role models. In his drive to become the American Bonington, or was it the American Messner, Roskelley responded to the newsworthy audacity of the undertaking; but he was also, in his cranky way, responding with the simple courage of his great mountainclimber's heart. Like Willi, Roskelley was on the smallish side; like Willi, he was a native son of the Northwest, a tireless and nearly fanatical seeker of climbing adventure in his youth, which he spent in Spokane. At the time of the Nanda Devi trip, he described himself as "hardly . . . physically impressive with my small-boned . . . frame. . . . I was strong, but so are many others who participate in sports. The difference was that I didn't know I could be beaten." Spokane, at the eastern edge of Washington, has a far different spirit and political culture from Seattle and Olympia, way over on the western edge; in the seventies, support for the war in Vietnam was intense in the Spokane area, which owes more politically to archconservative northern Idaho, only a few miles away, than it does to internationalist Seattle, with its great port and university.

Willi was of the left-leaning, froufrou, sensitive world of western Washington and the colleges and the youth culture and the protests. Roskelley, the son of a Spokane newspaperman, "had no deep-rooted feelings against the war, unlike so many of my generation," as he wrote in an autobiography published in '93. Describing a 1970 visit to Yosemite, he also wrote, "[My climbing partner] and I may have looked like flower children with our collar-length hair . . . but our down-to-earth, Spokaneite redneck philosophy oozed out every pore. . . . Real hippies shied away from us like we were DEA agents." And furthermore, "I found myself [camping] in a miniborough of Los Angeles. . . . We were supposed to stay in [Yosemite's] Camp IV . . . filled to capacity with transient climbers and drugged-out 'flower children.' . . . Theft was rampant throughout the park, but within Camp IV it was epidemic. And disease. Herpes was as common as love beads. . . . I was more than eager to [spend] some time with the ladies, but smart enough to know that some of them would give me the 'gift that keeps on giving.' "

Roskelley's upbringing was strict; his family was Mormon. His father made an outdoorsman out of him, and when John was fourteen his dad brought home a review copy of *Conquistadors of the Useless,* the autobiography of the great French mountaineer Lionel Terray, which Roskelley read with the same intense onrush of excitement that Willi felt when he read Tilman's book on Nanda Devi, or E. F. Norton's book about Mallory and Everest. By 1975, when the Nanda Devi trip was shaping up, Roskelley was the veteran of three international expeditions, and his hyperindividualist, hard-liner personality was fully formed. His behavior before and after Nanda Devi was remarkably consistent. First step: accept an invitation to climb some world-famous mountain, in some exotic foreign land, but immediately challenge the authority of the older male expedition leader. Second step: continue to challenge resident father-figure, if possible provoking him to outbursts of apoplectic rage. Third step: form a clique, a tight group of loyal diehards determined to get the summit; if possible, make the factionalizing so flagrant that the rest of the team feels not only excluded but insulted. Fourth step: get out ahead early, climbing higher sooner than any other possible counterfaction. Fifth step: climb brilliantly, absolutely brilliantly, leading all the hard pitches yourself. (On Gaurisankar, a previously unclimbed peak in Nepal, Roskelley led fifty-eight of the sixty pitches it took to get to the top.)

In '74, Roskelley accepted a spot on a trip to the Soviet Union. The team leader, Peter Schoening, was a climbing hero from an earlier generation, a man of dignity and legendary fortitude, who in '53 held five people in a fall on K2—one of the greatest acts of single-handed rescue in the history of mountaineering. During a training period on Mount Rainier, Roskelley so tried Schoening's patience that he risked being dropped from the team. "Pete . . . was becoming like a dormant volcano," Roskelley wrote, "a puff of ash here and a little rumble there. . . . I managed within two weeks to bring him to a boil." At Cadaver Gap, on the same slope where Willi Unsoeld would one day die in an avalanche, Roskelley unroped from his partners in a storm; this violated a cherished principle of mountaineering, and "this time Schoening hit the roof," Roskelley reported with glee. "But still, given his personality, that's like a koala bear getting mad. Nothing happened, and he buried it inside."

Roskelley unroped because he hated—*hated*—being tied to people who slowed him down. His attitude toward roping up was entirely practical, utterly unsentimental: "If we're not belaying," he explained in an article published in *Outside* in '83, "I unrope. That's rule number one. That way I don't kill them, and they don't kill me." Belaying means offering your partner protection over terrain where, without a rope for safety, a fall would likely be fatal. Roskelley thus is saying that he will never stop for lunch on an airy ledge, or for a rest going up a steep ice face, and remain tied to his partner just because they're pals and they're in this thing together, only to have that stupid partner fall and pull Roskelley to his death, too. The author of the article in *Outside,* David Roberts, concluded, "Much of Roskelley's instinct for safety comes from a distrust of others." And Roberts further noted, "[A] mark of Roskelley's excellence is that he's had surprisingly few close calls in the mountains."

Compare Willi's attitude toward the climbing rope. In his classes and lectures, Willi insisted that the rope was more than just a rope, it was a symbol, a metaphor; to connect to another climber in a relationship of mortal responsibility, each holding the other's life in his hands, is an act to be undertaken with grave awareness. The rope needs to be handled correctly, of course, but it serves always as the outward sign of an inward condition of connectedness, heart to heart and soul to soul. On Nanda Devi, where the severity of the route ultimately required the use of thousands of feet of fixed rope—ropes hammered into the mountain and left in place—Willi came to appreciate the relative ease of movement up and down that this permitted, but as he wrote in an essay afterward, "[W]e did notice some insidious side effects of such reliance on fixed ropes. It . . . tended to fragment the party. . . . [S]o much of your time was spent isolated from each other . . . you did not really have to adjust your pace to that of your companion," as is required when climbers carry the rope with them as they move.

"[Y]ou just naturally started setting your own pace," Willi went on, "and the [partners] became more and more strung out and separated. . . . When one member of a team of two was not feeling well or was traveling unusually slow[ly], the separation between team members could be as great as three hours. This amounted really to solo climbing. . . . The quickness with which we tended to drift apart when the wind blew and the snow flew and when one climber was much slower . . . was a distinct revelation to us of just how important it has been all these years to be tied in together on the same climbing rope."

It was important in a *psychological* way, maybe even in a *spiritual* way. On his world-beating first ascent on Everest, in '63, Willi climbed the hardest new route on the highest mountain in the world, harvesting enduring glory, but his memories were mostly of companionship. He climbed the mountain with guys he knew, guys whose friendship he cherished. "At six-fifteen that night," he told audiences at his slide shows, "suddenly just forty feet ahead of me I saw the flag. . . . I turned around and waved to Tom [Hornbein, his partner] and started coiling in the rope . . . when he got up to me we linked arms around each other's shoulders and marched up to the summit together. Some people said afterward it was to avoid arguments over who got there first, but *actually there are other reasons for linking arms with your buddy.*"

Earlier on the Everest climb, as Willi related it, Hornbein and he benefited from extraordinary support from other close friends. Climbing above Camp IV, they were accompanied by Dick Emerson, who, though suffering severely from the altitude, carried bottled oxygen for them to use later. When Hornbein told Emerson to just drop the bottle, he became confused, since his purpose for being on the mountain was to help them. Hornbein then instructed Willi to tell Emerson why he was *really* there: "Dick, we invited you along today because we like you," Willi promptly declared. Then the three of them "just broke down," according to Willi. "The emotions are very close to the surface at that altitude. . . . So we stripped the bottle out of his pack, and we stuck it in the snow. Then the three of us went on."

The ethos of camaraderie, so essential in '63, had evaporated by the midseventies. The Nanda Devi expedition was only one of many to signal a sea change, and several seventies expeditions have gone down as mold-breaking catastrophes, complete madhouses, fiascoes. As Tom Wolfe declared, it was the "Me Decade." There are many reasons for the remarkable change, but none quite captures or explains it fully; the great extent of the distance traveled can only be shown by comparing expeditions near in time, such as Everest '63 and Nanda Devi '76, and marking the profound differences between them. Certainly there were ego conflicts and glory-hogging earlier in climbing history, going all the way back to the first ascents in the Alps, in the 1850s, but the unavoidable *symbolism* of the climbing endeavor had seemed to guarantee that brotherly cooperation would remain the ideal. Here is that symbolism: Enormous, murderous mountains. Mortal men and women anting their way up the terrifying slopes, far beyond the world of running water and forests for which their physiology suits them. Forced to rely on each other for physical support, for moral support, for rescue in case of accident. And connected, literally *tied* to each other, by lengths of rope. If ever there was an effort that demanded an all-for-one mind-set, climbing would seem to be it, and Himalayan climbing especially, which adds the factor of extreme altitude to the dangerous mix.

By 1976, John Roskelley—an unusual climber, but one facing the usual problems of survival in modern society—was able to go on an expedition and to believe, not without reason, that he might even turn a profit by doing so. Prior to the 1970s, American climbers had no such hope. To climb the world's highest mountains meant personal sacrifice, months of earning time lost to an effort that, whatever else you might say about it, never helped anyone in his *real* career. Of the eighteen men who climbed on Everest in '63, three were medical doctors; one was a magazine editor; one a professional photographer; two professional filmmakers; four university professors; one a physicist; one an engineer; one a clinical psychologist; one a math teacher; and three the part-owners of retail businesses. None was by any stretch of the imagination what could be called a professional mountaineer, although some had worked as guides on occasion.

In America, high-altitude climbers made up a very small group, most of whose members knew each other personally. Nick Clinch, who organized the only American expedition ever to achieve the first ascent of an 8,000er—the year was '58, the mountain was Gasherbrum I (also called Hidden Peak), and one of the two men to reach the summit was Pete Schoening, whom Roskelley would later drive crazy in the Pamirs—wrote a charming and amusing book about the expedition, which itself seems to have been fairly charming and amusing. "The odds were so great that the climb would never occur," Clinch wrote about his early efforts at recruiting, "that to become a member just was not worth the risk to one's [personal] reputation. . . . I promised to keep the matter as confidential as possible." This suggests the esteem in which climbing was held at the time—someone like Clinch, who hoped to launch a legal career, risked being identified as an oddball should it become known that he climbed mountains for fun. "[T]he primary qualification for membership in the expedition was availability," Clinch further notes in his book, *A Walk in the Sky,* and he adds that the host country, Pakistan, was asked to nominate two men not just as a gesture toward international cooperation, but also because the American expedition desperately *needed* two more bodies.

No one imagined, should they actually make it to Pakistan and climb high on the mountain, that there was a financial profit to be taken, or a public career to be made; the best that could be hoped for was a relatively small personal outlay of funds to cover expenses, and an employer kind enough to welcome you back after your mad adventure. (Clinch did get financial help by snagging an assignment to write the trip up for the *Saturday Evening Post,* but this was nothing like a first step in a career as a professional mountain writer, nor did *A Walk in the Sky* ever earn significant royalties: like most American mountain books before *Into Thin Air,* Jon Krakauer's '97 best-seller, it appealed to a small specialty audience, something on the order of the audience for books on bow-hunting.) But by the midseventies, a few marquee climbers in America could actually expect to make a living from the sport, if they managed things well and worked very hard. Far less developed than the European version of the sport, American climbing was enjoying a modest boom, with improvements in gear and the remarkable exploits of a few talented, colorful climbers generating an upswell in interest.

In California, the Yosemite pioneers Royal Robbins and Warren Harding put up new routes on El Capitan and other vast granite faces; by 1971 their greatest ascents were behind them, but Harding, in particular, was photogenic and an ardent self-promoter, and his ascent of the Dawn Wall on El Cap (October–November '70) became "the most intensive media event ever portrayed in American climbing," according to Steve Roper, the historian of Yosemite's golden age. Asked by reporters why he and his partner climbed, Harding answered pithily, "Because we're insane," and his madcap glamour made his public appearances fun. For that matter, the much trumpeted success of the '63 Everest expedition, with Unsoeld and Hornbein and Jim Whittaker and three others all getting the summit, was a breakthrough media event in its own right, a vigorous boost to U.S. climbing. Newspapers and magazines tracked the team's progress, and after victory was announced, *National Geographic* devoted an issue to the heroic struggle, and a documentary film appeared on CBS. Tom Hornbein wrote a handsome coffee-table book, *Everest: The West Ridge,* and James Ramsey Ullman, the best-selling author of *High Conquest, The Age of Mountaineering, Tiger of the Snows,* and many other works, produced a four-hundred-page official history stuffed with photos, *Americans on Everest.*

President Kennedy handed out medals to the team in the Rose Garden, and Jim Whittaker and others gave lectures around the country, with the proceeds from their talks used to retire the expedition's debt. (Willi, from Kathmandu, where he was working for the Peace Corps, mailed in $33; Whittaker, the official "first American on Everest," handed in $8,000.) The point is that when John Roskelley, in 1975, made his fateful decision to live and support himself from now on as a professional mountaineer, the ground had already been plowed, and his leap of faith was in fact a sensible calculation, based on his understanding of how some Europeans were doing and on his thorough knowledge of the drill, the article-writing, photographing, and slide-show-giving that generated revenue. In his decision, as in all his adventuring in the seventies and eighties, Roskelley was supported by a loving, amazingly understanding wife, Joyce Bakes, who worked as a schoolteacher back in Spokane; their home and family, which came to include two children, were his emotional anchor. "Blood is more important than anything else," he told Dave Roberts for *Outside*. "If I go off on an expedition, I know I have a place to return to, people who care for me."

He also told Roberts that his highest goal was to "make enough money so that Joyce can quit her job and stay at home." His own jobs, before he declared himself a climbing professional, were often hard, physical ones: a construction worker building a new Sheraton in downtown Spokane, a steam-mold operator in a tire-retreading plant. At all times and in all situations he was aware of himself as a workingman with real-world responsibilities, one skating perilously close, despite his mountaintop heroics, to the simple dishonor of failing to provide for those he loved. Thus, when he argued and manipulated and bullied in the name of climbing Nanda Devi by a scary new route, not the old milk run, but a route that would rock the world back on its heels, announcing to all that a mountaineer from redneck Spokane, Washington, was the equal of the Messners and the Boningtons, he was playing a desperate hand. It was a hand that he'd dealt himself, out of his need to go on climbing high peaks, discovering just how great he could be, but no less serious for that. The consequences for him of failing to do something noteworthy would be *professional* ones, *family* ones, all the ones that really matter. He might observe about himself, "The difference was that I didn't know I could be beaten," but he knew perfectly well what failure would look like, what it would mean to fail as a man and a husband and a father in this place and at this moment.

. . . .

Limping on from Dibrugheta, then, Willi presides over the wreckage of a team. Peter Lev may never rejoin them, and Ad Carter has been seeming more and more of a wistful presence, disinclined to speak up about anything. With Marty gone, too, the balance tips that much more in the direction of the hard-man faction, Roskelley and Reichardt and States; as if to announce his intentions unmistakably, Roskelley barges out of the meadow at Dibrugheta like a steam engine, getting way out in front of the others.

Devi wears harem pants and a hippyish blouse, and her bright good nature goes along with the thongs she wears on her feet, and the full pack she carries, and the ongoing love affair she's having with the Garhwali porters. The weather improves as if to say that her sunny disposition has writ itself large. She feels the loss of Marty keenly, and for the next few days is quieter than usual; the other youngest team members, Andy Harvard and Elliot Fisher, become in consequence more important to her, peers she can count on to see things pretty much the way she does. In comments twenty-three years later, Roskelley was at pains to recall "a kind of deep goodness" about Devi, that she "wanted to be your friend" even though she might hate and oppose what you stood for and argue against you violently. "Marty was the great heartthrob, the one who could make all men fall in love, but Devi was the real *beauty*," Roskelley said, "more beautiful by far, I thought, but she didn't put out the kind of feeling that would allow an approach to her. Anything more than a *comradely* approach, that is."

The porters call the other climbers sahib, but Devi is *didi* to them, sister, someone mysteriously of their world. Devi doesn't know their dialect, but Nepalese is cognate with the language of the Garhwal, thus they can more or less understand each other, filling in the gaps with scraps of Hindi. The porters have left no record of their feelings about her. Their impressions of this warm, quietly joyous, intimate-yet-distant American girl are like the flight of wild birds—seen but then gone, leaving at most some trace on the soul. *Nanda* is a Sanskrit word meaning "joy," *devi* means "goddess," but probably they thought of her as *Gauri,* another local name for the goddess: *gauri,* as an adjective, means "bright, fair-complexioned, beautiful," which she was. One of the Indian team members, a tough-nut military officer not known to be especially devout, wrote after the expedition that "Devi . . . was the goddess personified," and the degree to which someone like him could be persuaded of this idea may suggest how the porters, active participants in the local cult, were inclined to feel.

In Nepal, not far from the Garhwal culturally or geographically, the goddess is worshiped intensely, and one of the most remarkable ways involves a goddess figure called the Raj-Kumari (literally, "royal virgin"). A local girl is chosen from a Buddhist family of the Shakya clan—the Buddha himself was of the Shakya—then brought to live in the main assembly square in Kathmandu at the age of three or four. Here she dwells for years sometimes, in a holy temple residence called the Kumari-bahal; as an incarnation of the goddess, she retains her divine status until she sheds blood, either with the onset of menstruation or from an injury, such as a cut finger. To prevent such accidents, the Kumari is closely guarded; she ventures out in public only twice a year, for mass celebrations, at which times the temple square may fill up with as many as fifty thousand ecstatic devotees.

Kumari is a "beautiful living child dressed in red," according to Vidya Dehejia, an art historian specializing in images of the goddess. "[Her] eyes [are] dramatically outlined with collyrium, a third eye painted prominently on her forehead [and] hair piled up in an elaborate topknot." Visitors to the temple square try to catch a glimpse of her, no matter how brief, at one of the upper windows of the palace; as it says in an ancient Sanskrit text, "Without a form, how can God be meditated upon?" This practice, this viewing of a god's image with devout attention, is called *darshan* in Hinduism; the devotee "sees" the image in the same way that a religious seer is said to have a holy vision. To stand in the goddess's presence, meanwhile—actually to touch her or be touched by her—means an encounter with true magnificence.

Trekking up the Rishi Ganga, carrying sixty-pound loads for fifteen rupees a day, the porters are thus having *darshan* in a way; those who joke with the pigtailed, good-humored American girl come to know her spirit, and this is both a momentous development, something capable of changing a man's entire life, and also the most ordinary sort of thing, for, as everyone knows, the gods are everywhere in the Garhwal. Ad Carter, the language teacher, will later write an essay about the etymology of the local place names, noting that within a thirty-mile radius of Nanda Devi are sites known as Nanda Khat (Nanda's bed), Nanda Ghunti (Nanda's headdress), Nanda Pal (gaze of the goddess), Kalanka (a name deriving from that of Kali, the most cruel, bloodthirsty goddess-form), and Gauri Parbat (fair goddess mountain—*parbat*, the word for "mountain," derives from yet another goddess appellation, Parvati).

Even Lata, the backward village the porters all come from, has a goddess connection: *lata* means "leg" in Garhwali, as the village is said to be the leg, or support, of Nanda's resting place. Who, then, should a Garhwali porter *expect* to encounter in a group of foreign climbers hiking up the Rishi Ganga, other than some form of the bliss-giving goddess herself? And if she actually calls herself, with sweetly unconscious effrontery, Nanda Devi—if she dares to bear this holy name—is this a wondrous marvel, inconceivable and strange, or is it simply something of the everyday? As it says in the *Devi Mahatmya,* the fifth- and sixth-century poem that the porters, though perhaps unable to read Sanskrit, have heard chanted all their lives, *all women are portions of Devi,* all partake of her to a greater or lesser extent. Some partake of her bloodthirsty, slight-avenging side, as for example the murderous Kali (and even touchy Nanda, who sprouts eight arms and slays demons when aroused), and some partake of her divine goodness, her incomparable sweetness and compassion, which is beyond comprehension. This American girl, then, with her forthright eyes and the nylon pack on her back, hiking along like the others, enjoying sunny weather for a change, sweating, joking, admiring the emerald foliage of the spectacular gorge, is she, after all, the goddess incarnate, does she embody her holy aspects, some or even all of them?

Well, yes, of course she does. Of course she is the goddess.

SEVEN

Willi hikes out of Dibrugheta slowly, still thinking about the Marty affair. His guts are in a knot, and as he notes in his journal, he has bloating, mucus in the stool, constant pain. He walks kind of funny, too, with his toeless feet packed into special-order mountain boots. (His favorites come from the house of Limmer, a 220-year-old German bootmaking concern now based in New Hampshire.) Willi has been talking up the serene beauty of the mountain to the others, recalling his first sight of Nanda Devi twenty-seven years ago, during his epic *Wanderjahr*, when he was just twenty-two, exactly as old as Devi is now. The other climbers are suitably hyped but still frustrated—they haven't had even a glimpse of it, on account of the swirling mists and the twists and clefts of the steep gorge-faces.

Willi's hip problems, and his back problems, go back to those nine and a half toes he lost on Everest. As Napoleon said, "Everything invariably turns upon a trifle," and the stress on his joints from adjusting the way he walks has accelerated the degeneration to be expected from a lifetime of climbs, heavy loads carried, all kinds of activity. Willi in his youth was not just a fine athlete, he was a *life-force,* a *dynamo,* someone given to leaping up on top of roofs, rappelling down clock towers, bridging his body up open doorways. His energy—a lot like Roskelley's—was not to be contained, an inexhaustible and awe-inspiring force. The deep pleasure to be gotten from using such a body to the utmost and beyond: this was his biological compass as surely as Christian doctrine was his ethical, with the same feeling of incontestable rightness involved. In a lecture he often gave in the seventies, on the subject of accident prevention, he said about climbing, "It is addiction," the extreme responses called forth from one's body having a quality and delivering a payoff hard to match elsewhere in life. Probably every healthy athlete knows this feeling to some extent, but when those exertions also bring medals and the materials for constructing an entire personality, and a fascinating career, the attraction has a special force.

In that same lecture on mountain accidents, published, after his death, in a newsletter called *Off-Belay,* Willi talked about the dangers of pride, specifically about the danger to the veteran climber who refuses to let go. "There is the pride of the daredevil who just wants to explode out and impress everybody. Then there is the established solid climber who has . . . been to the Himalayas or such and is published in the Journals. . . . Everybody looks at him with a certain degree of awe. He does everything he can to avoid [failing on easy climbs], because just think what would happen if [others saw him].

"Now I had to make a conscious decision years ago," Willi added in a personal vein. "That tendency towards pride would not be allowed to stand in my way, and I would exuberantly fall off all the beginner's pitches. . . . You give in to these little manners of trying to always appear the man that you have been saddled with, the appearance which you know is much better than fact and largely a fabrication of rumor and tall stories, many of them contributed by yourself. If you give in to that temptation . . . it can put you into positions from which you cannot extricate yourself."

The compelling dialogue a young climber has with his own body, and the associated feeling of rightness, of doing something *significant* with all this climbing, is almost always tempered as the years pass and frailties accumulate. Willi was perfectly at home with the irony and embarrassment of physical decline; those toes, which fell off one by one, auto-amputating as he waited out the painful process in a flyblown hospital in Kathmandu, ended up in a jar, to be produced at the Unsoeld dinner table on suitable occasions. His favorite older sister, Beryl, recalls a visit Willi made to San Francisco in the midsixties, not long after Everest. "We had a huge gathering," she says, "and ate dinner. . . . Mother [Mrs. Isabel Unsoeld] and Bill were at one end of the table, and I said, 'Bill, tell us what happened to your toes—I'm so distressed to hear about that!' And he laughed and took off his boots right then and threw his bare feet up on the table. It was shocking. It was—just shocking."

The Old Guide does not hide his crippled places; he does not pretend to be younger than he is, or more intact. If anything, he revels in his deformities, for, à la Bergson, the struggle is always with intractable physical reality, and by counting up your missing toes, you see the score that the *spirit* has racked up. There's nothing to be ashamed of in that; in fact, there's something to be proud of. "It takes a great many months for them to decide whether to [fall off]," Willi told his audiences displaying appropriate slides of frostbitten feet. "My eldest daughter [Devi, then aged nine] said, when she saw me in the hospital, 'But Daddy—those are wizard's toes!' Finally I just plain got bored, and one day I found an old pair of scissors . . . for a unique experience, I can't recommend it too highly. Like cutting your toenails a little too close."

The body, this splendid body capable of amazing feats, expends and wastes itself. That's the way of the immortal struggle, the spirit-vs.-matter struggle. To try to preserve the body in some ideal form, or pretend it isn't falling apart, would be pathetic, exactly the wrong way to go. Willi talks frankly about the hemorrhoids that afflict him when he climbs mountains, calling them his "Achilles' anus," and he reports that he enjoyed a great advantage over Hornbein on Everest because "I had an enormous bladder. . . . [Tom] was just filling and emptying all night [while] I could go on an easy fourteen hours. We had a fancy French urinal [for use inside the tent at night] . . . it turned out my bladder was larger than the urinal. You have to devise a means, way down deep in your sleeping bag, of monitoring the flow exactly, and if you underestimate, as I sometimes did . . ."

The attitude that Roskelley, a *professional* climber, takes toward his body could not be more different. At the time of the *Outside* profile, Roskelley was "quite clearly in fantastic shape," according to Dave Roberts. "A typical day include[d] racquetball before breakfast, a seven-mile run at noon, and an hour or two on the Nautilus in the evening," he reported. Roskelley also lost some toes (one and a half, to be precise); again recalling Napoleon's maxim, about everything turning on a trifle, his injury was the result of borrowing a pair of boots too short for his feet during the Dhaulagiri expedition. Forty days before getting that peak's summit, Roskelley frost-numbed his feet while picking up air-dropped supply loads; despite the constant discomfort, and the fear he'd end up a cripple, he climbed in his usual gangbusters style, telling himself that "mountaineering is the process of finishing what one begins. . . .To leave now, before completing the climb, would only sharpen and deepen the pain."

Like Willi, like just about every aspiring mountaineer the last half century, Roskelley had read and been profoundly influenced by *Annapurna,* Maurice Herzog's thrilling account of the first ascent in history of an eight-thousand-meter peak, in 1950. Herzog and his partner, Louis Lachenal, both lost parts of their feet to frostbite, and Herzog also lost most of both hands. Roskelley accepted the terms of the climber's contract—that horrific maimings might result—but for him the idea of proudly displaying lost toes, or seeking meaning in the destruction of his wonderful body, was entirely foreign. As he became more of a professional, he became ever more systematic in calculating his needs and powers. Since intestinal ailments could weaken you up on a mountain, and a case of the sniffles turn into bronchitis, he became obsessive about what he ate, whom he allowed to cook for him, the water he drank, whom he slept around. He was a finely tuned machine ever in danger of breakdown (or sabotage). For Roskelley, going to high mountains was more and more about *getting the summit,* getting it efficiently and then getting the hell out of there, before suffering any damage or decay. You had your future to protect, as well as your person: other summits, other awe-inspiring routes you might put up, as you built a world-beating résumé.

Nick Clinch, who climbed with Willi in Pakistan, says that older climbers often accuse younger ones of lacking the "spirit of mountaineering." "As you find yourself consigned to doing easier and easier climbs," Clinch says, "there's always the vague, indefinable feeling that something's lacking in anyone who climbs any better than you do." But the difference between Roskelley's instrumental approach, largely pioneered in the seventies, and Willi's open-ended adventure style was real, and the disapproval ran in both directions.

"There was a subtle philosophical split," Willi told his audiences after Nanda Devi. "It seemed to take this form:

" 'Well, why do you climb mountains?'

" 'Oh, to get to the top.'

" 'Just to get to the top? I was afraid you'd say that.'

" 'Afraid? Why, what else is there, besides getting to the top?'

"Now, that's a tough one to answer. The discussion would then take this form:

" 'It's hard to say what those more important things are. But they're more important.'

" 'Hey, what are you, some kind of namby-pamby character? Looks to me like you're not very *gung ho,* know what I mean?'

"And then you'd say, still trying to think of those important things, 'Well, India's important. The people on the approach march. All of that's important.'

"And then the inevitable comeback: 'Oh, I know about those people. They're what we call "porters." '

"You see the split? You begin to get the idea?"

For his part, Roskelley couldn't abide the endless search for meaning. He was not an unfeeling sort of person, he wasn't stupid, or unobservant, and although tending to take an "Are you useful?" approach to making friends, he was loyal and an excellent companion to those who won his favor. But this embrace of everybody and everything, all this social engineering (women on the mountain, no fixed ropes, decision by consensus, and so on) struck him as a lot of hooey. It was the kind of hooey that you could get away with down in the flatlands, where life was inherently messy, but not up high where things became elemental, where everything matters and really counts. Part of Roskelley's love for hard climbing, maybe the largest part, was his need for a realm of consequences beyond the ordinary, where fine margins were crucial and someone smart enough to calculate them, and strong enough to do what had to be done, found a true home. The very *nature* of this realm was that it crushed those who were ill-prepared or softheaded or "spiritual," and indeed, this was its glory. It was beautiful just *because* it was severe.

For Willi, the harshness was a given, the fascinating mask worn by the Absolute. The *mysterium tremendum* lay beyond and taught its most important lessons by means of its potency, its fascinating hiddenness. "This dangerous power," as he said in his addresses, "is the origin of that 'fear of the Lord which is the beginning of wisdom.' When one is acted upon with such towering finality, one is forced to say with Job that 'my mouth is stopped with dust and ashes' and 'I am as dust in Thy sight.' "

He wasn't inclined to get the hell out as soon as possible; on the contrary, every moment he had in this realm was precious, potentially the moment when *the* insight might arrive, the life-transforming revelation. He loved the harsh austerities as much as Roskelley, for themselves but also as intimations of something greater. "For me God was no longer to be found in His traditional steeple houses," he said, "but rather seemed to dwell more vividly among the bare austerities of His . . . high places."

The trail goes up from Dibrugheta, then down, into the fabulous gorge. Great slopes descend thousands of meters, clad in tangled greenery. At a place called Deodi, right at the narrow bottom, they cross the Rishi Ganga by planks laid over rocks; the torrent, squeezed between high canyon walls, has a fire-hose power and bears the muddy runoff of the recent rains. Tilman and Shipton stopped here. Nearby is the grandest stand of birch in the entire Himalaya, and a lichen-spotted forest that entranced Shipton and others.

Roskelley tells his teammates about almost buying it a couple miles back, when, hiking ahead of everybody as usual, he got caught in a fall of Volkswagen-size boulders in a gully. The clear sunny weather—an anomaly in the full-on monsoon—makes every-body cheerful, and maybe they're being nice to each other because they're all a little bruised from the Marty episode, it got so ugly there. They bed down in two packed four-man Bauer tents, looking really like a team for a moment. Shortly after dawn, Roskelley zooms on ahead, accompanied by Lou Reichardt, climbing up the south flank of the gorge through rhododendron stands. Reichardt doesn't have to struggle to keep up; he may be fresh from his Har-vard lab, he may be recovering from a recent shoulder injury, he may look geeky and Abe Lincoln awkward, but those legs of his are prodigious. Reichardt, the other greatest American mountaineer of the seventies, the only one to be mentioned in the same breath with Roskelley (and possibly Jim Wickwire, a terrier-sized titan also from the Northwest), is quite evidently a man of probity, stolid and not much of a talker. On Dhaulagiri in '73, Roskelley and Lou were caught in a storm at 24,500 feet; over that ten-day period, "we . . . talked only once or twice," Roskelley later reported, "and that to obtain food from one another. I didn't really get to know [Rei-chardt] despite months on the same team. To know someone takes at least some conversation. . . . We weren't mad at each other, we just didn't have anything to say."

Reichardt is not just "any" Harvard neurophysiologist. His youthful work on gene expression—the way cells know to turn into the right thing, a muscle cell where muscle is needed, a nerve cell where nerve is—became the foundation for modern understanding of the phenomenon. On the basis of this work alone, Reichardt in his twenties emerged as one of the leading medical researchers of his era. More recently, he's been working on the ability of brain cells to adapt to changing conditions, a quality known as neuronal plasticity; his move into neuroscience from cell physiology has been a bit of a stretch, sort of like a golfer deciding to take up swimming, then immediately qualifying for the Olympics. "Lou is the smartest guy I've ever met," Roskelley told Geoff Tabin, a climber/writer who wrote a profile of Reichardt; and other people who have met him and have somehow gotten more than two words out of him have come away with the same impression.

Descriptions of Reichardt always mention his dishevelment, the scraggly, ill-cut hair and the eyeglasses held together with tape. Rick Ridgway, whose book *The Last Step* recounts Reichardt's successful climb of K2—he and Wickwire were the first Americans to summit—describes "the beard matted with sunscreen, the tufts of hair sprung out between his ski-goggle straps. . . . [Reichardt] had been given a beautiful Gore-Tex jumpsuit, as [all K2 expedition members] had, but he had left it behind in Skardu, saying, 'My red parka still has lots of use left.' " Reichardt may also be "the only climber to lug a backpack to the summit of Everest," according to Tabin, "with the airline luggage tags intact," and even in his high school days friends were remarking on his unusual awkwardness and on those "thick, greasy glasses."

Ridgway came to admire Reichardt deeply. But on K2 he also found him to be petty, competitive, eccentric, and utterly unknowable. "Lou was no ordinary man with ordinary drives," Ridgway observed; "he had some kind of devils running around inside, which apparently were exorcised [only] by brilliant accomplishment." Reichardt talked to himself. He blew his nose in his hand. Like Roskelley, he was always out front, the first up in the morning and on the trail; "for two days straight, [he] had carried heavy loads from Camp I direct to Camp III," Ridgway notes, "descending to Camp I in a single day. That was twice the distance the others were [covering]."

Reichardt is on the largish side: about six foot one, two hundred pounds. Part of the myth that grew up about him in the seventies concerned the fact that he never seemed to train; he rushed out of his office building still wearing a lab coat and immediately began climbing the highest, hardest mountains in the world. Roskelley, the professional, ran seven miles before lunch, but Reichardt trained by *doing* the thing he was supposed to be training for, and doing so only once in a blue moon, every few years or whenever his work permitted. "His only regular training is a three-block walk to the bus stop," Tabin declared in the eighties, "[followed by] a one-flight stair climb to his office. . . . Some say he must be a physiological freak, a person whose respiratory system is perfectly crafted for work at altitude."

Be that as it may, Reichardt's astonishing strength is quite obviously *inner,* too, a capacity summoned by a formidable will. "I was still puzzled," Ridgway wrote late on the K2 climb, "by what inner drives could be responsible for [Lou's] almost unbelievable motivation . . . [but] I at least had had several weeks to observe the empirical results of those drives—such as [always] forging on, when the rest of us were so close to turning back."

Above Deodi, the two men hike through fog, traversing the flank of the gorge. The mist burns off, but still they can't see the mountain they're aiming for, and they descend to cross a tributary stream, the Trisul Nala, where it thunders into the Rishi.* Roskelley crosses the river on a bridge made of branches. He positions himself a few yards upstream to take photos of the sahibs and goats as they come across. Willi also takes photos, Ad Carter takes photos, Peter Lev

---

Trisul is Sanskrit for *trident,* and the reference is to a three-pronged weapon that Nanda wields against the demons. Words in European languages, such as the English *trident,* often resemble Sanskrit words because of a common origin in an ancient mother tongue. Thus *devi* comes from the same root as the English *divine,* and both spring from the proto-European *div,* which means "to shine."

takes photos, Reichardt takes photos, and States takes photos, too; at any given moment, a photographic record is likely being made, for good or ill, from this viewpoint or that. Willi, Carter, Roskelley, and States will later give slide shows, and Roskelley has known for at least a year that he'll be writing a book, an honest-to-God book about the expedition, just the way Messner and Bonington have been writing their popular books in Europe. Roskelley will write a book because . . . well, because it's the thing to do. A professional mountaineer is an author, a lecturer, a product-endorser—whatever it takes to survive. He'll also be writing a book because there's a new feeling in climbing, a new *truth* that many people are trying to tell, all at the same time.

Before the seventies, climbing books were largely about heroism. Descriptions of the brave, hardy team. Accounts of noble sacrifice, of the marvelous esprit de corps. Even books about conflicted expeditions—the best example may be Hornbein's Everest book, about the West Ridge ascent—are really about heroism in a semi-conflictual context. (Hornbein's great hero, made to appear even slightly greater than himself, is Willi Unsoeld.) This heroism is of an ideal kind, not marred by psychological complexity or the tragedy that sometimes grows from complexity; the accidents are all of the terrible-shame type, crevasse falls, avalanches, dire acts of God. By the late sixties, early seventies, though, heroism was a discredited idea, to judge from the books that were being published in the new decade. Climbers continued to regard themselves as heroic, in secret, but a tell-all spirit consistent with the iconoclasm and anger everywhere present in modern society began to make itself known. Mountaineering accounts suddenly became stories of selfishness, greed, slacking off, and even outright cowardice.

A "literary" tone went with mountain writing in the old days. Here are a few samples taken from *The Naked Mountain,* by Elizabeth Knowlton, a well-known expeditionary account from the early thirties, about an attempted ascent of Nanga Parbat:

"[O]ne afternoon the Rajah of Astor held a polo match in our honor."

"We found traveling with a hundred and seventy coolies never exactly dull."

"The high and solemn beauty of the snow world could no longer penetrate into the little closed circle of concentrated emotion where the climbers were living . . . bound all around by the one fixed purpose—the ascent of the mountain."

"[L]iving for most of us was stripped bare . . . of all the ordinary range of interests and desires; so that, without any distraction, all the vital force in us went to feed the one essential flame."

Climbing was a *high* endeavor: morally as well as physically elevated. *Annapurna*, Maurice Herzog's book, offered less of a high-flown style, but heroism remained its essential subject.* About reaching the mountain's airy summit, Herzog wrote using simple words and phrases, focusing on the private or psychological reality of the experience: "[W]e went forward now as brothers. . . . I felt as though I were plunging into something new and quite abnormal. I had the strangest and most vivid impressions, such as I had never before known. . . . I smiled to myself at the paltriness of our efforts, for I could stand apart and watch myself making these efforts."

---

*An interesting book published in 2000, *True Summit,* by David Roberts, deconstructs Herzog's version of the Annapurna expedition, showing the many ways Herzog controlled the story that emerged after the team returned to France. The three most important of Herzog's teammates—Louis Lachenal, Gaston Rebuffat, and Lionel Terray—were professional guides, unlike Herzog, and each wrote an account of the climb that cast profound doubt on Herzog's version. Those other accounts, however, were suppressed, in one way or another, for many years. Herzog's book remains the most successful mountaineering narrative ever published, with 11 million copies in print in forty languages.

Furthermore: "The snow, sprinkled over every rock and gleaming in the sun, was of a radiant beauty that touched me to the heart. . . . An astonishing happiness welled up in me. . . . Everything was so new, so utterly unprecedented. It was not in the least like anything I had known in the Alps, where one feels buoyed up by the presence of others. . . . An enormous gulf was between me and the world. This was a different universe . . . a fantastic universe where the presence of man was not foreseen, perhaps not desired."

Herzog writes about heroism because heroism is what he believes should be remembered. For writers of the Himalayan golden age, the period when all the 8,000ers were climbed at least once, a book about fear, trembling, wetting your pants, and backing off would have been a nonstarter, like writing a baseball novel about a mediocre fielder who also can't hit. Herzog had a great story to tell, made great by the terrible obstacles he overcame, but animated at every turn by what the adventure revealed about the heart of Man, its stoutness, its indomitability, its vast reserves of fellow-feeling. His subjects is always Man with a capital *M* (and especially, French Man), the pluck and the lordly disdain for death of the true adventurer ever to the fore. *This* is what climbing is about, and this is what climbing books are for—to tell the world about this heroic essence.

Consider, then, a description of a casual discussion held on K2, in '77, during the American expedition led by Jim Whittaker. " 'Those two guys [fellow teammates] weren't too impressive this morning . . . Chris could be doing a lot better.' " (The book is Rick Ridgway's, and the speaker is Lou Reichardt. The teammates, Chris Chandler and Cherie Bech, have been spending a lot of time together—some people think they've become lovers.) John Roskelley, also along on this climb, observes, " 'I'm afraid it might be a repeat of what I've seen on other trips. . . . Every time I go on one of these big climbs with women it's the same. . . . I've seen them kill them-selves trying to prove they're as strong as men. . . . I've never yet been on a big mountain with one that's worth a damn.' "

Roskelley also announces, " 'I don't want to go out and rescue anybody and risk my own neck just because they shouldn't have been allowed in the first place. Dianne [Roberts, another woman on the trip] should not be allowed to go to Camp IV. . . . Everybody here knows the only reason she's along is because she's [Jim Whit-taker's] wife.' "

The shock is to hear people talking just the way they might talk in a business office, or on a construction site, without any pretense or much Christian charity, either. According to Ridgway's version, the K2 climb was a matter of rampant egos, infighting, men bad-mouthing women, and women striking back as they could. " 'I'm tired of hearing all this stuff about [my husband] being upset,' " screams Cherie Bech when Roskelley gets in her face about her romantic adventures. " 'You're all bastards. Bastards, bastards, bas-tards.' " Dianne Roberts, not in Roskelley's class as a climber, but no weak sister either, writes to friends back in the States, "It's funny how when you spend too much time with them even the nicest climbers start to drive you crazy. . . . We have so many prima don-nas. . . . When Jim tried to name [a summit team] the others called 'foul' and more or less refused to carry loads. . . . When a bunch of independent s.o.b.'s get stuck in their tents [by bad weather] some-thing weird happens. . . . Rather than blaming . . . fate . . . [they] start feeling victimized."

Heroism has clearly gone missing. Cherie Bech, whose husband is along on the climb, insists on her right to sleep with whomever she wants, right in front of her poor husband if she wants; Ros-kelley fumes, "Incompetents. Why in the hell do I always end up

Willi, leading fourth pitch, East Buttress of El Capitán, Yosemite, 1952.

Photo by Allen Steck

Willi, guiding in the Tetons, Wyoming, 1950s. *Photo by Bob and Ira Spring*

Unsoeld and Hornbein, Mount Everest, 1963. *Photo by Barry Bishop for* National Geographic.

LEFT: Unsoeld and
Hornbein, West Ridge
of Everest, 1963.
Photo by James Lester

BOTTOM: Willi, his feet
frostbitten, carried off
Everest by Sherpas, 1963.
Photo by James Lester

Devi and Willi Unsoeld, Cascades, early 1970s. *Photo by Bob and Ira Spring*

Devi and Willi Unsoeld, before leaving for Nanda Devi, 1976.
Photo by Seattle Weekly

Rishi Gorge, with Nanda Devi summit to the east. *Photo by John Evans*

The avalanche chute before Advanced Base Camp, Nanda Devi.
Photo by Peter Lev

with incompetents on these trips [when] [t]here are so many good climbers who wanted to come[?]"

Another vivid, tell-all book from the seventies, Galen Rowell's *In the Throne Room of the Mountain Gods,* speaks of an earlier attempt on K2, by many of the same people. Here we have again the egos, the cliques, the gut-churning resentments; everyone is frankly out for himself. "Dianne gained membership . . . wholly within one of the expedition's rigid pairs," Rowell notes, referring to the ever-contentious Roberts's ever-controversial marriage to Whittaker. "None of the rest of us really understood how she had transformed her original role as a trekker and photographer into that of a climber." Rowell, the prolific photojournalist, gets especially steamed when Whittaker orders him away from the window on a flyby of K2 so that Dianne can take her own "exquisite aerials." "Dianne and I developed a strong antagonism," Rowell notes, perhaps unnecessarily. "[She] considered me a hopeless chauvinist, and I thought of her as a rabid feminist."

All appear to have been reading too many books of exactly the kind in which they're now characters: expedition stories where only one or two people will get the top of the mountain, and everyone else will go home feeling screwed. A summit clique, resentfully called the Big Four by the others, emerges and seems to be rigging everything in its own favor. "[N]ow we were having more personal difficulties than I had ever experienced in all my years of climbing," Rowell writes about the clique and reactions to it. "[W]e weren't out . . . for enjoyment [anymore], using climbing as an escape from the stress of normal life. . . . [The expedition] had all the seriousness . . . of an eight-to-five job. [We had] thought of ourselves as individualists [but] now we were suddenly thrust together into a situation more socialized than a Chinese commune."

Rowell's tone isn't especially literary; certainly, it isn't heroic. He's just tellin' it like it is, even when the testimony goes against him personally. (Lou Whittaker, Jim's brother, on Rowell as teammate: "I've never heard a guy talk so much about everything and nothing.") The new tone implies a critique of the old. "Expeditions [in the past] etched their way into recorded history not so much by what they accomplished," Rowell asserts, "as by their public relations at home. . . . Gentlemen did not discuss personality conflicts, and therefore expeditions composed of gentlemen [appeared to have] no such conflicts. [In] the fictional world . . . of [early] expedition literature . . . emotions are reduced to pleasant simplicities. . . . Petty squabbles are absent. . . . The violence that takes place is of the clean, cartoon variety." And then, to really nail the indictment home: "Like children's dolls, all the characters have a noticeable absence of genitalia."

In the seventies, climbers will have genitals, whether or not they use them on the mountain. They will certainly have their petty squabbles, and they'll report on them almost proudly. The idea of acting like "gentlemen" in print or reality goes the way of the puttee, of the pipe-smoking Brit climber in a wool jacket. From now on it's the Me Decade, the Watergate age, a time of ripping the mask off all pretenders; climbers, like other groups in society, will tell ugly truths about themselves, believing this to be tantamount to telling The Truth. Along with this impulse to a brutal honesty comes an exaggerated self-consciousness and a tendency to believe only the worst, most vulgar things about the other guy. In other words: welcome to modern times.

....

EIGHT

Ramani, the name of the next camp up the gorge, means "joyous" or "beautiful." Here, at the narrowest part of the great canyon, the Seven Rishis escaped the demons, coming at last under the protection of the goddess Nanda. As the porters pass through the spectacular area, they claim to hear sounds coming from the Rishis' encampment: trumpets, drumbeats, the barking of ghostly dogs.

The gorge walls, thousands of meters high, form a slot only about fifty meters wide, through which the churning river vaults. Roskelley picks up a load of rope and gear and, with energy to burn, pushes on beyond Ramani, anxious to find a route up these slippery, fractured cliffs. An hour or two later, a few thousand feet higher up, he still has no view of the mountain Nanda Devi. In places the route is marked by lengths of old rope; other climbing groups have come this way, most recently a Japanese team that left fluorescent-red lengths fixed over some traverses.

Nanda Devi—maybe it should be called the invisible mountain— has only recently become a possible goal for climbers. Between 1951 and 1974, foreigners were forbidden to venture anywhere close, and only groups led by Indian nationals, such as an Indian army expedition of 1964, enjoyed access. But in '74 the "Inner Line" restrictions to the Sanctuary of the Blessed Goddess—an area composed of high meadows, glaciers, rockfalls, the great mountain itself—were lifted. A reverse flood of trekkers and porters then poured up the Rishi Gorge, bringing economic relief to the Garhwal, but at a cost to the area's exotic ecology.

The Sanctuary is an evolutionary marvel, a kind of Shangri-la. An early explorer described it as an immense saucer with an inverted teacup in the middle (the mountain itself); a more accurate image, Eric Shipton's, describes the basin as a reversed capital *E,* a main north-south ridge with three arms pointing westward. Nanda Devi is at the end of the short middle arm. The two longer arms curve toward each other at their ends, and the area within their embrace is some 250 square miles of rugged Himalaya. The area closest to the mountain, called the Inner Sanctuary, held a special fascination for explorers by virtue of all the trouble and years it took to get in there at all, and by reason of the splendid meadows discovered up high, where herds of blue sheep greeted Shipton and Tilman, the first humans to show up, with curious glances and no fear.

The "peaceable kingdom" environment supports the idea that the Sanctuary is truly sacred ground, an abode of goddesses and gods. The nearby slopes are home to serow (a goatlike antelope) and tahr (a wild goat with stout, recurving horns), as well as to musk deer and eagles and snow leopards, not to mention black bear and brown bear and the more common kind of leopard. Exotic edible herbs and mushrooms, some highly valued, attract plant gatherers along the routes forged by shepherds. The ring of subsidiary peaks creates a special subclimate; the enormous bottom arm of the *E,* facing the warm foothills and sun-baked plains of lowland India, takes the full brunt of the yearly monsoon, but on the other side a permanent mass of cold, drier air creates unique conditions, reducing cloud cover even during the worst of the storms and lessening somewhat the amount of yearly precipitation. Elsewhere in the Himalaya, climbing teams must follow a strict pre- and post-monsoon schedule, never venturing high during the period of heaviest snows, but on Nanda Devi "the climate of the inner sanctuary permits a certain latitude," according to a book promoted by the Indian forest ministry, which notes in passing that Tilman made his ascent of Nanda Devi on a brilliantly clear day in August, when storms were raging elsewhere.

Because the surrounding mountains protect the Sanctuary, meadows thrive at higher elevations than normal, and wildflowers are astonishingly abundant in summer. Yet this rainbow-hued splendor, so suggestive of an earthly paradise, exists within a stone's throw of glaciers and ice cliffs, adding to the feeling of dislocation that visitors often have, especially after a hard slog up the gorge. Roskelley, returning to Ramani after his exploratory climb on the cliffs—and still frustrated because unable to see the mountain—reports that the way ahead looks okay; all they have to do is follow the route he's just picked out, making use of ropes left in place by other parties. As darkness comes deep down in the gorge, Peter Lev walks into camp, along with Andy Harvard and Jim States. They've arranged for Marty to be coptered out (Ad Carter has remained behind to see to the details), and the crisis is officially over, for better or worse. "Even Peter admitted that he now felt sending her out was the right decision," Roskelley reports in his book, adding that Marty's symptoms hadn't abated in the few days since the decision.

Roskelley further notes, "We were all glad to see [Peter and Andy and Jim]. No matter the past differences, the anger, and the harsh words. The comradery [reduced] the loneliness and fear. Our relationships were tentative [however] . . . only during the expedition would we crave one another's company. Once back into the world, these relationships would trail off . . . [they were] fleeting."

The next morning, Roskelley, Reichardt, and States get out ahead again, following the route up the southside cliff. Roskelley tops out on a ridge ahead of his companions and sees a view that "I was not prepared for. . . . Dominating the entire skyline was the gigantic form of Nanda Devi. . . . Here was what we had come so far to attempt. The . . . Rishi Gorge framed the mountain's broad northern base, but she . . . reached up another ten thousand feet" above the Inner Sanctuary wall, itself over sixteen thousand feet in height.

The spectacular mountain announces itself as it wants, when it wants. With maximum drama, showing its profound power. While they were bickering their way up the gorge from Lata, *this* was waiting for them all the while. A great mountain seen at close quarters induces awe, fear, squirrelly excitement; it communicates to the very cells of those who would approach it, who dare dream of climbing it. Something about *mass* not learned in any physics course, some quality of *thingness* becomes shockingly evident. Nanda Devi seen from the northwest (Roskelley's perspective, and now Lou and Jim's as they join him on the ridge) shows a vast snowy wall, the Northwest Face, and atop this wall a camel-backed ridge with a vertical bite taken out of it: this bite has left a long, near-vertical rock wall very high up the mountain. Incomparably beautiful. Terrifyingly awesome. The minimal distortions of ten miles of thin atmosphere give the mountain a hyperreal quality, an aqueous vibrating *presence*, and the three men pay it respect for long moments.

"God," says Jim States at last, "God, that's impressive!" And then: "That's our route right there!" meaning the snowy face topped by the scary vertical cliff.

Roskelley has already been translating this vision into a doable climb, a series of discrete maneuvers. There are rock bands to surmount and a great deal of steep snow and ice, and finally that huge vertical bite, with the rock wall having the look of a buttress supporting the snowy summit pyramid. "The Buttress was clearly the crux of the climb," he will later write, hard technical climbing on mixed terrain at an elevation of over twenty thousand feet. And then, in stiff-upper-lip understatement: "Our work would be cut out for us."

Roskelley doesn't quail—no, he *thrills*. This may well prove to be a great route. An unclimbed, at-the-extreme-edge, true Himalayan challenge. Few people in the world stand a chance on such terrain, he believes. Oh, probably Messner could do it—the famous team of Messner and Habeler. (Peter Habeler, an Austrian, has been Messner's favorite partner since the death of Gunther Messner, Reinhold's younger brother.) Only last year, Messner and Habeler electrified mountaineers everywhere with a two-man ascent of an eight-thousand-meter peak done in only a matter of days. This obsessively prepared-for feat made a tremendous media splash, rewriting at a stroke the standards and possibilities of Himalayan climbing.

Among Americans, only Roskelley himself could lead this ground with confidence. (Maybe a couple of other guys, but they're not here, are they?) The elevation will make everything more difficult—prohibitively difficult for anyone not extremely fast and secure. Has this kind of technical ground ever been attempted before at such altitudes? Is there anything like it in the entire annals of climbing?

"We've got to send back for the fixed line," Lou Reichardt says, acknowledging the seriousness of what he, too, sees before them.

The others agree: this is not a route to be slogged up by duffers, by anyone capable of putting one foot in front of the other. Willi's golden dream of a fun route undertaken by a bunch of pals out for a lark must yield, because there's just no way to climb faces like this except by fixing thousands of feet of rope.

They set to scheming—they simply *must* get their hands on the spools left behind in New Delhi. By all means, they hope to avoid another massive group breakdown over all the maddening issues, fixed rope vs. climbing free and toilet paper vs. using your hand, and at just that moment Peter Lev heaves himself up onto the ridge-top and, just like them, registers with jaw-dropped astonishment what's before them. For Lev, in that instant, all of Willi's talk about Nanda Devi's beauty and spiritual intensity is borne out, but the vision has an unsettling effect on him. The palpable emanations from the Great Goddess Mountain are evil, he feels, not at all benevolent, and almost the first words out of his mouth are about how uncomfortable the sight makes him.

"I don't like the looks of it," he says flatly. "No, I don't like the looks of it at all."

Roskelley gets right to the point: they're going to need a ton of fixed rope, everything they left behind in New Delhi—it'll take every foot to give them any kind of a chance. A late-arriving member of the expedition, John Evans, a respected Colorado mountaineer and Outward Bound director, will be passing through New Delhi any day now (Evans delayed his departure for India to attend the birth of his second child), and maybe they can get a message out to him in time, and he can arrange for porters to carry the other spools in. Lev has been an enemy of fixed ropes since the group's first discussions, and all his career in the world's high mountains will demonstrate a peculiar mix of strength and skill and quiet dependability with something that looks to Roskelley like sheer laziness, or maybe stupidity: though he loves to be up among the world's great summits, going for the top, he *hates* fixed-rope climbing with a passion. "To me it was incredibly boring to string ropes up high," Lev later explained. "It was like being a construction worker, and I'd done enough of that . . . if you can't walk up it in the Himalaya, I'm just not interested. Piton after piton after piton, and standing around for hours belaying . . . no, I'm not interested now, and I wasn't then."

Yet Lev, seeing what awaits them—reading the features of Nanda Devi's great Northwest Face—changes his tune. "I hate to say it," he tells them, "but I was wrong, gang. Plain wrong. We're going to need all the fixed line we can get."

Roskelley rejoices—this is a crucial change of heart, and if Lev can be made to come around, maybe there's hope for all the others, Carter and Harvard and even Willi and Devi.* In short order, Elliot Fisher and Andy and Devi arrive on the ridgetop, and conversions break out all over—no one can look at that icy shadowed face, that severe snowy immensity, and *not* want a whole bunch of rope for fixing. Too damned scary. Too darned huge. Lev understands that they're in for the "climb of their lives," as he puts it to himself, and though he's a mountaineer through and through with the same kind of competence as Roskelley or Reichardt or Willi, this idea leaves him feeling strangely morose. Devi, like her father an opponent of fixed-rope ascents, takes one look and immediately understands Roskelley's point of view in a new way. She'd wanted to climb the mountain in classic style, with partners roped together and moving upward and downward in tandem, but the Bliss-Giving Goddess has revealed new aspects of her power, its true *dimensions,* and only someone without eyes to see could fail to understand.

---

*Lev, speaking to the author in 2001, recalled that he was still, at this point, hoping to climb the mountain by the 1936 route. What appeared to Roskelley to be a change of heart was only a concession about the technical nature of the northwest approach.

Unlike Lev, Devi feels excited. Incredibly eager. She's never encountered the mountain before except in photographs; she's lived
an entire life preparing for this moment, one might say, and the
impressions she takes now are richly thrilling. Like Roskelley,
though for different reasons, she's attracted rather than repelled:
she only wants to get closer, yes, as close as possible! And quickly!
An extraordinary thing happens: she who opposed the fixed ropes
sternly, who wanted an ascent au naturel or not at all, flies two
thousand feet right back down the cliff, aiming to catch Willi back
in Ramani, where he's paying off the *bhakriwallahs*. And she does
catch him before he sends the goatherds off, and she yells out to
him, "Dad, Dad—wait! Wait! We've decided we need more rope!
Yeah, the whole group's decided! We've got to get our hands on
the spools we left behind, and we need to send a message out with
the *bhakriwallahs!*" Willi greets this unexpected communication,
coming as it does from his radiant daughter, with bemusement but
with an open heart—if it were Roskelley hurtling down the cliff at
him, yelling about the fixed ropes again, well, that would be a different story.

Willi writes a note out for John Evans, ordering him to bring in
the extra spools. Another four thousand feet of line, enough, Willi
will later joke to audiences, to string a web over the whole mountain, like a cargo net on the side of a ship. But it's a group decision,
with even Devi behind it, and that's good—at least there's that to
be said for it. The goats and goatherds depart, and Willi slowly
begins climbing up the cliff that Devi just came down. His guts are
all aboil, bursting with the usual low-grade expedysentery—if he
didn't have all this suffering, if he had somehow escaped it this time,
he wouldn't really know what he was up to. Traveling in another
foreign land, eating funny food, and aiming, for the usual lack of
any sane reason, to climb a great mountain.

....

NINE

July 22: In sparkling weather, on a true blue-sky day, the Nanda Devi expedition enters the Sanctuary of the Blessed Goddess. To the left as the climbers follow a trail up through boulder fields and into the region of fabled, bee-buzzed meadows, a wall of dark cliffs guards the snowy upper reaches of the mountain. These cliffs, an ugly dripping mass of broken schists and other unstable garbage rock, rise four thousand feet straight up. There appears to be no way to climb them. For good measure, the headwaters of the Rishi race along the base of the cliffs. There appears to be no way to cross it, either.

For the moment, though, a kind of sweet lethargy overtakes the hardy mountaineers; they loll in the fragrant grass, by the babbling brooks, flower-struck and sun-demented. At a place called Sarson Patal they make Base Camp. This lovely, flowery, brooky place has collected a remarkable amount of trash in the mere two seasons since the Sanctuary was opened to foreign expeditions: a kind of mini-Everest South Col dump has formed with metal and plastic and paper and every other kind of junk offering the usual ironic commentary: "Here where the work of Nature is most divine, Man leaves his shameful corruption." The altitude, close to fourteen thousand feet, slows everyone down a bit. For once, Roskelley doesn't climb the farthest the fastest; no, it's Pete Lev who traverses a slope beyond the camp and, from a lookout at about sixteen thousand feet, examines the dark cliffs and the icy wonderworld above.

His verdict: there's no way through, none at all. Certainly there's no way to get the porters up those harrowing cliffs, carrying their bulky loads. To have a fair chance on this massive face, the expedition needs to get its supplies, about a ton and a half of stuff, up beyond the cliffs and onto the snowy ground above. Up there, at close to eighteen thousand feet, they can establish another camp, Advanced Base Camp; only from such a launching pad is there a chance of success on the heights above.

And not much chance. From Lev's lookout, it seemed that the top of the cliffs ran directly into a sheer ice-wall. No comfortable ledge or platform up there, no place to catch your breath and build a depot. A nearly hopeless proposition all around.

Roskelley, who hasn't blown his stack in at least a day or two, hates this sort of defeatist talk. In one of the four-man Bauer tents, all of them lying around, discussing options, he gets steamed when Willi points out that it isn't written down in blood that they have to climb Nanda Devi by *this* route, up *this* particular daunting face. Hey, not so fast there! Roskelley wants to say. No one's going to snatch this beauty away from him if he has anything to do about it; they've come here to try something noteworthy, something suitable for writing up in the journals, and by God, they're not going to give up so soon. "Bullshit!" he roars at the very idea of pushing on farther into the Sanctuary, then climbing the south side of the mountain by the tired old anniversary route, the one from 1936. All very well for these others, these superannuated specimens like

Willi and Ad Carter, and these mountain-huggers like Devi and Andy, who only want to get up on the slopes a ways and then have some kind of "experience"—but for him, John Roskelley, climb professional, anything less than an extreme objective won't do.

"You can never tell from a first view of a mountain," Devi says soothingly, hoping to prevent a full-scale blowup but also speaking simple wisdom. "We're too far away to know if the cliffs are unclimbable, and for that matter, exactly what's up there on top of them." The mountain has a mysterious face, off-putting at first but containing possibilities. She already saw this about it, when she first glimpsed it from afar.

In the morning, under low clouds, Roskelley and Reichardt seek the impossible, a way across the Rishi and up the cliffs. And as if a playful Providence were chiding them for their foolish fears, everything falls into place. Avalanches cascading down from above have deposited snowy debris in the river chasm, forming a plug that serves as an icy but adequate bridge. They cross, hardly believing their good fortune. On the other side they choose a steep gully not full of avalanche leavings—therefore less likely to be a deadly trap as they climb it—and ascend on steep, broken, but passable rock up and up into the low-hanging clouds. The gully ends, but just in time they find a way to traverse out of it, to a rib of rock separating the gully from another one alongside, and by climbing an airy rib they discover another godsend of a feature, a narrow walkway heading up and into yet a third gully, a broad, easily angled one, a veritable highway to the top. After only three or four hours they've solved the great problem, passed the impassable cliffs! Onward they push, after making radio contact with Willi thousands of feet below. O ye of little faith, rejoice: all is not lost, and the doubters have been confounded.

"Great! That's just great!" Willi cries into the radio, relieved and, despite what he said the night before, excited to be making headway here, on this fabulous unclimbed face, and not on the old route from '36. "Aw, that's just great, Lou, really great! Good work, John! Terrific!"

"We not only have a route," Roskelley adds, "we have one for the porters. We only have to fix a few steep sections and they can climb it, too." Everyone agrees that this is great, wonderful and truly great.

For Roskelley, "the route was too easy to believe," as he later noted in his book. In the mountains, hopelessness and danger can resolve in a moment; things do sometimes magically work out. The challenge is to know how to interpret such strokes of fortune. The rational, utilitarian way is to credit yourself with having done something right, persevered when the going got tough, used good judgment; in the current situation, having pushed on, refused to despair, refused to give up without seeing if it just might go—this, obviously, was the right thing to do.

But a shadow interpretation often slips along in the wake of this rational, defensible one. Am I favored—are my steps being marked out by Fate? Is some special destiny guiding me, have I been granted this break so that I may feel encouraged, will persevere and realize my sweetest, most fantastic dreams? Even the most rational climber or long-distance solo sailor or Himalayan para-glider registers during a difficult and possibly fatal adventure the signs of metaphysical favor (or its absence). You don't have to believe in destiny, or the hand of God, to notice when things are falling in place incredibly well, when "something" is on your side and you can do no wrong.

Probably the most fiercely rational—certainly the most scientific—member of the expedition, Lou Reichardt, was once the beneficiary of an act of God as perplexing as any in the history of mountaineering. In 1969, on an expedition to Dhaulagiri, Reichardt was climbing with seven companions in the icefall of the mountain's Southeast Glacier, installing a bridge across a crevasse; surrounded by his companions, he began taking photos, then, as he later described it in his diary, "[T]he noise of an avalanche [reached us], then a mutual realization that it might hit us." Reichardt dove for a shallow depression in the snowfield. The avalanche passed over him, merely roughing him up a bit. He got to his feet, ready to laugh about it with his companions, but there was "just silence. . . . I was not hurt [so] it couldn't have been that bad[I thought]. Then came the discovery that nothing was there—no tents, no cache, no ice ax, and no friends. . . . Hey, Boyd! Hey, Dave! Hey, Vin! I'm alive and OK. . . . Just let me know where you are."

The snowfield had been swept clean. Reichardt's seven companions, with all their gear, had vanished from the face of the earth. The crevasse they'd been building a bridge over, using logs, had filled with tons of snow and ice at precisely the point where they'd been trying to cross it; as if the mountain, or avalanche, were an evil jokester, it had done their work for them in one monstrous, mocking stroke. Reichardt searched frantically by himself and later with other expedition members who had been at Base Camp. Nothing was ever found. The expedition collapsed, understandably, and Reichardt returned to the United States in a "pretty blown away" condition. Unable to resume his scientific work, he spent months crisscrossing the country, visiting the families of his lost teammates.

Reichardt has said, "The Himalaya weren't really in my life plan." A lab rat, a powerful thinker, someone at the threshold of an epochal research career, he fell into climbing while a grad student at Stanford, going on jaunts to Yosemite and other Western rock-playgrounds. He climbed a few times in Alaska, but his inclusion in the '69 Dhaulagiri expedition was a last-minute, fluky thing—"I think I got to go because I was the only one without a real job," he once told an interviewer. Deeply remarkable, then, that four years after the awful tragedy he chose to return to the Himalaya—and to Dhaulagiri, its southeast side. The '73 climb—the personnel included Roskelley, Harvard, and Lev—was for Reichardt a gesture toward his lost friends, whose shrine he visited on the trek to the mountain, but it was also an embrace of a radically redefined "life plan," one that included the Himalaya most emphatically, as talisman and defining focus.

As far as Himalayan summits go, it's certainly true that "many are called, few are chosen." But what does it mean to be chosen—or, rather, to *feel* chosen? For someone of Reichardt's temperament, climbing the world's highest mountains presents an abundance of the kind of problem that research scientists (and chess players and computer programmers and crossword puzzlers) relish, multifactorial conundrums where each element depends on the others in complex and novel ways. The thrill, for such practitioners, comes from teasing out a possible solution at the very border of knowledge, counting on some basic lawfulness of the physical world in one of its most chaotic, most threatening forms. Will this slope avalanche—how tired am I—will my partner have the guts for this—how much food is left at Camp VI, and will the monsoon arrive tomorrow—how long I have been up here at twenty-five thousand feet, and does that mean that my brain's dying, therefore all my calculations are off? The great pleasure, for many who love the high peaks, comes from engaging with these knotty questions, then having to act immediately and in the most direct and consequential way, betting your survival on the belief that you've come up with a good answer. As Reichardt told an interviewer, "You live on the edge, figuring out what you need to do to stay on the right side of the line. Science is sort of similar."

But what about that feeling of being "chosen"? Even the most scientific head, the most antimystical or atheistic type, by virtue of going to the high mountains at all evinces faith in a kind of destiny, a feeling that he won't be among the one in ten Himalayan climbers who dies, among the hundreds lost in modern times. The belief in special destiny can take many forms: a sense, or desire to prove, that one is made of the toughest physical material; an intuition about glory to be won; a feeling that your true character, wonderful and exemplary, will at last be revealed up high, to yourself and the world. Not everyone climbs to fulfill a sense of destiny, but for most mountaineers the effort to get to the Himalaya at all, and then to have an actual chance at a great summit, is so extreme that thoughts of "something" guiding one's wayward steps are inevitable.

And for another type of climber—one not opposed to meta-physical speculation—climbing can be *largely* about the encounter with destiny. I am here because I love the sport, I worship the heroes of the past, and I've paid my dues, mastered the necessary skills; I intend to prove myself a dependable member of this expedition, but in the meantime, isn't that the cosmos sending me a signal? Revealing the special path that's always been marked out for me? All truly extreme efforts, in extreme environments, are attempts to get right up into the face of God—to give it only one of many possible names—in hopes of catching a flicker of recognition. Daily, the high-altitude climber or transoceanic solo sailor deals with discrete problems, attacks them directly and survives or fails to because of his clearheadedness; but in a larger sense, such endeavors always pose another question: Am I unique? And is this my unique, my providential way?

Ernest Hemingway, in his story "The Snows of Kilimanjaro," about a man dying of gangrene, wastes no breath on ideas like destiny or God and instead locates the fate that each man has squarely in his own character, in his willingness to cheat on the things that really matter. The universe is replete with tragic out-comes, and the mystery is how we sometimes avoid them for so long. Hemingway's hero, an aging, rueful writer much like Hemingway himself, succumbs in an atmosphere of all hope destroyed, illusions shredded, wisdom won but deeply bitter in the mind. But the story begins with a remarkable epigraph, one that posits an alternate view—one that insists on seeing life as inseparable from the urge to find one's way in it, to puzzle out one's unique path:

> Kilimanjaro is a snow covered mountain 19,710 feet high, and it is said to be the highest mountain in Africa. Its western summit is called the Masai "Ngàje Ngài," the House of God. Close to the western summit there is the dried and frozen carcass of a leopard. No one has explained what the leopard was seeking at that altitude.

Following the great breakthrough, the ascent of the cliffs, the team mobilizes to get the porters and all the supplies up to what becomes known as Ridge Camp, at 17,700 feet. All the gear is repacked, and then the porters have to be cajoled into carrying loads up the broken rock of the gullies. Willi, in Ad Carter's continued absence, directs all the efforts. He carries heavy loads up himself, as do most of the other sahibs.

July 24: Toward the end of a day of carries and exploration, Ad Carter walks into Base Camp. The sixty-two-year-old is in splendid form, having walked from Dibrugheta in a mere forty-eight hours. The Inner Sanctuary, with its fabulous flower fields, has inspired him to take many photos, and at a team meeting that evening he reveals that the expedition's finances are in better order than expected, so not to worry on that score. Marty went out in the chopper, and maybe attending her these last few days has put Ad in mind of his own dear companion, Ann Carter, whom he last saw weeks ago in Delhi, laid up with a bad back. Maybe he misses her or is worried about her. At the meeting, Willi announces that Ad has decided that "his usefulness to the expedition is over at this point," and that he will be "leaving the Sanctuary in a week or two." In other words, good-bye to everyone, and good luck.

Expeditions sometimes lose climbers, to accident or sickness. They lose porters all the time, and teams may split apart and work against themselves, sabotaging the group effort. But expeditions abandoned by a team leader are extremely rare—almost unheard of, in fact. Not to mention that the team leader in this case is a towering figure, an honored elder of North American mountaineering. Someone in apparent good health and of sound mind.

Ad's decision is shocking. No one likes it, and no one really understands it. Is it simple petulance? Does it go back to the early arguments and Roskelley's big mouth? Does Ad secretly despise these modern climbers with their soulless disregard for classic style, their obsession with career-making routes? But he's been the editor of the *American Alpine Journal* for years, he knows everything that's going on in climbing, and he hasn't shown himself to be a retrograde critic.

And what about Devi? A year ago, she returned from travels in Asia and landed in Ad's living room in Massachusetts, where together they hatched this idea for a Nanda Devi ascent. Devi and her siblings and Willi and his wife are close friends of the Carters'— the two families, one New England, the other Pacific Northwest, more or less bracket the country and the possibilities for Americans passionate about the mountains. Ad's a little older than Willi and starchier, but the yodeling, bearded, slouch-hat-wearing wildman from the West has always awakened an affectionate response in the Milton Academy schoolmaster, who sounds, even sort of looks, like the British actor John Mills. They understand each other. What's not to understand: they're both educators, Protestants, ironic idealists; they both can talk, with amused earnestness, about things that really matter. Indeed, Willi, for all his dusty-vagabond ways and counterculture style, has always registered well with Eastern establishment types—this is why Sargent Shriver, head of the Peace Corps, could talk to him for an hour on a plane flight once and immediately name him deputy director in Nepal.

But again—what about Devi? Carter stands in relation to Devi almost as a fond uncle, and it was Ad with whom she felt sufficiently supported to propose this expedition. Ad himself climbed (but did not quite summit) Nanda Devi at exactly the same age that Devi is now; the Bliss-Giving Goddess has been an important theme in his own life, a source of meaning for him. How does Ad then simply back out on her?

That Me Decade stuff, that new "I've gotta satisfy myself" ideology, keeps popping up in the strangest of places. In the actual essay by Tom Wolfe, published in *Mauve Gloves & Madmen, Clutter & Vine* (1976), the new American selfishness emerges as a consequence of the post–World War II economic boom. The vogue for talking about me, obsessing about me, *my* needs for once, forget about yours, is deplorable but also oddly spiritual, according to Wolfe, the basis for a new godly refulgence. The common man in America at last has enough money and leisure to do what privileged people have been doing all along, looking to their own satisfaction, and the explosion of encounter groups and UFO cults and hippie communes and psychedelic drug-taking has led to a typically American eruption, a Third Great Awakening.

The first two Great Awakenings came in the eighteenth and nineteenth centuries, when ecstatic Holy Roller–type revivalism swept through American communities like prairie fire. Wolfe argues that the social innovations of the late sixties and early seventies add up to much the same thing. Sexual liberation, Gestalt therapy, Jesus-freakism, transcendental meditation: as different as they may seem, each is an example of the relentless, not to say demented, American search for authenticity, for an ecstatic mystical core.

Ad Carter, of all people, would seem a poor candidate for inclusion in a such a frenzy. His life has been about responsibility, services rendered and duties shouldered without complaint, to the benefit of large numbers of people sometimes (whole generations of Milton students, all the readers of the *AAJ*). Yet here he is, perplexing his friends and his enemies alike. Especially in view of what's to come for the expedition, Ad's decision to deprive them of his steady head and hand at this juncture looks deeply wrong—surely the atmosphere of the times, the self-indulgent seventies, has *something* to do with it.

Wolfe's essay says that Americans, regardless of age, are much alike: we tend to be believers, not atheists; individualists, but joiners, too; above all, sinners looking for a way out. Central to our quests is the belief in a divine spark, something irreducibly good within each of us that partakes of overarching heavenly glory. This is an idea common to almost every religious cult ever founded, from gnosticism through medieval antinomianism to the Methodism of John Wesley. Primitive American sects—the talkers-in-tongues, the Shakers, the Mormons under Joseph Smith—sought a direct hookup to the cosmos, and sometimes all that writhing and stomping led to sin. Too bad, but the point was to open up, drop the repressive social conditioning and become gloriously brimful with spirit.

Willi is well schooled in all this. He's had the benefit of a seminary education, and he himself has felt the call: but for the objections of his wife, who came from a religious family and had had enough of churches, he might well have ended up a Methodist or Episcopal minister, an open-collared, let's-have-fun type pastor in the suburbs somewhere. As he once said to Allen Steck, a well-known California climber, "We're on good terms, God and I." Willi understands that inner-spark business, the search for direct experience of the mystery on high. His faith is fundamentally Christian despite his early encounters with Eastern religion, and like John Wesley he's a believer in salvation through faith rather than election, in the possibility of Christian (or Buddhist or Jewish or Zoroastrian) perfection. He's impatient of orthodoxy and ritual ("I really concentrated at the altar rail, staring up . . . nothing, just nothing") and has always put more credence in personal experience than in received doctrine.

A believer of Willi's type enjoys a giddy, but also terrifying, freedom. He makes his own religious practice, relying on feelings and intuitions to establish a higher truth. But intuitions and feelings may be faulty. More to the point, how do we distinguish "correct" religious experience from "incorrect"? How can we prove, for example, that your ecstatic heavenly insight, which came to you after years of prayer, is valid, whereas mine, which came to me after I drank a fifth of Scotch, is an illusion? How do we know that the fiery idea you have of God, which includes the belief that He reveals Himself in nature, in the glories of the snowcapped, mystic mountains, is genuine and not just some shopworn idea you got out of a book? Religious revelations *always* feel original, they *always* seem intensely true, but that doesn't mean they are.

Carter, abandoning the expedition, probably wasn't thinking about all this; but his unexpected decision, like Willi's freestyle orientation toward faith, ended up being powerfully relevant to all that was to come. "The route was too easy," Roskelley wrote later, but too easy is surely better than too hard; and for those inclined to find omens in such things, the break they've just gotten on the shattered cliffs is full of meaning. Maybe their way to the top has been "revealed" to them. Maybe success has been written for them all along, and they've only needed to claim what was always gloriously theirs.

TEN

Elliot Fisher, Ad's young protégé, the Harvard Medical School student, is in a dark mood. All along he's been secretly doubtful about the expedition, bothered by thoughts of catastrophe, and now that Ad has announced that he's turning back, the whole point of the thing seems lost. Back home in Cambridge Elliot has a girlfriend, a future; here he has . . . a chance to die. On his first carry up to Ridge Camp he's gloomy, and Jim States points out the positive features of the route, that the slopes up above Ridge aren't as steep as they looked from below, that climbers will be safe from avalanches on this broad terrace. But Elliot doesn't cheer up. He talks again and again about going home. For States, and for Roskelley, this is bad news not because they're so fond of Elliot, but because another defection at this point could destroy team morale.

They need load-carriers—live bodies for the assault on the upper slopes. The delicate psychology of factionalized seventies-style expeditions works something like this: the hard-men get out early, impressing everyone, including themselves, and establishing their superiority. They self-select for the summit in two main ways: first, by showing just how physically and mentally superior they are, and second, by generating an intense esprit, a feeling within their little group alone that everyone else senses and comes to resent. Feeling excluded and implicitly put down, those not accepted in the lead faction pull back—after a while they'd sooner cut their own throat than ask to be included.

This odd pattern marked any number of expeditions, especially American ones, in the seventies. Two attempts to climb K2, in '75 and '78; the Pamirs expedition in '74; Nanda Devi in '76; an international Everest attempt ('71) on the Southwest Face: again and again the same dynamic, with the anger and self-righteousness often achieving blastoff level around the issue of women. In these same years, some people also climbed amicably, even enjoyably. In '74, Nick Clinch, with whom Willi had climbed Masherbrum, led a friendly trip to Paiyu Peak, in the Baltoro region of the Karakoram. Clinch's presence on an expedition, and his organizing talent, worked like a magic charm from the early fifties into the seventies; with Clinch adding humor and unstuffy decency to the mix, teams enjoyed success on Hidden Peak as well as Masherbrum (the two highest first ascents ever by Americans). Also in these years, as noted before, women were succeeding on respectable Himalayan routes—the Polish Ladies' Expedition in '75 included men as well as women, and its successes included three ascents of Gasherbrum II, by three separate routes, in thirteen days. (One of these climbs was the first ascent of an 8,000er by women alone.)

The monsoon of '76, as it affected the Himalaya, was peculiar. It was late in coming, and articles in the *Times of India* wondered what in the world had become of it. On July 7, an article in the *Times* introduced the Indo-American Nanda Devi Expedition, then passing through New Delhi, to the newspaper's vast readership. Devi Unsoeld was the focus of the report. "For the twenty-two-year-old American blonde," the article began, "the very idea of setting foot on Nanda Devi is a dream come true." "I feel a very close relationship with Nanda Devi," the blonde is quoted as saying. "I can't describe it but there is something within me about this mountain ever since I was born." Amidst articles about the hijacking of an Israeli jetliner to Uganda, the death of a great Chinese military hero, and a visit undertaken by the Indian prime minister, Indira Gandhi, to Afghanistan, the *Times* report rehearses the remarkable story of an American girl named after an Indian mountain, one that she now aims to climb. "Devi's father, Dr. Willy Unsoeld, will lead the expedition to the peak which he first saw in 1948," the article explains. " 'He was so impressed by the beauty of this mountain,' says Devi, 'that he decided then to name his first daughter after the peak. He got his opportunity in 1954.' "

July 26: The late monsoon meant drier conditions on the long hike up the gorge. But a few days after Ridge Camp is established, the first monsoon tempest arrives, dropping a foot of snow. On this second day of heavy rains down below and warm snow above, Roskelley and Reichardt carry loads between Ridge and Advanced Base, along a path marked out by Reichardt and Lev. Both camps are at about 17,800 feet, but they're separated by half a mile of unique geography. Ridge Camp is on a great, broad, broken ridge running almost all the way up the mountain. Advanced Base is also on a kind of ridge, vast and discontinuous; the two ridges veer slightly away from each other, and the area between them, a rough square mile of steep terrain in the shape of a titanic V, contains the entire Northwest Face. Snow falling high up that face sloughs downward through the V. Not far from its bottom is the snout of a steeply angled glacier: this feature consists of ice cliffs over which the snow from the upper slopes relentlessly pours. The short walk between Ridge and Advanced Base, an easy scamper in terms of distance and terrain, unfortunately passes right beneath that snout.

Crossing on the twenty-sixth, Roskelley feels "creepy" but notes an absence of movement above. Reichardt and he leave their loads and return to Ridge Camp. That evening, during a radio call to Willi at Base, an avalanche, a *monster,* thunders down and over the snout. Reichardt has to pause in his radio transmission because of the noise. And go on pausing. It takes fifteen minutes for the whole thing to cascade through.

That same evening, a second monster roars and crashes and un- nerves as it sweeps the face, to be followed by lesser avalanches throughout the night. "By the next morning," Reichardt wrote in an article for the *AAJ,* "these ledges [where the climbers had crossed] were under twenty feet of avalanche debris. Suddenly, we understood how that mysterious ice bridge across the Rishi Ganga had been formed. The avalanches had traveled down four thousand vertical feet of rock below the glacier to cover flowers on the Sanc- tuary floor."

"Never again," Roskelley declares in his book, "did we feel safe carrying to Advanced Base." The climbers have crossed on the very day when the gully becomes hellishly dangerous, when the simple scamper turns into a desperate writhe through giant snow blocks. The monsoonal schedule, a thing of planetary systems, vast storms, the convulsions of entire mountain faces, operates this time with a kind of eerie precision, as if Nanda Devi were offering a demon- stration of its moodiness. "My gut response," Reichardt wrote in his article, "was queasy. Crossing the slide zone took twenty minutes each way. Virtually everyone tried to run. Coming back was always the worst. 'There is no choice at that point. You are left with the horrible suspicion [that] you made a bad mistake that morning.' "

Because John Evans, the missing team member, still has not ar- rived, Willi names Reichardt the climbing leader on the mountain.

This involves deciding who carries when, who occupies the next camp up, and so forth, and in practice it means that Reichardt must from now on negotiate between the factions, resolve the irresolvable, square the circle. Willi's choice is an inspired, if inevitable, one. Only from Lou Reichardt, that stalwart driven character, lost in arcane thought while climbing like a colossus, will the others accept such potentially fatal decrees as "Six carries for everyone"—six carries, in however many days it takes, across that nightmare stretch, the jumbled death-zone under the snout.

July 27: After Reichardt and Roskelley carry, in great fear, early in the morning, Jim States and Elliot arrive again at Ridge, with porters. Jim has attached himself to Elliot by a sort of instinct: troubled youths, souls in torment, anyone on the verge of a nervous breakdown finds in Dr. States a compassionate answer. Back home in Spokane, States is a counselor to kids with big problems, junkies and others out on the street, but Elliot's suffering is real, too—he's painfully torn between a desire to get the hell out, save his own neck, and a sense of responsibility to the others. Every day now, usually in midafternoon, it snows, a heavy warm snow that accumulates and then breaks free, in capricious, terrifying cascades. Elliot is shaken down to his toes by the magnitude of some of them, the way the whole world seems to be crashing down on their heads. He shares his fears with Devi and Willi as well as States, and Willi opines that the best thing for Elliot to do is just to tough it out— the mountain's a character-builder, a way to discover who you *really* are, and if he bails out now he may never forgive himself.

July 28: In the morning Elliot carries a load down to the edge of the avalanche gully. States, Reichardt, and Roskelley also carry down to the edge. No one can make himself move out on the ice, though. As Roskelley described it later to Laurence Leamer, he was more frightened than he had ever been before on a mountain. The feeling was of having no control: "I've never turned around and not done something because I was scared. But the fear of the avalanches had me. I knew nothing I could do about it."

Reichardt moves out at last; hurries across. There's a downside to being the climbing leader: you must do what must be done, in front of all. But no one follows him. It's just too damned scary. They leave their loads at the edge and go dejectedly back up to Ridge Camp.

Roskelley's book, published five years after Leamer's, amends this account slightly. "I carried down to the gully alone an hour later, ashamed of myself for not forging ahead that morning with Lou," it says. "I made the crossing and returned to camp with some dubious self-respect restored." In the version he gave Leamer, however, Roskelley recalled that for several days he was unable to cross. The point is not that John Roskelley, as determined and bold a climber as America produced in those years, airbrushed his behavior for the sake of readers, but that even *he* might fall into a petrified state when confronted by the gully. *Not* to experience a crisis of some sort would have been a sign of ignorance or possibly dementia. And in the end, Roskelley does carry cross, many times, with many loads; he tries to do so early in the morning, when the upper face is in its most frozen condition, thus less likely to avalanche.

Elliot's unable to cross, though, and remains so for days. His moral crisis has been given a precise physical form: it's a patch of mountain terrain about four hundred yards wide, a few hundred yards deep, and directly beneath the snout of an active glacier. Not so far across, really, and if you sit on the rocks at the edge for hours at a time, as Elliot does, an infinite number of moments pass when it *would* have been safe to hurry across, and you feel stupid as the others seize those moments, quietly suppress their panic, and carry safely to the other side. Devi goes across, Pete Lev does, States does; on the morning of the twenty-ninth, Jim crosses with a load, then crosses back in the other direction and sits down next to Elliot, puts his arms around him, and urges him to do what he's capable of, what the situation requires, what will make him feel much better to have done.

Devi hauls her loads without much fuss. She isn't in Roskelley or Reichardt's league as a gainer of summits—after all, she's only twenty-two—but she's been climbing since early childhood in the Cascades, Nepal, Wyoming: yes, she's Willi Unsoeld's daughter, all right. This kind of situation makes sense to her, as unnerving and uncertain as it is. Avalanches make sense to her, because she's seen what they can do; living in windblown tents, climbing in miserable weather make sense, because she knows them. She's solicitous of Elliot, hoping he'll continue; playfully she tries to voice his deepest fear, telling him that the roar of the avalanches is the sound of the mountain itself, saying that there's no escape, that he must climb across or die. But Elliot can't be shaken out of his crisis.

The Indian team members, Captain Kumar and Sergeant Nirmal Singh, of the Indian Mountaineering Federation, cross the zone late in the day sometimes; like everyone else they hurry but have a hard time picking their way through the jumbled ice debris, expecting at every moment to see an avalanche pouring over the snout. Roskelley reports a crossing when, with the expedition cook, Surrendra, in tow, the two officers exit the zone just as a big one roars down, wiping out their newly made tracks. But the most cavalier crosser of the mind-bending gully is Willi, there's no contest. He carries many times, yodeling as the spirit moves him. Not hurrying so much; appearing not to be afraid at all. Pete Lev, an avalanche expert, can't believe what he sees. One afternoon, with several porters following, Willi sets out just when Reichardt, at a higher camp, is radioing down that a great avalanche is sweeping the face. According to Jim States, who witnessed events from Ridge Camp, "Willi waited for the big one to pass, then walked on through that mad shooting gallery. The porters had minimal training on ice and snow . . . they were lowlanders, inexperienced. . . . Willi's attitude was that he *knew,* he simply knew, in the way that a perfect master knows. I found that questionable."

At who knows what expense of effort—because one man's hill is another's Everest—Elliot finally does cross, after days of torture. Part way over he suddenly hears and feels it: an avalanche, a real one, roaring down the face. Why at *this* moment, among the infinity of moments that he didn't choose—moments that turned out to be perfectly safe? He starts to run as fast as he can. At over 17,500 feet, to run all-out is to bust a lung, maybe kill yourself that way, and as ice blocks and a plume of white roar over the snout he throws himself behind a rock, and the avalanche engulfs the spot where he was, who he was, just seconds before. He laughs. He laughs and laughs.

Why Willi wasn't afraid, why he trusted *his* selection of moments, goes to the heart of who he was. It can be explained in terms of forty years of climbing and paying attention to conditions and learning what works, or it can be explained by saying that he was a woolly-headed madman who was very lucky.

It remains mysterious. What was he really doing, yodeling and sauntering across at the wrong time of day, in the monsoon season, with the litter from dozens of avalanches all around? To say that he was tempting fate doesn't really answer, because to be on the mountain at all at that time was a temptation. Willi was a teacher, Ad was a teacher, Devi and Elliot and Andy were students, and

they had chosen to climb Nanda Devi during their summer vaca-
tion. Tilman's expedition in '36 climbed the mountain at about the
same time of year, so they knew it was possible. (But Tilman's
group faced ordinary monsoon conditions and may have benefited
from the protective effect of the Sanctuary's wall of outlying peaks.
The monsoon of '76, though late, was the heaviest in over a hundred years.) Willi's boldness made an impression on the others,
some of whom were appalled. Pete Lev has noted that "everything
Willi did was a statement," that he "created a persona that wasn't
exactly equivalent to the person underneath. He was a public figure
when there was an audience out there, even a small one . . . one-
on-one, though, no posturing."

Furthermore: "It was always great to see Willi. His arrivals in
camp, his appearances up on the face . . . his presence made you
feel strong. I had some of my best days in the mountains climbing
with him. . . . I came to look up to him, which I don't say about
many men."

It was a gesture, then—a statement. But a statement directed at
whom? In *The Merchant of Venice,* a character named Gratiano
remarks to Antonio, the merchant who will end up owing a pound
of flesh to Shylock:

> *You look not well, Signior Antonio,*
> *You have too much respect upon the world:*
> *They lose it that do buy it with much care . . .*

Willi's jokes and yodeling and harmonica-playing suggest a spirit
inclined not to make that error. The *encouraging* nature of his presence had something to do with not losing the world through excessive care, responding to peril with a certain insouciance. We who
are about to die will now play the "Colonel Bogey March." Speak-

ing of an incident later on the climb, at a site not far below the summit, Lev said, "Willi arrived at the high camp in great spirits. Everyone looked at him and immediately felt better."

Or maybe Willi wanted to die. In the months before his departure for India, he often mused about what it would mean not to return. As reported by Leamer, he told friends, "I have a fantastic body, and I've made ultimate use of it. And now it was beginning to rebel as it had every right. And so . . . it seemed appropriate . . . to cast off the booster rocket. I was ready. I saw nothing particularly reprehensible about going out with honor."

Devi worried about her father, as his attitude made itself known in the family. Her mother was confident that Willi *might* come back from the trip, just might. Devi's brother Regon also picked up on Willi's endgame frame of mind; according to Willi, "[M]y eldest son is very sensitive to these things. . . . And he sensed this, was desolate, just most suspicious. . . . [He said,] 'Dad, you don't have any screwy notions now, do you?' [And I replied,] 'Ah, you mean my not coming back? The thought had crossed my mind.' [Regon then said,] 'Yeah, I thought so. Just like you.' "

There would be a certain rightness to it: the Garhwal, heavenly snowy realm, was the crucible of his Himalayan career. Here he'd met Swami Jnanananda so many years ago, here he'd encountered Christian missionaries whose lives of stirring good works remained a lifelong influence. Devi's mother told her that she wouldn't hold Devi responsible for whatever befell her father, no matter how unfortunate. To be absolved this way, while reassuring, must have raised questions about what was to come, but Devi appears to have known her father well: he was only acting like Willi, showing an amused contempt for death, treating it like a disreputable rogue. Refusing to have "too much respect upon the world." His great competence as a mountaineer, not entirely separable from her awe and love for him as a father, fed the belief that he would know in every situation how to save himself (and others). He was preeminently the sort of father to talk about mortality—to talk about any philosophical topic, any enduring human issue—but he was also a man who had led her on adventures, who in ten years as a professional guide on the highest peaks in the lower forty-eight had never lost a client.

She watched out for him, but from the start of the trek it was clear that he was fully equipped, emotionally in tip-top shape. Infused to his fingertips with the old mountain spirit. He was not some pale poetical type, half in love with easeful death; despite his bad hips and his intestinal gas and his other pains, he was stoked to do this wonderful thing again, his favorite thing in the world. If die he must, then let it come after—after they'd climbed this glorious peak. Walking out into the avalanche chute at the wrong time of day, sauntering over and whistling "Dixie" was a bit of showing off, but it was also a sign of feeling deeply glad. He was happy to be here, facing something complex and enormous. Happy to be feeling the mortal peril again.

ELEVEN

Willi stands squarely in the most American of traditions: for want of a better word, it can be called transcendentalist, after the movement associated with Emerson and Thoreau. The tradition is very much of this world, nature- and humanity-loving; at the same time, it is high-minded and metaphysical, because it sees evidence of a divine order in the ordinary world. Emerson and his circle emerged during the Second Great Awakening, a time of strong reactions against received opinions; they borrowed freely from German Idealism, British Romanticism, and Eastern religions as they put together a homegrown American answer to the doomful, drenched-in-sin inheritance of Puritanism.

This earnest, hopeful movement endorsed self-reliance, as in Emerson's famous essay of the same name. It proposed that man, rather than being sunk in ignorance and error, was capable of understanding the highest truths through the exercise of simple intuition. A faith suited to these American shores would be democratic, individualistic, and grounded in the one experience that distinguishes us from our European forebears: our encounter with raw wilderness. "[I]n the woods we return to . . . faith," Emerson wrote in "Nature";

likewise Thoreau, in *Walden,* advised his readers not to "underrate the value of a fact [as] it will one day flower in a truth."

Willi understood this sort of thing. When he climbed the Three Sisters in Oregon as a boy, he felt intimations of something higher; like Thomas Cole, the landscape painter who inspired the Hudson River school, he saw that in nature "the associations are not of man but of God the Creator." Willi was a sophisticated thinker about questions of faith, critical of easy formulations in his youth. The consequences of even small errors of belief were always interesting to him; when he studied Bergson, for example, he was troubled by the question of mysticism's relation to morality, finding that having insights did not necessarily lead to living correctly. If working out a philosophy is the most urgent labor to be undertaken by a thoughtful man or woman—because our beliefs, broadly conceived, are what allow us to live—then it pays not to be offhanded about the effort. Willi, in the years when he was thinking about such things, had a good understanding of what was required: reason *and* faith; love of mankind *and* self-interest; morality *and* vision; a desire to tame the passions and live decently, as well as an urge to lose the self in fiery consummations.

Aside from the problem of how to compare different people's truths—yours that come through prayer, mine through a bottle of whiskey—transcendentalism, being so hopeful, offers but a sketchy response to an element unfortunately present in most lives: tragic suffering. Emerson locates his God in nature, with intimations of a transcendent unity above, but he pays scant attention to nature's apparent indifference to our pain. "Nature stretcheth out her arms to embrace man," he writes, "only let [man's] thoughts be of equal greatness. Willingly does she follow his steps with the rose and the violet, and bend her lines of grandeur and grace to the decoration of her darling child."

The Puritan view of existence was so punitive, so bleak, that Emerson may perhaps be forgiven his attempts to rescue us from further despair. But the sunny transcendental attitude strikes a false note—writers like Melville, at about the same time, were making nature's *malevolence* their great subject, with tales of violent, implacable whales and ruthless ship's officers. Hawthorne's idea of nature, to take another example, was very dark: in stories such as "Young Goodman Brown," the wilderness is presented as a place peopled by demons, where a man may lose his immortal soul. The heart of man is itself a wilderness for Hawthorne, paradoxical and forbidding; yet Emerson, Hawthorne's exact contemporary, was at the same time writing cheerfully, "No law can be sacred to me but that of my nature. . . . The only right is after my constitution, the only wrong what is against it."

If we recruit Willi to argue against Emerson, we can see Willi ending up much closer to Melville, maybe even to spooky Hawthorne. About the sacred, the mystery at the heart of the world, Willi liked to say that it had "something of the ghastly about it. . . . It comes dangerously close to the graveyard"—a sentiment that Melville might have endorsed. Willi cherished the power of nature because it reminded him of his own insignificance, whereas Emerson, with his high-flown talk of man as Nature's darling child, hardly seems to notice his own mortality. Somehow, though, Willi ended up a believer in Divine Nature. He proclaimed the "spiritual values of wilderness" to student audiences, urging them to come to know those values directly, through adventure. And as he settled in as a revered college lecturer, a thinker of deep spiritual thoughts, he became ever more Emersonian: the idealism of the tradition made for successful public appearances, he found, cheering sessions for wilderness.

Jon Krakauer, in *Into Thin Air,* suggests the esteem that Willi enjoyed when he writes that an "ascent of [Everest] helped establish the trajectory of my life. . . . On May 22, 1963, Tom Hornbein, a thirty-two-year-old doctor from Missouri, and Willi Unsoeld, thirty-six, a professor of theology from Oregon, reached the summit of Everest via the peak's daunting West Ridge. . . . I was nine years old at the time and living in Corvallis, Oregon, where Unsoeld also made his home. He was a close friend of my father's, and I sometimes played with the oldest Unsoeld children. . . . A few months before Willi Unsoeld departed for [Everest] I reached the summit of my first mountain. . . . Not surprisingly, accounts of the 1963 epic on Everest resonated loud and long in my preadolescent imagination. While my friends idolized John Glenn, Sandy Koufax, and Johnny Unitas, my own heroes were Hornbein and Unsoeld."

A hero is someone who transcends the ordinary—a man or woman marked by extraordinary courage and skill. The pursuit of honor is valued above all else, and reputation is regarded as something worth dying for, as it alone may survive death. Classical heroes, Achilles for example, are often of semidivine parentage; their adventures are on such a scale that they may find themselves transported into the world of the dead or that of the gods.

In the late sixties, an ABC-TV series, *The American Sportsman,* became interested in filming a mountain-climbing segment. Scott Ransom, a filmmaker for ABC, had read Hornbein's West Ridge book, and Willi's name came up. ABC at first proposed using Devi, then just sixteen, as a mountain guide in the show; she refused, finding the whole thing vaguely distasteful. Shot in the Tetons, where Willi leads David Ladd, one of the sons of the actor Alan Ladd, up his first multipitch climb, the film reveals Willi to be completely at home in front of the camera. Ransom remembers him being "instantly at ease . . . he ignored the camera, and a personal quality took over, a grandness of personality that we might have expected from him, given what he'd achieved in the Himalaya, but that you're never really prepared to meet in ordinary life. He was enormously calming. David was scared out of his mind, see . . . it became this poetic and enjoyable thing, to be out there on a high cliff where you didn't belong—you felt something instantly about him as a man, that he was *capable* and *trustworthy*, in the deepest meaning of those simple words."

Willi bestows *confidence*; in his hands, you (or David Ladd) feel capable of doing things only dreamed of before. The TV segment, shot in super-16 and first shown nationally in the early seventies, brings into play a set of dramatic values not often found these days; the Tetons, where the climb takes place, show forth in their lucent majesty, and the whole encounter has the same calming effect on the viewer that Willi is said to have had on Ladd. Willi looks like somebody out of the past, a Jedediah Smith or a Kit Carson. Good humor radiates from his brushy beard. He's doing something he's done thousands of times before, taking a scared greenhorn up a mountain, but he does it with freshness and generosity of spirit and a lot of smiles. Ladd asks him about the historic West Ridge climb; Willi refuses to preen and instead introduces the philosophical note, saying that when they reached the summit, "Hornbein and I added up to about a half a mote in the eye of that great immensity," which feeling was perhaps the essence of the thrill.

Striving to explain the quality Willi has that impresses him, Ladd offers for him the highest praise: "My *father* was like that when he worked . . . always so natural that it was relaxing just to watch him. He had nothing to prove." The hardscrabble mountaineer and the glamorous star of *Shane* and *Hell on Frisco Bay* share an ability to captivate, to inspire. The funny thing is that the hero-worshipful tone seems justified, and Willi appears unaffected and not for a moment distracted from the complicated business at hand, which is to get someone with no experience up a serious climb in front of cameras. "Willi turned it into an essay about a man finding his way," says director/cinematographer Ransom, "encountering fear and dealing with it. He hardly had to say anything. It was all there in how he was, how he moved . . . always implying larger things."

Real heroes: Are there any, do they exist? Looking pretty good on film isn't being heroic, and maybe mountaineering shouldn't be considered heroic at all, since the whole effort is "useless" and in no way to be compared with sitting down at the wrong lunch counter in the early-sixties South, or going into battle. Nevertheless, situations arise in the useless enterprise of mountaineering that present people with choices, that make emotional and physical demands that few can meet. One example: In 1960, near the end of the Masherbrum climb, foul weather threatened several team members descending from the highest camps. Willi and George Bell had already reached the summit four days before; Nick Clinch, organizer of the expedition, and a Pakistani army officer had also gotten to the top, but they woke up two days later in a blizzard feeling severely weakened, needing to descend immediately along a slope continuously swept by slides. The third climber descending that day, Dick Emerson, later described what happened:

"[T]here was no way to wait this one out. We cut the tent cords free in order to break camp fast. . . . I was about to suggest to Nick that we abandon two of the packs in the interest of a speedy descent, when *the strains of a harmonica* came up through the whiteout below. . . . Down at Camp V [Willi] and Tom Hornbein had figured out exactly what our situation was. . . . They moved up fast with no packs; they measured in rope lengths the size of the ice face, which they knew would be invisible on the descent. They took two of the loads and we flew down slope, with small slides brushing our heels. At the appropriate [marker] Willi turned us down the fall line for exactly eight measured-out rope lengths, and a flat traverse brought us straight into the tent at Camp V.

"So Willi probably saved my life," Emerson concludes. "So what? My belay definitely saved him [on an earlier climb in Wyoming]. But there is a big difference between a routine belay and his extraordinary rescue! Willi *sought* the opportunity to protect and nurture. It fed the shepherd in his soul."

Willi's version of the rescue, in an article published in the *AAJ,* is more succinct: "Having relieved Nick and Jawed [the Pakistani officer] of their packs, we carefully counted rope lengths downwards. . . . After a soup stop at V, we five climbers trudged on down in the developing storm." What's notable about this rescue is that Unsoeld and Hornbein put themselves at great risk—climbed over a thousand feet in whiteout conditions without packs, without gear to save themselves—and did so in fine Unsoeldian style (*"the strains of a harmonica* came up"), a style that, while insouciant, was also professional and precise ("Willi turned us down . . . exactly eight measured-out rope lengths"). No one could see in the blizzard, yet in short order they were all eating soup in a tent. Readers of *Into Thin Air,* which tells of climbers doomed to death because they were unable to find shelter a few yards off in a storm, will appreciate the forethought. The image of a madcap, risk-besotted Willi, waltzing out under avalanche snouts, must be considered in the light of stories like this as well as his general record in the mountains: six Himalayan expeditions survived, hundreds of clients and companions brought safely home.

That he had a special feeling for risk, a *passion* for it, is also the case. Allen Steck, who pioneered the East Buttress route on El Cap with Willi in the early fifties, says he was "remarkably daring, and completely calm." Nick Clinch recalls another incident from Masherbrum: "Willi and George had already gotten the top, and Jawed

and I then came up for a shot. We had lost all our climbing hardware, and I found myself at a spot where I had to make a long step
onto a downward-sloping slab with crampons on. If my crampons
didn't hold, both Jawed and I would surely die. I suddenly saw,
right in front of my nose, an iron ring. I knew that Don Whillans,
on the English Masherbrum attempt, hadn't gotten up this high, so
it had to be one of our guys [who put it in], and I thought, 'Thank
God Willi was conservative for once,' and gratefully clipped the
ring. Now, why did I think Willi and not George? And why 'conservative for once'? It wasn't a rational thought but it was immediate. . . . I knew that in certain moods Willi might *not* have put
that ring there. He just pushed harder."

Willi's great climbs, those of the fifties and sixties, came at a
turning point for American climbing. "If you don't go beyond, you
get nowhere—nowhere," Clinch says. Before the fifties, American
mountaineers, while recognized as masterful on rock (as opposed
to snow), were known internationally for "funking" it in dicey situations. "In pre-WWII America," Galen Rowell has written, "the
cardinal rule of mountaineering was to turn back before taking
risks. Few Americans died while climbing, but even fewer achieved
successes . . . comparable to those [of the] European climbers.
[Fritz] Wiessner's first ascent of Mt. Waddington in Canada was
a . . . case in point, since it followed on the heels of fourteen consecutive retreats from the peak by the top American climbers of the
time." (Wiessner, a German immigrant, brought technical brilliance
and a bold attitude when he came to the United States, and in the
postwar period climbers like Pete Schoening and Willi followed his
example and were strong enough to accomplish grand things.)

The West Ridge, more than any other climb, broke the mold for
Americans. It was not only the first ascent of Everest by a route
other than the one pioneered by Hillary and Tenzing, via the South

Col, in '53; it was also a climb that put two young Americans far, far out on a limb. It was a *daring* climb, unmistakably a "going too far" type of thing. It was also the strongest possible rebuke to the idea that great summits aren't worth risking your life for.

The expedition, under the direction of filmmaker Norman Dyhrenfurth, was an all-American effort, a true summoning of national purpose and will. In scope it was unique among climbing ventures in this country. Never before had the highest circles in Washington given such support to the attempt to climb a mountain—a foreign mountain, at that, and at a time when mountaineering was thought to be the province of a tiny coterie of unwashed eccentrics. Dyhrenfurth worked hard for years to pull together an enterprise that resembled nothing so much as a Cecil B. DeMille production crossed with a military invasion. His brilliant work, often slighted by climbers allergic to hierarchy of any kind, and obscured by the National Geographic Society, a sponsor that hoped to take the credit for itself, was an organizational equivalent of Unsoeld's ascent—breathtaking, one-of-a-kind.

It was also very much of its moment. The Kennedy administration wanted bold, memorable gestures for foreign and domestic political consumption. Fifty-mile hikes, touch-football games, and climbs of mountains seemed to strike the right note. In accounts of the Kennedy years, and of the attitude that JFK brought to Washington in '61, the launch of *Sputnik I* (October '57) never fails to be mentioned, and this shocking demonstration of American backwardness was undoubtedly upsetting. But more relevant, perhaps, is that the Soviets retained a commanding lead in space exploration well into the sixties, with each anticipated American breakthrough preempted by another slick triumph in the Soviet Luna series. (The Soviets first crashed a probe into the moon in '59; the Americans, after a series of failures, did so only in '62.) So hungry were U.S.

leaders for success that in the years after *Sputnik* a team was tasked to prepare for an ICBM moon launch, with an atomic bomb as payload. The ensuing nuclear explosion, timed for best possible viewing from earth, was to demonstrate America's ability to retaliate should any terrestrial opponent launch an attack.

Dyhrenfurth wasn't thinking of all this when he planned his trip to Everest—or was thinking of it only generally. But people in Washington had caught the mood of the vigorous young president (with his spinal injuries, and his chronic Addison's disease), and bold gestures carrying compensatory messages about American prowess were in favor. Dyhrenfurth, German-born, son of the renowned Himalayan geologist Gunther O. Dyhrenfurth, had been mad about mountains since his youth. In '33, Gunther, to finance an exploration of the Karakoram, developed a film project and ended up playing himself in a movie called *Der Dämon des Himalaya (Demon of the Himalaya).** Norman, a *Gymnasium* student at the time, became fascinated with moviemaking, and in '35 he assisted the German mountaineer Hans Ertl on a promotional shoot for the '36 Winter Olympics. Then he got out of Germany, fast. By the early fifties, Norman was established in southern California, teaching cinematography at UCLA and serving as head of the film division in the theater department.

In '52 he went on a Swiss Everest expedition, for which he made

---

**Demon of the Himalaya* was one of many films with a mountain theme produced in Germany after World War I. Probably the best known is *Blue Light,* starring the shameless opportunist and gifted filmmaker Leni Riefenstahl, who directed *Olympia* and *Triumph of the Will* for Hitler. Why there came to be a rage for romantic mountain-climbing films in the years when Hitler was just coming to power is an interesting question. The mountains are posited as an ideal realm, and handsome ski-instructor-type men and fiesty, spiritualized vixens of the kind that Riefenstahl herself portrayed are offered as attractive Teutons living at one with nature.

a documentary film. In '55 he led an expedition to Lhotse, one of Everest's subsidiary peaks, and in '60 he produced an award-winning documentary about the first ascent of Dhaulagiri. By then he was already thinking about an *American* Everest extravaganza, a big project because only the biggest seemed to succeed on the highest (the English on Everest in '53, the Italians on K2 in '54). He applied to the government of Nepal for permission. He began to court sponsors, meanwhile inviting the best climbers to join him; Willi's name came up, and Dyhrenfurth tendered an invitation in early '61.

Dyhrenfurth's approach to expeditions bespoke his background. He was European, therefore mountaineering was a normal endeavor in his eyes, eminently deserving of government support. But he was also a film producer, thus the expedition developed in a certain Hollywoodish way, with the assembling of a first-rate "cast" and "crew" and the simultaneous launch of sophisticated fund-raising efforts. Norman displayed the relentless, string-pulling savvy of a genuine mogul; he had good connections in the press, in book publishing, and in the entertainment biz, and his movie-star good looks and upbeat demeanor made him many friends. On a typical visit to Washington, in July of '61, he had audiences with twenty-two "men in high places" in three days—Edward R. Murrow (head of the U.S. Information Agency), the director of Aerospace Research (USAF), and top officials with the President's Council on Youth Fitness were the kinds of figure he sought out and inevitably won over.

The first order of business, considering American indifference to climbing, was to make a case for going to Everest at all. Dyhrenfurth answered the question he kept coming up against—"Why climb it when it's already been climbed, won't that be sort of boring?"—by invoking the hallowed space program, pointing out that the same thing could justifiably be asked about our attempts to get above the atmosphere. "Russia's Yuri Gagarin was the first to orbit our planet," he wrote in a formal prospectus he circulated among decision-makers, "but does this stop our own efforts to soar up from earth?"

An ally of Dyhrenfurth's, the newspaperman Jim Murray, wrote that "Norman starts this project on a week [in '61] when the papers are full of a sea-level swaggerer named Khrushchev labeling American kids . . . as good-for-nothings . . . sons and daughters of parents with money in their pockets leading a dissipated life! . . . Dyhrenfurth . . . feels it is altogether too prevalent a feeling abroad about Americans and feels that [Everest] would do much to destroy the image of the soft American." Thus, the idea of American vigor being in need of defense was there from the start. Dyhrenfurth added, in his prospectus, "If we succeed, it will . . . be a feather in our cap, a booster to our prestige, a refutation beyond argument of our detractors' taunt that we are a nation gone soft and gutless."

Also there from the start, because of all the space talk, was the idea of the expedition as a *scientific* effort, a gathering of invaluable data. Expeditions were always trying to justify themselves this way, and indeed the National Geographic Society, when first approached for support, pooh-poohed the whole idea and let Norman know that they were onto him. (National Geographic had never before underwritten a pure mountaineering attempt, as distinct from an exploration.) But Dyhrenfurth was serious—or as serious as he had to be—and understood that he needed to link the effort with a larger national concern. "In addition to illuminating certain features of human nature," he wrote, "and thus adding to the basic store of knowledge about Man, it is anticipated that the results of these studies will be of particular usefulness to America's Space Program," offering answers to questions such as "What kind of man will make the best astronauts? . . . Which astronauts will be best suited for which job? . . . What factors determine the effectiveness of a team of men isolated in a space-exploring rocket and capsule?"

In the end, the expedition *did* amass an impressive amount of data, some of it even scientific. None was of any use to the space program, but because Dyhrenfurth had recruited first-rate people who carried through on their research proposals, Everest '63 was the most exhaustively studied expedition in history. James T. Lester, a clinical psychologist based in California, came on board early and in a dogged, good-natured way gathered precise information the whole time, beginning with personality assessments made before the climbers left for Asia and including dream reports and confidential ratings of other team members before, during, and after the climb. (Willi ridiculed all the psych stuff; because of a scheduling conflict, he escaped the early personality assessment, and in his lectures after returning from Everest he complained that "we filled out forms all the way up the bloody mountain, *and* a diary . . . this was all printed in a day-to-day book, waterproof, that weighed two pounds. You had to carry it *all the way.*")

Dick Emerson, Willi's friend and fellow Masherbrum team member, undertook a study entitled "Communication Feedback in Small Groups Under Stress," a boondoggle-sounding bit of sociology. Emerson was an assistant professor at the University of Cincinnati, a powerful climber, and no kind of intellectual faker: out of his love for the mountains and legitimate interest in how groups like this got along, he produced a case study that remains penetrating forty years after the events. Emerson discovered that climbers remain involved in a project to the extent that the outcome remains unknown; they work to promote uncertainty to keep their own heads in the game, answering bad news with optimism and good news with fear and doubt. (The process is known as negative feedback—

meaning, to give back the opposite.) Dyhrenfurth, when he first promoted the trip, sold it not as a simple ascent via the South Col, but as a three-pronged attack on Everest, Lhotse, and Nuptse, with the West Ridge scarcely mentioned as a possible route. But once the team began the long trek to the mountain, the West Ridge became "an increasingly frequent and engaging topic of group discussion," according to Emerson's report. "By the time the Expedition had moved twenty days along its march . . . the Ridge had a firm hold on the climbers' imaginations," mainly because it was *so* outlandish and unlikely—the most mysterious possibility of all.

"Lhotse and Nuptse had drifted to peripheral interest," Emerson noted, "and the group had formed into two [factions], one for the West Ridge and one for the South Col. . . . Group conflict became a built-in feature of the expedition." Willi and Hornbein were the strongest proponents of a West Ridge reconnaissance. *"But what would the outcome of such a reconnaissance very likely be?"* Emerson asks in his report. "The outcome would be inconclusive, through uncertainty-maintaining processes [the same processes his study had identified]. . . . A reconnaissance was [in fact] conducted up to 25,100 feet. . . . [T]he uncertainty of outcome . . . was sustained through long and repeated discussion [and] was not resolved until two men saw the summit of Everest forty feet ahead of them after ninety-two days in the field."

There were other, more ordinary scientific studies. One aimed at measuring the amounts of radioactive hydrogen in the layers of glacial ice. Another measured changes in the rate of red blood cell production at altitude. William Siri, a biomedical physicist, looked at hormone production of the adrenal cortex; team members provided him with urine samples taken at specified altitudes and times.

("[T]he quest for urine was pursued," Siri wrote in his report, "over the faces and ridges of Mt. Everest. The Sherpas could well understand our using bottles in camp at night, but carrying the bottle while climbing perplexed them, and carrying the full bottles back to Base Camp was beyond . . . comprehension.") The Office of Naval Research, the National Science Foundation, and the Air Force Office of Scientific Research underwrote a broad range of experiments, and Dyhrenfurth's venture soon achieved critical financial mass. But the biggest contributor, at close to $120,000, was the National Geographic. The Society overcame its doubts about the research when Dyhrenfurth, Siri, and Maynard Miller, a Cambridge-educated geomorphologist, came to Washington and poured on the schmooze and the *bona fides*. Dr. Melville Bell Grosvenor himself, Society president, was won over, and that was all that needed to be said.

Willi campaigned hard to get to go. His wife was at first opposed; they had four young children at the time, Willi was just getting established as a professor in Oregon, and he'd told her that his Himalayan career would be over with Masherbrum. Then early in '62 the Peace Corps tapped him for service in Nepal; he prepared to move his whole family to Kathmandu, then put in for a leave of absence almost before reporting for his first day of work. Peace Corps director Shriver's willingness to grant this request owes something to Dyhrenfurth's strenuous lobbying, but Willi's personification of the Peace Corps ideal probably had as much to do with it: if anyone was a heroic *doer,* a virile achiever of great things in remote, primitive places, it was Willi Unsoeld, and to deny his request to climb the highest mountain would have seemed churlish, if not anti-American.

Even so, Shriver acted only at the eleventh hour, granting Willi's release just as the expedition was setting forth from Kathmandu.

The expedition's true, indispensable friend in the circles of power wasn't Shriver, who only occasionally lifted a finger, but Stewart Udall, Kennedy's secretary of the interior, who enlisted Senators Warren Magnuson and Clair Engle in support and who welcomed Dyhrenfurth to Washington with a two-hour interview in front of an audience of journalists. Udall declared, for all to hear and the reporters to record, that the American Everest proposal was a winner and ought to be supported federally.

The final budget was $403,307, a heroic amount in '63 dollars. (The State Department alone contributed $82,000 in Indian rupees, for transportation costs.) For this great sum of money Dyhrenfurth secured an expedition that was fully equipped, if not overequipped, with state-of-the-art materials donated by some two hundred manufacturers; the gear sent from the United States weighed in at fifty-four thousand pounds and required 909 porters for transshipment to the base of the mountain. "The joke," Willi liked to tell his audiences, "was that the head of the line reached the next camp before the end left the one before. Sometimes the line of porters stretched out over three miles . . . our real challenge," he told people, "was to come up with a challenge worthy of our inventory."

Willi was thirty-six at the time of the expedition. Most of the other climbers were younger, while Dyhrenfurth and Siri (deputy director) were older authority figures. Willi, with his fund of Himalayan experience, was expected to serve as a sort of deputy-deputy, making strategy with Dyhrenfurth yet taking an active role on the mountain, and this is how things worked out, more or less. "[Willi] was the philosopher of the trail, the peacemaker, the younger elder statesman," wrote James Ramsey Ullman, author of *Americans on Everest,* the definitive account, "[the] moderator when, as sometimes happened, [West] Ridge versus South Col routes became a subject of warm debate." Tom Hornbein, in contrast, was the "high apostle of the West Ridge . . . forever thinking and planning ahead, working on problems of routes, schedules, and logistics with almost mathematical precision."

In Hornbein's book, the author offers an astute account of an expedition split at the root. As on Nanda Devi thirteen years later, factions formed and deep enmities arose, yet vicious mutual denunciations never became the order of the day. The old *expeditionary idealism* was still intact, if on aging and unsteady legs; the idea of a team as a group of like-minded men with a common goal, that of putting somebody on top, anybody, lived on in the hearts of climbers. Mountaineers were so scarce in America in the early sixties that the best of them tended to know each other—Willi had climbed with seven of the twelve chosen to go high on Everest, and several were his close friends. Hornbein, talking about a period when competition between the factions first heated up, writes that "opinions were stated more forcefully—and less charitably—than they were felt. . . . [I]n the privacy of my tent I could readily admit my understanding of the South Coler's point of view. . . . Others must have faced the same problem of achieving compatibility between their goals and that which they knew was just." That what "was just" remained a consideration at all suggests how far we are on Everest '63 from Nanda Devi '76; a clique of superclimbers has not selected itself, is not maneuvering to turn the others into pack mules, and a degree of common ground can still be assumed.

Willi was named the climbing leader on the mountain, by general acclamation. That he was closely identified with the marginal West Ridge try gave no one pause: people simply liked him, and they trusted him. Hornbein became obsessive about the Ridge and hypervigilant against attempts to drain away supplies, and one night, lying in a small tent with Willi, he wonders if maybe he's gone too far:

"Willi, do you resent my talking on the radio when it's supposed to be your job as climbing leader?"

"What? Where did you get that idea?"

"Well, Dick [Emerson] thought I might be stepping on your toes as leader. He thought you might resent it. Do you?"

"Well, son, as long as you remember who's the leader of this affair, go ahead and talk on the radio all you want."

"No, seriously, you baboon, how do you feel?"

"Well, I'll tell you. As they said, you're a fanatic. With you around, I don't figure I have to worry about all the things my old guide's instinct has had me doing for years. . . . I can hear you lying awake over there at night, with the gears grinding out new ideas. I figure all I've got to do is wake up in the morning . . . filter out what sounds good, and keep you from starting a civil war with the Colers. And just keep the old Unsoeld talents ready [for] when you finally crack."

Aside from suggesting the lovely quality of their friendship, this passage indicates the strategy that Willi hit on, a strategy that allowed him to pursue his personal goals while also serving the expedition effectively. He let Hornbein scheme and maneuver and in group meetings argue the West Ridge route vehemently, meanwhile lying back himself and showing tolerance toward all. He was a model climbing leader, smart about logistics, fair, and in his own performance almost unbelievably tireless and powerful. Indeed, Hornbein, a first-rate high-altitude athlete in his own right, has a hard time keeping up; about some early days of hauling loads to the lower camps, he observes, "[T]he incredible Unsoeld . . . appeared to have gone maniacally awry, threatening to demoralize the expedition by his extreme hyperactivity. . . . What was Willi trying to prove? Soloing half the Icefall unroped and beneath an eighty-pound load. . . ."

This is Willi in his prime, a man of modest size and physique able to leap tall buildings. There's just no accounting for him. He loves to compete, making arduous carries into contests to see who can do it best, and when he occasionally loses he sincerely admires the other chap. But he almost never loses. It almost seems unfair for someone so bold—"On the front points of his crampons, Willi led up a tiny fissure diagonally transecting a bulge of glare ice"— also to be so smart about the mountains, and *also* phenomenally gifted physically. And animated by a radiant, welcoming spirit. No one's talking about Bergson out here in the Khumbu, but the élan vital captures the feeling, the idea of a miraculously potent energy inhabiting mortal human flesh. There's a feeling of going beyond, of "creative evolution" happening before your very eyes.

Roskelley, thirteen years later, recognized this same quality when Willi was already well past his prime. "If we'd been young together," he said, "we would've torn up the mountain," and in his book he describes a day of hard carries on Nanda Devi, Willi full of youthful enthusiasm and enjoying the heck out of everything, and declares, "I liked Willi [despite our disagreements]. I saw his drive and success as similar to my own—he was a part of me in a white beard and laughing eyes. [If born at the right time,][w]e would have made an invincible partnership."

Because of Lester's research, we know exactly what Willi's Everest teammates thought of him. Everyone filled out those questionnaires "all the way up the bloody mountain," then back down and back at home as well. Willi's results were highly positive throughout, despite the struggle over whether to support the West Ridge (and fears this attempt might jeopardize the South Col). Most remarkable were the results of the final assessment of the study, when team members were asked whom they would most like to climb with on a future expedition, whom they would wish to be led by, which member of the team had exercised the most influence, who was most important to morale, and so on. Lester was surprised by what he got: "I knew that Willi was held in high esteem, but these were extraordinary results . . . far beyond the range we could expect . . . no, they weren't predictable.

"This was a group not easy to snow, either," Lester says, "scientific and logical in thought," and including three medical doctors, five Ph.D's, and five men with master's degrees. Their idea of a valuable leader was someone alert to and subtle about other people's psychologies, someone who endured physically and emotionally and who exercised fine judgment. Whether they were thinking about it or not, they were thinking about an ideal hero, someone who led others in a loving and generous way, who possessed skill and strength far beyond the ordinary, who displayed courage and who persevered. They were thinking about a personality motivated by considerations of honor, someone whose goal (if he had a goal beyond the satisfactions of the game) was to augment a reputation worth virtually nothing in the wider world, but of precious value within an intense peer group. As it happened, when the members of Everest '63 conceived of this ideal figure, they tended to think of only one man, and probably no other such considered opinion of an individual under conditions of challenge and mortal danger has ever been so scientifically, and incontrovertibly, rendered.

Lester came to know Willi well on the trip. Lester wasn't much of a climber himself; still, he was strong and young and found he was able to go fairly high, and his presence must have proved agreeable, because no one threw him and those two-pound waterproof notebooks down a crevasse.* While reporting their dreams, the climbers reported many other things to him besides. "Emerson and I rated everybody twice in relation to some personality dimensions," Lester says. "We called these Field Trait Rankings, and we ourselves put Willi first on complexity of personality, maturity, emotional control, disposition, inviting manner, sensitivity to his impact on others . . . there was maybe some 'halo effect' after the success on the West Ridge, but Emerson knew him well before the expedition started, while I didn't know him at all, and still we agreed remarkably.

"Willi wasn't *too* sensitive to others, which is probably good . . . he knew how to evoke things in people, and, you know, I have to say that he reminded me of no one else I've ever known in my life. He was loud—laughed a lot. After the expedition he always wore a huge beard . . . wore leather shorts and boots, often in venues where they were a bit noticeable—he got people's attention one way or the other. There was a look on his face that somehow encompassed all. He beamed—and you wanted to be in that beam.

"Willi knew a lot about things, and he remembered what he knew. He had an organized mind and stuff was available to him . . . he felt strongly about his personal ideals, while we others had a *loose* attachment to ours and could be persuaded, perhaps, one way or the other.

"Even at the best of times, I'd say that he had an agenda that you didn't necessarily know about. Was he a bullshitter? No, I wouldn't call him a bullshitter by any extension . . . still, he could use his philosophy pretty much as he wanted. His characteristic

---

*In 2001, Lester insisted that those two-pound notebooks were "part of Emerson's project, not mine. I had forms for them to fill out, but I . . . collected them when I needed them."

effort was the effort to inspire other people. Fortunately he was completely unself-righteous, while being full of conviction . . . you remembered his eyes, his big laughs, his slightly deliberate way of talking, slower than most people's. Some of the other members, when we asked them to expand their comments on him, said some interesting things . . . I remember one [comment]: 'Willi is very selfish, but selfish to the benefit of the team.' And another: 'He has a tendency to hide his own infirmities, perhaps even from himself.' "

TWELVE

On the morning of May 22, 1963, Hornbein and Unsoeld wake at 4 A.M. The oxygen tank they've been breathing from, to help them through the night, has hit empty. They're at an altitude of 27,200 feet (8,290 meters), in a tent anchored by a single piton driven "half an inch into the rotten rock of the Yellow Band . . . our axes buried to the hilt in equally rotten snow," according to Hornbein. After eight weeks of climbing at great altitude, they have a single day to make it to the top of Everest.

Three weeks before, on May 1, Jim Whittaker had become the first American to bag the summit. He went up the South Col way, in a classic demonstration of siege mountaineering technique: great loads of equipment hauled up by Sherpa and sahib, camp after camp established in a ladder of support. With Whittaker (and Nawang Gombu) summiting, the expedition was officially a success: Dyhrenfurth could now relax, the National Geographic Society could relax, there would be photos for the magazines and books would get written. The temperate, nonautocratic Dyhrenfurth had finally run out of patience and had ordered all resources thrown into the South Col effort. "We have—almost *have*—to have a success," he noted in his journal, and he judged in the end that their two-pronged approach might have resulted in failure on both fronts.

Willi thought of the West Ridge in terms of absolute value. Hornbein quotes him speaking of the "spiritual, moral, and moun-taineering correctness of the only route worthy of our efforts." But because of his position as climbing leader, he felt obliged to support Dyhrenfurth's decision, even though it meant the end of his own hopes. Still, he declined Dyhrenfurth's offer to make Hornbein and him members of a second assault team via the Col; he preferred to persist in a reduced West Ridge effort, which would effect a recon-naissance of the route as high as possible, for the benefit of expe-ditions that might come in the future. "[W]e came awfully close to tossing in our chips and joining the stampede [on the Col]," Willi wrote about the offer of a ticket to the top. "Our chances for the summit are tremendously decreased [with the end of support for the West Ridge], but surely mountaineering is more than a matter of summits—even when the summit is that of Everest."

But on May 22, against all odds, there they are. Above them are almost two thousand vertical feet of extreme terrain never before trod by man. They're in pretty good shape, good spirits; by eating at every opportunity they've avoided the debilitating weight loss that normally goes with weeks spent up high ("we stuffed our-selves . . . we would neatly clean the leftovers of those whose ap-petites were jading," Hornbein wrote); and they trust each other implicitly. The problem is that even if the icy couloirs and down-sloping snowy slabs and rock pitches above can be climbed, there's good reason to doubt they can be *down*-climbed as well, in the event that retreat becomes necessary. And if they somehow manage to climb what has never been climbed before and reach the summit late in the day—what will become of them then? They're carrying no sleeping bags or tent (their packs are already too heavy: about forty pounds apiece), and no human being has ever before survived an unprotected bivouac at the altitudes of Everest's summit zone.

They do have a plan, though. In retrospect, it seems almost the most audacious part of the whole enterprise. While Unsoeld and Hornbein are climbing the West Ridge, a second summit team will be climbing the other side of the mountain, and a top-of-the-world rendezvous has been planned, after which all four intend to descend by way of the Col. The other two climbers, Lute Jerstad, a Rainier guide and speech instructor from Oregon, and Barry Bishop, a mountaineer and photographer on assignment for *National Geographic,* will know the route down after having just climbed up it; presumably, they'll be able to lead all of them safely back. Willi's account, published in the *AAJ,* is, like his other mountain writing, humorous, clear, and absolutely without self-puffery; we have to look to Hornbein's version, or to Ullman's, for revelations about Willi's remarkable performance. For instance, after four hours of climbing, mostly up a narrow, snowy couloir, on the morning of May 22, Willi takes a rest from leading and asks Hornbein to go first on the rope, up a sixty-foot cliff of snow-dusted rock. "The rock sloped malevolently outward," Hornbein writes, "like shingles on a roof—rotten shingles. The covering of snow was no better. . . . It would pretend to hold for a moment, then suddenly shatter and peel, cascading down on Willi [belaying below]." Struggling to make hard rock-climbing moves up a steep wall at close to 28,000 feet, on chalky schist that crumbles in his unmittened hands, Hornbein completely exhausts himself after less than an hour; defeated, he rappels back down to Willi.

Now Ullman's account: "Willi took the lead . . . at last, using Tom's piton, [he moved] beyond [Tom's highest point]. For the topmost part of the pitch he had to take off his mittens and climb barehanded, clawing and worming his way up [an] almost holdless surface . . . In the end he came up over it. Tom came up after him. At a height of almost twenty-eight thousand feet, [Willi had led] the most difficult stretch of climbing that the expedition encountered."

And now Willi's version, in its entirety: "Well over an hour was spent on one hairy forty-foot rock pitch requiring two pitons and bare hands."

Safely above the crucial pitch, the key to the whole climb, Willi calls Base on the walkie-talkie. He describes the climbing through the Yellow Band as "a real bearcat" and mentions that the going is too hard to reverse: there are no rappel points, no way to lower on a rope, and he announces simply but clearly, "So it's up and over for us today." Hornbein, listening in to this conversation, concurs: "An invisible barrier sliced through the mountain beneath our feet, cutting us off from the world below. . . . The ethereal link provided by our radio only intensified our separation."

With no real options, they climb on. "[The] oxygen shortage was our one serious worry during the climb," Willi wrote, "and I frankly cannot remember being too nervous even about that." He jokes that "problems arose even as we left. As I stood at the foot of the first pitch, an ominous hiss warned of an oxygen malfunction. Tom quickly installed our spare regulator—but the hiss continued. Together we . . . decided it was only a small leak and nothing to worry about—a decision which fully demonstrates the dangerous effects of a combination of altitude and enthusiasm on the minds of even experienced Himalayan veterans." Rather than return to the tent, only a few paces off, to pick up a bottle that won't leak, Willi climbs for the rest of the day on a much restricted flow, turning off his supply completely at belay stances. His performance is phenomenal, regardless of how much oxygen he is or isn't getting, but oxygen taken at extreme altitudes is not only an aid to performance, it's a crucial protective element. As Charles Houston, M.D., one of the Nanda Devi climbers of '36 and an expert in high-altitude medicine, has written:

> As climbers are unable to maintain an average oxygen uptake greater than 50–60 percent of their maximum . . . metabolic heat production . . . may be [barely] enough to balance thermal demand. . . . It is not surprising, therefore, that cold injury . . . may occur in fully clothed mountaineers. . . . This means that heat production is very limited and the climber at extreme altitude is never far from hypothermia.

In other words, bottled oxygen functions as antifreeze, promoting heat generation at the cellular level. Indeed, when oxygen was first prescribed for climbers, early in the last century, the aim was to offer protection against frostbite, not to enhance athletic performance. It would be foolish to conclude, though, that the damage to Willi's feet suffered on this ascent was the result of a casual decision not to go get that other bottle. Too many factors are involved, and Willi's loss of nine of his toes can as plausibly be laid to the decision to be on Everest at all, to be a climber in the first place, to be going for a summit via an unknown route.

Maybe more significant is Willi's statement that "oxygen shortage was our one serious worry . . . and I frankly cannot remember being too nervous even about that." Recent research in high-altitude neurophysiology, some of it conducted by Tom Hornbein himself, suggests that the people blessed with the ability to climb powerfully up high may be at greater risk for neurological impairment. "[P]ersons with a high hypoxic ventilatory response," write Hornbein et al. in an article in *The New England Journal of Medicine*,

". . . appear more impaired after exposure to extremely high alti-tude . . . [and these] are the ones who seem to perform best physi-cally at great heights." Hypoxia is oxygen starvation: what happens from being up in the thin air. A "high ventilatory response" means deeper or more rapid breathing and more efficient use of available oxygen. According to Hornbein, climbers with a high ventilatory response may be sending more oxygen to their exercising muscles, but correspondingly less to their brains; during sleep they may also experience longer spells of not breathing at all, moments "sufficient at extreme altitude to injure the brain."

In a letter to the *New England Journal,* in response to Hornbein's article, a researcher at the University of Utah, Robert D. Herr, the-orized that high-response climbers may actually owe their physical superiority to this dangerous trade-off. The mechanism that sends more oxygen to their hardworking muscles, and less to the brain, may result in decreased cerebral function, including a decreased ability to recognize injury and fatigue as they develop. Though in pain, such climbers may fail to understand; where others might fal-ter, they push on.

We can't know what Willi was really thinking—or failing to think—on his ascent. But to say that "I frankly cannot remember being too nervous" about a malfunctioning oxygen system at the very start of a day when he will ask his body to do unprecedented things—climb Everest by an unknown route, then traverse the whole mountain to descend—suggests *some* sort of dissociation from reality as most of us know it. A degree of nervousness might even have been called for. Recognizing and thinking less, he may have felt capable of more—capable of almost anything. "Altitude and enthusiasm" accounted for his lack of worry, he wrote, but the full implications of this probably accurate insight escaped him, as indeed they had to, given the understanding of cerebral function then current. This is in no way meant to detract from the boldness, the toughness, the genuinely *heroic* quality of his performance over the next twenty-four hours (and in the weeks leading up to this day). To say that a climber encountering severe terrain at over eight thousand meters on an unknown route is less clear in the head than usual is to say something both obvious and terrible; and Willi's presence in this unforgiving realm, where he may well have felt like a "sick man walking in a dream," as the old saying has it, was the product of a series of decisions and preparations made at lower elevations and in full possession of his wits.

At about 4:00 P.M., the men crest out on the West Ridge. Peering down the South Face they see Advanced Base Camp eight thousand feet below, just a few specks of tent. And above them—the South Summit of Everest. "We were within four hundred feet of the top!" is how Hornbein records this exhilarating moment. Willi has been kicking steps up frozen faces and steep couloirs for close to nine hours by now. His first oxygen bottle, which lasted just six hours (Hornbein's lasted ten), was discarded long ago. He leads up four pitches of blue-gray rock, which present "quite delicate moves on moderately small holds." (At slide shows, Willi would often show a shot of Hornbein following him on these limestone crags and would say, "Here's one of Tom on a thin arête; on his left there's an eight-thousand-foot drop, on his right a drop of about five thousand feet. If you look closely, you can see him leaning just very slightly to the right.")

At 6:00 P.M., Willi halts. He turns, coils in the rope, drawing Hornbein to him. Forty feet ahead of them is the tattered flag left on the summit three weeks before by Jim Whittaker. There's nowhere else to go, nowhere higher in the world. The two men embrace and walk the last few yards together. They don't speak.

Someone had given Willi a crucifix, and among his first acts is to wrap it in a Buddhist ceremonial scarf, a *kata,* and bury it at the base of the flag. "Buddhist prayer flags ... the American flag ... the cross of Christ all perched together on the top of the world— [t]he symbolic possibilities rendered my summit prayer more than a trifle incoherent," Willi records. He thinks of the great figures in mountaineering history who have inspired him, "Mallory, Norton ... Shipton, and Tilman," all of whom dreamed of standing where he now is. "Control is thinned by the altitude and the tears came readily—called forth by a wave of gratitude and burst of comradely feeling. . . . Twenty minutes of emotional flux such as this and the marvel is that we still had the starch to even start the descent."

Amazingly, the two South Col climbers, Jerstad and Bishop, *had* made it to the summit that day, coordinating their own ascent with Tom and Willi's. Despite the lack of radio contact between the two teams, and the unpredictable mountain vastness covered by each, they arrived on top only three hours too early for a perfect linkup. Unsoeld and Hornbein see their footsteps leading down and follow them. The sun sets. Willi, who had led the whole day, going "first on the rope because Tom was having oxygen trouble and hadn't felt well till he switched over to his second bottle," after ten hours, is now pretty much done in. On the South Summit he runs out of oxygen for good. "It was now pitch-dark," Willi would say in his lectures. "You just feel your way down the mountain. I couldn't describe it, because I don't even remember it ... just pure craziness ... I can only talk about it because I've dreamed up this story to tell," meaning that in his hypoxic state, he wasn't really aware.

Hornbein feels pretty good, though. He still has oxygen and, despite his own great exertions that day, has not been cutting steps and leading since seven in the morning. Willi goes first on a belay as they descend, using their only flashlight to spot footprints in the snow. "There was pitiful humor as Willi probed, holding the light a few inches off" the surface, it says in Hornbein's account; then the flashlight fades in the cold. The night is moonless, the stars shed no useful light: "You could order your eyes to see, but nothing in the blackness complied," according to Hornbein. The two men call out in the void, and after a while something seems to answer them. David Dingman, one of the expedition's doctors, and Girmi Dorje, Sherpa, are supposed to be in the highest camp on the South Col route, prepared to come up and render assistance to anyone able to stumble down far enough. Willi thinks, "Wow! We're saved! We're saved!" and the suicidal descent promises to have a happy end.

They see two darker shapes ahead: it's hard to tell them from a pair of rocks against the snow. Then the rocks speak: "Easy, easy! Over to the right! Careful!" Willi and Tom descend and throw themselves into the arms of their rescuers, only to discover not Dingman and Girmi, fresh and able to lead them down to Camp VI, but Jerstad and Bishop, terribly weak and "just as lost as we were . . . those cats had just been wiped out," according to Willi's account. Hornbein says, "They were near exhaustion, shivering lumps curled on the snow. [Bishop] in particular was far gone. . . . Determination [had] got him to the top, but now he no longer cared. Lute was also tired. . . . His eyes were painfully burned. . . . From sheer fatigue they had stopped thinking."

It's now nine-thirty. The temperature on Everest that night was estimated at minus eighteen degrees Fahrenheit, with powerful gusts of wind in the early hours. Willi and Tom, sorely in need of rescue, become rescuers themselves; Hornbein, still with bottled oxygen, realizes, "We had to keep moving or freeze," and he ropes in with Jerstad and leads off. All four men are now essentially climbing blind, descending by feel as much as by sight. "The track was more sensed than seen" is how Hornbein puts it, and with Jerstad trying to remember which way to turn, at which half-visible landmark, they inch painfully down a vast vertiginous face, keeping to the east of a snow crest below the South Summit. Willi ropes to Bishop, and he picks up the nearly comatose climber when he repeatedly falls. Everyone gropes and stumbles; Jerstad falls once and starts sliding off toward oblivion, only stopping "when his chin hooks over the rope stretching between Tom and me," according to Willi's version.

"Finally, at around 12:30 A.M.," Willi writes, "the arête becomes indistinct and Lute thinks it is time to get off the ridge before turning left toward Camp VI. The turning point is crucial—a mistake could land you [eight thousand feet down]—and it is too dark to be certain. [Therefore] we bivouac. A simple maneuver—just take off your pack and lie down. . . . Tom fusses with his feet, complaining of the cold. I report no discomfort in my feet [feeling] secretly proud at my superior cold tolerance."

No one has ever bivouacked before—slept out, without cover— at such an altitude and survived. Walter Bonatti, the great Italian climber and guide, spent a night out at over twenty-six thousand feet on K2, and Herman Buhl, the brilliant Austrian mountaineer, bivouacked on Nanga Parbat after his solo first ascent in '53, also at about twenty-six thousand feet. Twenty-six thousand feet is very high, but importantly less so than the rocky, unprotected perch on the Southeast Ridge of Everest that Hornbein and the others have chosen. The terms *jet stream* and *upper troposphere* become relevant to understanding the unendurable bitterness of conditions at twenty-eight thousand feet; without bottled oxygen to breathe, humans have less of the lifesaving, limb-preserving gas present in their bloodstreams than they need, and hypothermia and death are almost inevitably the result. Of the four climbers, only Hornbein, most recently still on gas, has the presence of mind to remove his crampons—the frigid metal conducts heat away from a climber's boots, just as lying out on cold rock, or on an empty backpack on rock or snow, lowers core body temperature dangerously.

In his *AAJ* article, Willi mentions nothing about the cold. Nor does he say anything about his feet beyond the single sentence quoted above. In Hornbein's book, we have a moving account of what Willi was prepared to do for a partner in trouble, and in his lectures, Willi himself sometimes offered a more complete, less stoical version:

"A *long* night . . . fading in and out of consciousness. Tom and I snuggled up together, but he began to twitch. He was *so bony*, even through four layers of down his hipbones just *lacerated* me . . . so we rolled apart.

"Bishop was only five feet above me . . . somewhere on Mars. If he had screamed I couldn't've reached him. The only thing that did reach me was Hornbein: 'My feet are cold.' [So] we took off his overboots, his boots . . . this was strictly instinct, I wasn't really thinking . . . it's a guides' tradition in the Tetons, when a client has cold feet, you warm 'em. You pull up your down clothes and you stick them on your hairy stomach, and then you massage them, for *hours* if you have to. 'That feel better?' 'Nope . . .' "

Hornbein adds: "I slid my feet back into socks and boots, but couldn't tie them. I offered to warm Willi's feet. Thinking that his freedom from pain was due to a high tolerance of cold, he declined. We were too weary to realize the reason for his comfort."

Too weary—too hypoxic—Willi fails to recognize his lack of sensation as dangerous, disastrous. The night passes, each man suffering within his narrow scope of occluded consciousness. During the blind descent the normal winds of Everest's summit zone had died, and throughout the long night they blessedly forget to blow. "In a whole year's cycle of Everest nights," Ullman says in

Americans on Everest, "there are no more than a handful in which unsheltered men . . . could conceivably live to see the morning. But this was one of them." Will Siri, the expedition physicist, later wrote that on forty-nine of fifty nights on Everest the winds would have frozen anyone exposed to them, as his four teammates were, at over twenty-eight thousand feet.

Seven o'clock the next morning, Dave Dingman and Girmi Dorje, ascending from Camp VI to search for survivors, call out ahead, and in response to their shouts two figures slowly stagger into view. "I was so astonished, so absolutely dumbfounded," Dingman told Ullman, "that the significance of [Tom and Willi's] being there didn't dawn on me for another half hour." Dingman had expected to find Jerstad and Bishop, or their bodies; that Unsoeld and Hornbein are still alive, and on *this* side of the mountain, means that they've accomplished their monumental traverse of Everest. (In the ensuing forty years, no climbers have repeated this ascent, up the West Ridge and down the Southeast, despite continuous improvements in equipment and mountain technique.) Rising shortly after dawn, Tom and Willi had roped together, leaving Bishop and Jerstad behind; their aim was to descend as quickly as possible to Camp VI, to summon help. Dingman offers them his bottled oxygen but they decline: Jerstad and Bishop need it more. So Dingman and Girmi continue up the face, and only a hundred feet farther on they come upon Jerstad and Bishop "lying prostrate on a little shelf of snow. As they spoke to me, it was very slowly and with much effort," Dingman reports, "and their faces were a deep ashen blue," from hypoxia.

Everyone survives; everyone gets down safely. Norman Dyhrenfurth, who produced a stirring documentary film, *Americans on Everest,* about the '63 expedition, captured images of the tired summit climbers arriving at Camp I, just above the Khumbu Icefall.

Tom Hornbein, a small man with a noble nose, looks like an exhausted, sunburned Ratty from *Wind in the Willows,* but Willi looks pained and saddened: vastly older, no longer handsome, ruined in some more than physical way. By now, having hobbled down over two thousand meters, he knows what he's done to his feet. But he also knows what he's accomplished: something unbelievable, one for the record books, possibly the most impressive effort yet in the Himalaya. Dyhrenfurth, who in the end chose to push the South Col and not the West Ridge, himself said of it: "For years it [had] been the dream of mountaineers to do a major Himalayan traverse. We [were] particularly happy and proud that this was not only the first Himalayan traverse, but that [it] was on Everest."

THIRTEEN

Americans on Everest, a film seen by 20 million viewers when first aired in the United States, has the heroic tone of other preseventies mountaineering accounts. Orson Welles narrates in his orotund style, reading from a script by Ullman that only occasionally resorts to purple passages on the order of "After three weeks Jim Whittaker's maypole still stands fast, with Old Glory streaming in the winds of space." Welles earned $7,000 for three hours' work in a recording studio in Rome. Dyhrenfurth, who directed but was given no director's credit by National Geographic—and who earned not a dime because, in his eagerness to get the expedition going, he'd accepted a bad contract—commented, bitterly, "Nice work if you can get it!" In addition to his work as expedition organizer, Dyhrenfurth labored on the mountain as principal cinematographer, constrained at all times by a National Geographic contract that required that he be looking through the camera on every shot. ("Look, it doesn't work that way out here in the Himalaya," he told his National Geographic overlords in Washington. "I can't be everywhere at once! I have to use an assistant!")

Ullman's script for *Americans on Everest,* like his book of the same name, belongs to the same school of mountain writing as Elizabeth Knowlton's *Naked Mountain,* Herzog's *Annapurna,* and just about everything else written before the end of the sixties. Both book and film hate to report bad news, and in fact, never knowingly attribute unworthy motives to any climber; by the same token, they love to find evidence of heroism, self-sacrifice, and team spirit in the complex story of the expedition. That story, thoroughly researched by Ullman, who had access to the climbers' diaries and other intimate writings, is told with clarity and admirable completeness. The book amasses a mini-Everest of facts about the trip, from the contents of a two-man summit ration package ("2 pkg. Metrecal cookies . . . 2 6-oz. pkg. Jell-O . . . 1 meat bar . . . 1 12-oz. can mixed nuts," etc.) to the kind of camera supplied each member ("Nikon F single-lens reflex . . . 50-mm f/20 Nikkor lens . . . 28-mm f/3.5 Nikkor wide-angle lens thoroughly tested in a cold chamber"). At the same time, we encounter passages like this:

Eighteen we were—with a great bond, a single purpose. In short, a team. But still, as with every team, the basic component was the individual. . . . [T]here was Jim Whittaker, six feet five inches of long bone and lean muscle, with shoulders that looked capable of nudging aside a small house. . . . Lute Jerstad, Whittaker's longtime guiding partner on Rainier, who was five foot eight including vertical crew-cut hair, and was a maestro on the ukelele. . . . Dr. Tom Hornbein, he of the oxygen gear and five children . . . who looked, in climbing rig plus mask . . . as if he had just emerged from a flying saucer. . . . Dr. Gil Roberts, one-third physician, one-third mountaineer and one-third existentialist, with paperbacks of Sartre and Kierkegaard oozing from his sleeping bag; and Dick Pownall, quiet, gentle, powerful.

Everyone, as in a nineteenth-century novel, has an identifying characteristic or two ("Unsoeld . . . a professor of philosophy and religion . . . [t]hat he was a man of action went without saying"), so that when he appears in a scene, we remember who he is by his admirable qualities. This kind of writing was old-fashioned even in '64, when Ullman's book first appeared; nowadays it reads almost like a Horatio Alger story.

But even as we smile at the period tone, we respond to the idea of a real team. The thought of a bunch of hardy fellows working together, holding each other in high regard and giving up their selfish desires when required, seems plausible as Ullman tells the story. And there *are* genuine moments of self-sacrifice. Willi, and to a lesser extent Tom, yielding to Dyhrenfurth, refusing to sulk too much when the West Ridge seems abandoned. Barry Corbet, one of the original West Ridgers, also the best rock climber on the team and fully the equal of Unsoeld and Hornbein in strength, quietly stepping down, giving up his chance for the summit so that Tom and Willi can have theirs. Dave Dingman, also very strong, also giving up an excellent shot at the top to help Tom, Willi, Jerstad, and Bishop down from Camp VI. Every expedition, in every era, is full of acts of selflessness and support of the other man, most of them undertaken without much fanfare. What differs over time, though, is the *attitude* brought to the act of self-abnegation. In '63, the idea that one was a sucker for giving up a summit bid had not quite taken hold; and to claim that one had a "right" to stand on top of a mountain would have seemed absurd.

Partly, this was the result of reading books much like *Americans on Everest*. Climbers are readers, and we've seen how Willi and others in the small fraternity of American climbers had thrilled to idealistic stories of daring and danger. Though we can't know, many had probably read earlier books by James Ramsey Ullman himself (*The White Tower, High Conquest, Banner in the Sky, Kingdom of Adventure, The Sands of Karakorum,* etc.) and, finding themselves on an expedition with a writer already attached to it, were more than able to fill in the blanks, imagine themselves as characters in his next one. If Ullman had been a writer ahead of his time, instead of slightly behind, and prone to write shocking exposés such as became commonplace in the seventies, these same reader/climbers might well have gone to Everest expecting a drama of egotism and resentment, rather than the mixed group experience that actually transpired.

It matters what myths we tell ourselves—which ideals we choose to honor. Hornbein, with *Everest: The West Ridge,* goes a long way toward writing an anti-Ullman, because the truth he wants to tell is almost entirely different from the one in *Americans on Everest*. For Hornbein, the expedition was *about* the conflict between bold, scrappy, big-dreaming West Ridgers and the dull, play-it-safe South Col contingent; though he credits Dyhrenfurth with first suggesting a West Ridge attempt, Hornbein's book is notable for all that it fails to say about the incredible organizational effort that put Willi and Tom in a position to make history. (Dyhrenfurth, a close student of expeditions throughout the twentieth century, had thought carefully about the proper time of year to get to the mountain. After consulting with Lionel Terray, leader of a recent ascent of Jannu, and Albert Eggler, of the Swiss Everest team of '56, Dyhrenfurth worked hard to get to Base Camp quite early, with ample time for multiple assaults. Everest '63 climbers thus reached the South Col on April 16, a full six weeks ahead of the schedule of the '53 expedition, which had put Hillary and Tenzing on top.)

Hornbein accuses Dyhrenfurth of double-dealing: "I felt let down on something that I thought had been agreed upon by the entire expedition . . . that we should push the two routes simultaneously." While Willi and Tom are out one day, reconnoitering the Ridge, the rest of the team holds a meeting and votes to throw everything into the South Col, then presents this decision as a *fait accompli*. Dyhrenfurth remembers the expedition as being a pretty wonderful time, all things considered: "There are always exchanges of strong views on a climb, strong disagreements. . . . Tom wanted to scrap the South Col, only go for the Ridge, but I told him, 'Look, I've been working on this thing for three years now. We have three hundred sponsors. We need to get someone on top because of that—we *owe* them that, don't you think?' " Hornbein's book takes a crucial first step in the direction of unmasking, of telling an expedition's story mainly in terms of a struggle between two factions (rather than the classic struggle between bonded men and a mountain). Even so, we're a long way from the brutal enmities and raw mutual disregard of books from the seventies. Nor is Hornbein's story a retreat from climbing ideals per se: like Ullman, he remains largely uncynical, honoring selflessness and heroism wherever he finds them.

The great hero of Hornbein's book—if not quite of Ullman's—is Willi, "the incredible Unsoeld." Hornbein's portrait is of a salty, earthy, ironic guy who never puts on airs, who merely climbs harder than anybody else and inspires with his bravery. When Jake Breitenbach disappears under shifting ice-blocks, Willi's the one to race up into the Khumbu and climb "down into the cracks, shouting into the [highly unstable] glacier." Willi manages that impossible jujitsu of serving the whole expedition yet keeping the West Ridge flame alive. Hornbein knows him too well, and on too equal a footing, to write anything worshipful or sycophantic, yet the message comes through strong and clear: here, indeed, is a *man*. Invaluable friend. Goofy joker. Relentless competitor. One for the ages.

Ullman, who also respects Unsoeld, fails to distinguish him from the many other heroes on board. In Ullman's opinion, everyone on the climb was remarkable, from Dyhrenfurth on down. Ullman stresses how these guys are also regular Americans, ornery, democratic, amateurs who climb for love of the game, not fame or reward. His book is amply seasoned with slighting references to Red China and the Soviet Union and includes a mocking account of a Chinese ascent of Everest in '60 ("no . . . proof . . . that the climbers had actually reached the top"). The tense politics of the era, as seen in a series of grave crises—Bay of Pigs, Berlin Wall, Cuban missile— lead him to cast the expedition as an assertion of American decency against Communist totalitarian oppression. Our boys are free men, self-sacrificing and loyal because they *want* to be. That they also happen to enjoy a series of spectacular successes on Everest, putting America at last in the top rank of mountaineering nations, only goes to show what true team spirit can do.

Having returned to the United States, early that July the expedition troops over to the White House, where President Kennedy bestows the Hubbard Medal on the group as a whole. Only Willi is missing: he's back in Kathmandu, at the Shanta Bhawan United Mission Hospital, waiting for his toes to drop off. (After four months of treatments, amputations, and often excruciating discomfort, he developed hepatitis and had to be flown to the Naval Hospital in Bethesda, Maryland, for further medical interventions.) Dyhrenfurth had campaigned hard, during his fund-raising period, for a personal audience with JFK, reasoning that a presidential blessing on the expedition would open the funding floodgates. But

Kennedy, busy with the above-mentioned crises, and careful about aligning himself with an effort that might not succeed, waited till after Whittaker, Unsoeld, Hornbein, and the other Americans had gotten to the top before signaling his approval. Upon their triumphant return he became generous with public praise, all but acknowledging what had been the case all along: that this was an *American* endeavor in more than the usual sense, that the federal government had been behind it, had helped fund and shape it.

"In presenting this award," he tells the assembled climbers and dignitaries, "I carry on a great tradition . . . demonstrating that the vigorous life still attracts Americans, and also particularly mountain climbing, which is a special form of the vigorous life." Nawang Gombu, one of five Sherpas flown to the United States for a tour, drapes a *kata* around the handsome young president's neck, and Dyhrenfurth presents Kennedy with an American flag that was carried up and back from the summit on May 22. The president seems pleased. "Thank you," he says, "thank you. We will hang this in the White House . . . then give it to the Archives. That is wonderful. Thank you." The ambassadors of India and Nepal are present, and Kennedy invites them up to the podium to share in the glory. Among the other luminaries in the Rose Garden this morning are Melville Grosvenor, Gilbert Grosvenor, and assorted lesser officers from the National Geographic Society, plus Interior Secretary Udall, Senator Magnuson, and high officials from the State Department. Dyhrenfurth, as he accepts the Hubbard Medal—previously given only to famous adventurers such as Admiral Peary and Charles Lindbergh—thanks the president and asserts that as far as he knows, this is the first time a group of American mountaineers has been so honored. A raft of photographers records the proud moment. The American Everest Expedition, in every measurable way a success, is now officially over.

FOURTEEN

In a preface to his West Ridge book, Tom Hornbein writes that "Everest was not high on [Willi's] list," that his friend had more significant aspirations, nonmountaineering ones, both before and after. "[Everest was] another good climb, an essential seasoning to life, but not an ultimate challenge. . . . [It] provided Willi a visibility that he used to help accomplish [his other] goals"—goals related to his work as an apostle of the mountain experience.

Willi was seriously wounded by Everest. Hornbein walked off the mountain under his own steam, but Willi had to be carried out of Base Camp in a basket on the back of a Sherpa. (And when the basket proved too painful, he was borne off the mountain piggyback.) His feet were "dead white, hard as iron, and icy to the touch," according to the first doctor to examine them carefully. Himalayan climbers often lose a toe or two, and we may be tempted to think of this sort of injury as unimportant or commonplace, but for a climber to suffer amputations to his feet is more or less equivalent to the same thing happening to a dancer—afterward, he or she may still be able to move, but new techniques must be invented, and the old fluid expressiveness will probably never return. In

Willi's case, adjustments to his stride may have contributed to the degenerative hip condition that eventually required replacement surgeries. He remained vigorous and often got out into the mountains, but his tenure as the world's strongest Himalayan climber—a tenure begun, and a status asserted, the day he succeeded on the West Ridge—was cruelly short. By succeeding so well he guaranteed that he would likely never climb so well again.

Willi also claimed to have suffered brain damage on Everest. Thirteen years later, during the Nanda Devi expedition, he "admitted losing a good part of his mental acuity on Mount Everest in 1963," according to Roskelley, and although Willi made this statement in the middle of a big argument—the one about whether to evacuate Marty Hoey—he may well have been serious. Climbers often report mental problems after long spells spent up high. Gil Roberts, a hardworking climber/doctor on the Everest trip, said that "we all lost brainpower . . . I was above twenty-two thousand feet for six weeks, and it was like a postconcussion syndrome. . . . I remember after the expedition was over reading a medical journal article, and as I got to the end of a paragraph I was aware of having completely forgotten what it was about. It's sort of like a high school football player who gets a blow and then has to drop calculus. It comes back, but it takes time."

Sometimes it may not come back. Hornbein, as we've already seen, has been prominent among researchers trying to pin down whether and how climbers suffer lasting brain damage. In some of the most interesting studies to date, Hornbein and others have tested climbers after and during high-altitude ascents and hypoxic simulations, noting memory loss and aphasia (impairment of language ability). Climbers often report persistent problems with concentration after trips, and some have depressions for a long time afterward. Jim States, the Nanda Devi doctor, says that "mostly things come back, but I think that there are permanent changes, or at least it's a possibility for some people. It's hard to measure . . . you, as a climber returning, have to sort out the effects of normal time-passage from neurological deficits. Going there isn't the culture shock: coming *back* is . . . and now you've had a three-month time-out, time in which to forget names, numbers, etc. But I do think there may be permanent effects. Of course, this is the report of my *own* brain, a brain that's been up high a lot."

Complex events, such as ascents of Everest, are hard to pinpoint as the cause of ambiguous human outcomes, such as feeling depressed or not quite up to snuff. Still, it may be meaningful to note that the eighteen members of the '63 team lost a collective 567 pounds of body weight. Dick Emerson alone lost forty-eight pounds. Several of the climbers also divorced after their return, among them Hornbein, Jerstad, Whittaker, and Dyhrenfurth. The average age of the Everest team members was thirty-three; thirty-eight years later, as this book is being written, over half have died, a statistical anomaly for men of their educational background and social status. Will Siri, in his medical report, concluded that the "climbers were physically debilitated by the time they left Mount Everest. . . . The expedition . . . seems to have been the victim mainly of semistarvation," possibly because food isn't digested well no matter how much you eat up high. Months after the expedition, "many members . . . have reported subjective signs of memory impairment [such as] frequent difficulty in recalling once familiar names, and a need now to search out words that formerly were often and easily used." A number reported bouts of depression.

Willi had climbed as hard as anyone, or harder; he had stayed up high for a very long time (including twelve hours over twenty-eight thousand feet without oxygen). Maybe we need to credit his claim of having lost significant mental horsepower: only he was the final judge of that. Gil Roberts found him to be "phenomenally smart" on Everest and in the twelve years Roberts knew him before; Willi was "seldom wrong and never undecided." Still, if we're to take him at his word, see him as firing on only a couple of cylinders after '63, we have to account for his excellent impersonation of a Peace Corps director, a college philosophy professor, a lecturer appearing in front of audiences in many venues, always making a hit and generally being asked to come back. In other words, though he may have felt brain-damaged, this effect was entirely lost on the rest of the world, which responded to him as an inspired, committed teacher and a spellbinding performer and raconteur. If there was a mental deficit, it was marginal and undetectable—a cause without palpable effects.

The way Everest affected him—the way it *wounded* him—was more complex and can't be separated from the great boon it also was for him. Although Hornbein says that Everest was just "another good climb" for Willi, it represented a consummation as perfect as could be imagined for that historical period, when only six people had yet reached the summit. (The Chinese claim of putting people on top in '60 remains uncertain.) Willi had been reading about Everest since his boyhood, and he admired especially George Mallory and the other English pioneers of the twenties. Willi and Tom had now climbed Everest in a style to thrill even a Mallory. They had risked all, they had forged an extreme new route; they had become the climbers in their own most ideal visions of their sport. Hornbein returned to the United States and was immediately taken up with the responsibilities of a university-based career in anesthesiology, not to mention the effort of writing his book. Willi languished in hospitals for many months, then went directly back to the scene of his great triumph, Nepal, where he lived and worked for the next four years.

Hornbein has written that he feared being seen afterward as the "doc who climbed Everest," and he claims that "[f]or many years I tried to separate my [professional] and mountain worlds." For Willi there was no such separation, or only the thinnest kind. Nor did he appear to want one. He ran the Peace Corps program in Nepal, by most accounts, inspirationally but inefficiently, and his identity as the hero of the West Ridge was central to his leadership style. Peace Corps people, upon arrival in Kathmandu, were often sent out on a stiff mountain trek. Volunteers, in their often-remote village postings, enjoyed a remarkable degree of autonomy, courtesy of the program director's philosophy of encouraging spirited independence at every turn. To climb a mountain by a desperate new route required something like the same qualities as did service in the rugged backcountry: that, at any rate, was the theory, and Willi acted to promote the possibility of adventure for his team, sometimes at the expense of real accomplishment. (Willi wasn't appointed to a second tour as director. After his replacement, a Peace Corps analyst said of the Nepal program, "It has outgrown its mountain-man phase and [now] acquired leadership based on something more down-to-earth than a mystique of the Himalayas.")

It would be misleading to say that Willi's leadership was a function only of his Everest experience. But his success in an effort where he had followed his own nose and clung to impossible ideals reinforced tendencies long present in him, and surely his belief in himself only grew stronger. Laurence Leamer describes Willi's Peace Corps service as an absolute disaster: the program, just getting off the ground in '62–63, was crippled by Willi's absence on the climb and long recuperation afterward, and the Willi who returned to service on damaged feet, after months of being trotted out in front of adoring audiences (the Peace Corps used him as a stateside recruiter), after being written about glowingly in *National Geographic* and other major publications, was a man much invested in his core myth about himself. Just as it matters which ideals we believe in (if any), it also matters how we narrate our own stories, and Willi after Everest was often the impresario of his own identity, giving slide shows and honing the Old Guide routine with ceaseless repetitions.

He had wanted to make a life based on the mountain experience: inspired by, centered upon, mountaineering and the wisdom he felt it led to. As a historic hero of Everest he now found himself fully qualified for this procedure, if not overqualified. "This was a complex man who was going to have trouble finding where to fit in life," Jim Lester has said about Willi, describing him as a seeker whose principal need was for "a home for his soul where he could exercise all that charisma in a big way." The outcome of Everest sent him down a path already chosen long ago. Getting to the top, in those last daylight hours of May 22, 1963, was a blessing for him, and also a dangerous turning; unlike Hornbein, and unlike most of his other Everest companions, he would be subject to the influence of that glorious day for the rest of his life.

. . . .

FIFTEEN

Nanda Devi '76: Advanced Base Camp, beyond the awful avalanche snout, is well stocked by the end of July. Above it is the best-protected line on the Northwest Face, a broken ridge that skirts the left (northern) edge of a snowy immensity. The rocks of the broken ridge provide opportunities for climbers, shielding them from slides and giving them something to cling to or rappel from.

July 30: Reichardt leads out of camp early, heading up with States and Roskelley. In their packs are ropes and lots of climbing hardware: they're actually doing it now, climbing, forging the route, the real thing at last. Reichardt writes about this exciting and uncertain moment, "I made the first tentative sortie up the face. One thousand feet of ice-covered scree and slabs led to the foot of a series of scalloped cliffs. . . . This rock was far too soft to hold pitons convincingly. The climb abruptly ended at the furthest outcrop. A constant 'hiss' to our right revealed these rocks were our only protection."

Avalanches keep slipping down, through the sleet and rain. Mist and cloud obscure the route, and sizable rocks also hurtle past. This is the same morning that Elliot Fisher, after days of petrifaction, succeeds in crossing under the glacier snout and almost gets clipped doing so; in his excitement he then climbs up above Advanced Base to greet the other three, just as they're starting out past the scalloped cliffs. The climbing is dangerous, a mixed bag of steep uncertainties: sometimes slogging up through heavy snow, sometimes front-pointing on high-angled ice, sometimes half-climbing the crumbly rock. This will be the bill of fare for the next three and a half weeks, a period during which the combined manpower of the team, operating in hopscotching small groups, succeeds in advancing the route only an average of about two hundred feet per day.

Aside from the avalanches and the broken terrain, the principal problem is the weather—huge monsoon storms that make any movement out of camp unwise. The different factions and mutually offensive personalities thus have to pass days on end in their little tents, sleeping near one another, smelling one another, staring daggers at one another on occasion.*

At the end of the first climbing day, the three route-makers return to Advanced Base to find Devi cooking supper, her "smiling face [popping] out of Jim's tent door," as Roskelley describes it. In their exhausted, soaked-through condition this is good to see. Roskelley's simple affection for Devi, especially when she's cooking him a meal or doing something else wifely, is evident despite their differences, and Jim States's fondness for her is equally plain. She's capable,

---

*At the time of the Nanda Devi climb, dome tents had not yet become widely available. The tents used on Nanda Devi were mostly orange-colored nylon A-frames—glorified pup tents. They were less stable in storms and shed snowfall less efficiently, thus often collapsed.

Another bit of technical gear not yet in play in '76 was the spring-loaded camming device—the "Friend"—invented by Yosemite rock climber Ray Jardine. The climbers on Nanda Devi relied for protection on older-fashioned gear such as ice screws, pitons, and tie-offs to natural horns of rock or snow bollards. Reichardt, Roskelley, and Unsoeld all mention using tubular aluminum snow-pickets in an unorthodox way, pounding them into deep cracks until they deform and can be tied off.

thoughtful, friendly, fun—what's not to like, and why were they so concerned to have no women around? Devi's full-hearted approach to the climb—that it means so much to her—puts her on the same wavelength as Dr. States. He's not so mystical, but he works with troubled kids looking to find a way, seeking a nod of recognition from the cosmos. Then you only have to get to know her a little, as States, in the next few days, tries to do, sharing a tent with her and Elliot, to feel the force of her refreshing goodness. With some people you're immediately on a different plane: it doesn't mean they've got their head in the clouds, only that they're searching, embarked on something greater.

In the night many avalanches. Advanced Base, beyond the dangerous snout, shouldn't be at risk when they come down, but sometimes the big ones overrun the normal path, pushing powerful winds ahead of them, like the gusts of wind that roar out of a tunnel ahead of a train. Roskelley writes about this and other stormy nights in a tent:

> How terrifying an avalanche in the dark . . . the grating, rasping sounds—the blackness. Each avalanche seemed intent on roaring into camp and burying us alive. . . . I would jerk into a sitting position . . . strain desperately to hear where the cold death was heading, but the sound was deceiving. . . . Then the blast of wind . . . would hit the tent and the noise would shoot by. My breathing would return and my heart would pound as if it wanted out of my chest.

In the morning, with the storm still going strong, they stay indoors and radio Willi not to carry below the snout today. But a few hours later he does, with porters and most of the other members of the team. Now just about everyone's at Advanced Base, pinned down by the dismal weather. Amiable Dr. States finds Willi's presence hard to bear: their clash at the time of the Marty crisis, when Jim spoke with full medical authority, and Willi pretty much laughed in his face, has never resolved, and Jim thinks he overhears Willi mocking the way he's been counseling the troubled Elliot. In the discussions over the next few days, about whether to wait out the storms or abandon the route, go climb something easy, Jim is alternately peevish and barely in control of his anger, steaming with all the things he wants to scream at Willi.

About these times of tension, uncomfortable closeness, doubt, and fear, Lou Reichardt will write in the *AAJ*, in a passage unfortunately not atypical of that esteemed journal:

> Forced rest days are a chance to meet your neighbor. For me the best part of a Himalayan adventure is the sharing of the experience with other dedicated climbers. Your best friends are made in adversity. [Andy] Harvard has a firm grasp on Himalayan logistics [for example]. He is an easy substitute for a "How to Do It" book. States relentlessly tries to cure sahibs of lowland ailments . . .

and so on, and so forth.

Willi's account of the stormbound days likewise looks hard for the positive, but hints at darker feelings, too:

> That we had to wait for seven or eight days: that was tough on some of the more gung ho members. There was talk of getting off this route and going somewhere you could actually climb . . . We did a lot of reading out loud, much of it from *Doctor Dogbody's Leg,* Ad

Carter's favorite expedition tome. . . . Devi'd whip out her harmonica, play endless out-of-tune versions of songs. . . . I'd whip out a recorder, and you know it's really pleasant to have a week to do nothing, just lie there in bed. But you have to be attuned to it.

August 1: A giant avalanche blast catches Devi outside the tent, dressed only in her underwear; she grabs a rock, waiting out the suffocating swirl of snow and ice. The support poles snap in Roskelley's tent, and the second one, the one where Devi's been sleeping with Elliot and States, tears apart and blows thirty feet and over a cliff edge. "We rushed over and peered down in horror," Willi told his audiences, "and then this head came out of the wreckage," which had snagged below the top. "Jim had been cooking a pot of Roman Meal mush . . . it was all plastered down his front and his beard, and the pot was empty."

From so many avalanches so close to hand, they become weirdly used to them: "We could predict how much blast was gonna result from which sort of sound," Willi said. "You'd . . . you'd hear the rumble high on the face, and you were pretty blasé by now, and you'd say, 'Nah—that's just a little one,' and you'd wait till it rumbled down over the snout. But when it was *really moving* you could tell that, too, and you'd go fast for the tent poles."

August 2 and 3: A window of good weather permits more climbing up the face. Roskelley locates a spot for the next camp at 19,100 feet, on a little snow ledge protected by an overhanging wall. When the sun comes out, as it does with tropical power, they sweat and suffer as they flounder up through the mush. The four to make it to Camp I on the second—Roskelley, Reichardt, States, Devi—are the four strongest, on that day at any rate; no one's fully acclimated, even Reichardt's moving like a snail, but they do some good work, and the young female keeps up just fine, bearing a bulky pack. Here, too, Devi somehow conjures a homey moment: as they collapse under the rock overhang, sheltering from the sun, she puts together a lunch of beef jerky and crackers and odd bits of this and that. Roskelley records approvingly: "We passed the tidbits . . . while enjoying the beautiful scene of mountains rising before us."

Three years earlier, Devi had traveled on her own in the Himalaya. On that memorable trip, she had adventures such as even these stalwart mountaineers, these cutting-edge ice- and rock-jocks, might have found a bit much. Her journey, inspired in part by Willi's similar vagabondage in his twenties, began when she was just eighteen.

First she hitchhiked in the United States, then she traveled and worked her way across Europe, a spell spent in a factory on Crete being her equivalent to Willi's Swedish foundry. Her trip is unthinkable today, partly because of political and cultural changes in some of the countries she traversed (Pakistan, Afghanistan), partly because it seems to belong to a different historical era entirely, a time when the authority of youth warranted bold pilgrimages, and an exaggerated hope attached to women's assertion of new freedoms. Often on her own, negotiating different cultures without much in the way of money or other resources, she made her way to Kathmandu, where she looked forward to renewing the impressions of her childhood.

A climber and novelist, Keith Hillsbury, who knew Devi at Evergreen, where they were both students, spent a year and a half in Nepal in the seventies. Before he went out to Kathmandu, in a program organized by the college, he took basic cultural instruction from Devi, who could speak Nepalese passably well and write the script. "Our language study was minimal," Hillsbury told me, "but Devi said, 'Don't worry, as soon as you get there, go to the Temple

Square and show the local kids that you can write the script. They'll be impressed, and *that's* where you'll learn the language.' So when we arrived, we did go to the square . . . the kids immediately came up chattering to us in Nepali, and we wrote our names in the dirt. From that moment on we were learning. . . .

"Devi talked a lot about the Kumari, the 'living goddess,' " Hillsbury says. "This was a kind of subtle way she got many important messages into us. . . . Kumari's the girl who's housed in the main Temple Square, considered a divine incarnation but only until she has her first period, or somehow sheds blood. The way they pick this girl: some high-caste Hindu, some Brahman, has an inspiration about where to go look for her. Then they gather up the little girls in the region and submit them to a sort of Halloween-style freakhouse ordeal, and the one who shows no fear is the one chosen. Devi told us about Kumari while speaking on menstruation. It's very taboo in Nepal, the women are isolated during their periods . . . she was talking to these politically correct American college girls, and they were appalled, of course. But she pointed out that if they didn't disclose their status to the families, the men in the houses they were living in would always wonder about them, and this would prevent them from ever getting close.

"Devi also told us about the Teej, a celebratory festival just about women, for women. You'd be invited only if you got with the program on menstruation. . . . About the idea of the living goddess, she said, 'I cannot describe it to you, you have to *see* it. See and then maybe you'll understand—maybe.'

"We went to the festival. Fifty thousand people packed in the Temple Square. A scene of intense fervor such as I'd never experienced before . . . we Westerners, benefiting from the kindness that was shown us all over the country, were pushed right up front, exactly where the carriage would go by, where the girl would get on it. Then they carried her out of her palace on a litter. . . . To see Kumari was good luck, but to be able to touch her meant astonishing good fortune, maybe for an entire lifetime. She was about eight or nine years old I guess . . . kohled eyes . . . she radiated a vibrant spirituality—I guess *holiness* is the only word you could use for it. All the yearning and belief of those fifty thousand people was focused upon her, and she *became what they wanted.* . . .

"Since we'd been pushed up front, I was able to touch her, lightly, on the shoulder. The look on her face was remote, enormously reposeful . . . as Devi had said, she *was* the goddess. And you couldn't've understood that back in a college class in America."

Devi on her own in Kathmandu was like other Westerners, in some respects. She wore "Tibetan dresses of thick feltlike wool," Laurence Leamer says, and also "flared billowing white pants covered with a sheathlike dress," the costume of some women of the Punjab. She was there to have an exotic experience, as were other young travelers in those years, the beginning of a period of extraordinary influx from the West, with longhaired tourists trekking and "looking, looking" everywhere, often enjoying the abundant hemp and other drugs. It would be a mistake to see Devi's time in Nepal as typical of the day, however. She wasn't really a drug taker or sexually relaxed; she "definitely wasn't part of the hippie drug thing," according to Al Read, a Foreign Service officer posted to Kathmandu (now co-owner, with Peter Lev, of Exum Mountain Guides, Wyoming). Read knew Willi from climbing in the Tetons, and he'd known Devi as a child, when Willi guided for Exum and his family lived with him during the summers. Thirty years later, Read's impressions of Devi remain singular and vivid: "This very *alive* young person . . . beautiful, poised. You felt a powerful and unusual spirit that reminded you very much of Willi's, although subtler and sweetly female . . . just a lovely person. One of the most captivating young people I've ever met.

"I saw her when I was at the embassy," Read says, "and also when I trekked in Langtang [National Park, a mountain zone north of Kathmandu]. What was she, nineteen, twenty years old? Amazing when you consider how poised she was, how acute. Very much at home there. I mean in Nepal, the Himalaya—very much at home."

Devi worked for a reforestation project near Everest. She also worked in a place called Tiger Tops Lodge, a nature-viewing resort inside the borders of Royal Chitwan National Park, in the subtropical lowlands west of Kathmandu. Chitwan attracts wildlife biologists from all over the world because of its remnant populations of rhino and Bengal tiger, and in the early seventies a Smithsonian zoologist, John Seidensticker, was just beginning some fieldwork on leopards and tigers in the park. Seidensticker, now the curator of mammals at the Smithsonian, remembers, "Devi was something special. . . . Al Read [had] suggested that Devi and Krag [her younger brother, who joined her in '74] come down and help out. And they did a great job. Very self-assured and completely competent. . . . Languages are not my thing [but] Devi took some time to teach me how to learn a local language just by talking with people about everyday things around a cooking fire. By the time they left, I could run a tiger-catching operation in Nepali.

"We organized a project for them," Seidensticker told me, "looking at ungulate habitat utilization . . . [t]hey just ran with it. They would put one person in a tree on the lookout for rhinos while the [others] did their plots. When I wanted to radio-track a female leopard that had three new cubs, we put them in a [treetop observation post] for two weeks at a time, and I mostly kept them supplied and checked in on them twice a day. This remains the best data sets ever obtained for a female and leopard cubs, or for nearly any big cat with young for that matter."

Seidensticker once saw Devi climb down from her tree platform, at dusk; they had been observing, from different posts, a group of twelve rhinos grazing in the nearby bush. She walked out among the group and then returned. This was at a time—her second year in Chitwan—when she was entirely aware of the risks she ran by doing so. The Asian rhinoceros, too large and powerful to be threatened by any land predator, nonetheless often charges, tramples, and gores. Another biologist at work in the park, Andrew Laurie, once saw Devi run through a grassland with grazing rhinos about. One of the great animals pursued her and narrowly missed her with its charge.

In his book about Nanda Devi, Roskelley praises Devi's work ethic on the mountain, but slights her pure mountaineering skills: "Her experience as a climber was limited," he says, "[and] [s]he believed mountains were more to feel from the heart . . . than to tread with the feet." Keith Hillsbury, her Evergreen friend, disagrees with this assessment categorically. He grew up in Washington, where he climbed often in the Cascades. In '75 he participated in an international Everest expedition, with Chris Bonington and other renowned climbers; as a son of the Northwest, he was familiar with snow and ice, a strong mountaineer adept on many kinds of ground. "Devi was one of the best climbers I knew," Hillsbury says, "cautious but also very game. Way beyond average in a technical sense. Remember, as a single woman she'd twice traveled the overland route to Asia alone. I traveled it myself, but not *by* myself . . . there were several women in our group, strong, independent feminists, who couldn't cope with traveling there alone, for good reason.

"There's a story people told about her fending off a guy with an ice ax in a bus once in Afghanistan. Maybe that's apocryphal, but what I know about Devi as a mountaineer I learned from climbing hard routes with her. I went up to do one on the northwest side [of Rainier], but there was too much avalanche danger so we climbed Mount Index instead . . . our first time on Rainier, we were in Paradise [a settlement midway on the mountain], and she looked up at the Nisqually Ice Cliff above and said, 'Hmm, that looks good— let's do it.' She said, 'A hanging bivy in the icefall isn't so bad if you have to get an early start'—someone she knew had bivvied on the wall and then gone to the top the next day. Then we got up into it and it was really *hard* route-finding . . . Devi found the way. I may have been better on Yosemite granite, but she knew ice and snow better . . . how to place ice screws maximally . . . there were sections of about 5.8 [degree of difficulty] on a lot of extended, very rough terrain. Many objective dangers—rockfall, and the glacier's always moving. You constantly had to look out for five things at once, in the meantime doing the hard ice work. I would have said, except that it would've sounded patronizing, 'You're as good as a really strong guy.' She carried it off talking Hindu theology all the while. And had a good time."

August 3: Devi feels sick and so doesn't join Roskelley on the route above. Still, she carries a full pack to Camp I in the afternoon. (Lev and Harvard, in line to push the route that day, are too sick to leave Advanced Base.) Then the bad weather returns, and no one goes anywhere for a long time. Elliot Fisher decides to leave the expedition: according to Leamer, the deciding factor for Elliot was "a rock ten inches in diameter" sailing past his head. Well and good—everyone has, by this point, become tired of holding his hand, trying to talk him through the process of either going home and not feeling guilty, or staying and not being crippled by fear. But most of them like him and it's hard to see him go. It's hard to see anybody go: with Ad Carter's imminent departure, the team is now down to a scarily scant number. Roskelley fumes about the perfidy of an expedition's leader turning tail just when the hard climbing's getting started. Though he'd loudly criticized Carter for his leadership at the start of the trip, now he rues the loss of another competent hand.

"Ad, you can't leave the expedition just like that!" Roskelley cries into the radio one afternoon. "You came in with intentions of helping and carrying on the mountain. . . . I asked you several times in the States to add another strong climber, but you said no because in your opinion the team was strong enough. With Marty gone and John Evans not here, your leaving could mean the difference. . . . None of us feel like being here in these conditions either, but we're going to give it all we have."

To which Ad replies, "Well, I appreciate your wanting me to stay, John. That's good of you. I . . . wish all of you all the luck in the world. I know you can do it. . . . Over and out."

And that's it. Carter leaves, accompanied by Fisher, on the seventh of August.

SIXTEEN

Slow, grudging progress; then no progress for days on end. If John Evans doesn't arrive, they'll be without the spools of rope he's supposedly bringing in from Delhi, in which case just forget about it. Mountaineering expeditions are often afflicted with uncertainty, but Nanda Devi '76 is a model of apprehension, insecure on so many levels and in so many ways that the whole endeavor verges on parody. The climbers don't know whether they can trust each other. Many are sick, with lingering bronchial and intestinal infections that lead Lou Reichardt to order them down to Base for recuperation. (They ignore his order.) There's the rope problem, and as the team members spend long days pinned down in high camps, they consume so much high-altitude food that it becomes a question whether enough will be left for a summit attempt. The storms are not only frequent, they dump amazing amounts of snow—in a single day at Camp I, a full nine feet accumulates (fresh snow plus deposits from avalanche blowby).

Then there are the uncertainties of the route itself. The face is turning out to be immense, unending; and should they ever get to the top of it, there's the Buttress. Reichardt tells Elliot, when he's still anguishing over leaving, "Only John and Jim are indispensable," meaning that only those two are capable of leading this kind of extreme terrain. (This is probably untrue: Lev and possibly also Reichardt himself possess the necessary technical skills.) Should they actually surmount the Buttress, there's still a long way to the summit proper—another one thousand six hundred feet of vertical gain, over unknown snowy ground.

Himalayan climbers cherish uncertainty, to some extent. If we can trust the books they write, epics are some of the best things that ever happen to them, as long as they survive. The extremism forces a stripping away of all softness, all inadequacy; part of the gratification is to discover who *really* belongs on the A-team. As Dick Emerson showed in his study of Everest '63, climbers will even manufacture uncertainty if things become too predictable. But an outside observer of such efforts, noticing how small the team on Nanda Devi had become (just nine members, several of them sick), how uncomfortable some of the people were with the others, and how vast and serious is the mountain they were attempting (just short of eight thousand meters high, and by an unknown route), must conclude that Fisher and Carter were acting rationally, if *rational* means removing oneself from a terrible situation. Certainly they were right to leave if they felt truly unlucky; if you *really* think your number is up, even your responsibilities to your teammates are trumped, since the bad luck you'll bring may be visited on them, too. Elliot agonized for so long, felt so genuinely bad about leaving the others, that we have to consider the possibility that he knew more than he consciously knew, that he sensed some "fate" awaiting him on Nanda Devi. Even if he believed that he was just playing the percentages—counting the number of avalanches, measuring the insane amount of snow, taking a cold, hard look at his teammates— he may have been responding to something less tangible.

Both Leamer and Roskelley record an unusual conversation that took place on August 7, when Fisher was descending from Ridge Camp for the last time and ran into Roskelley, who was on his way back up from Base. In Leamer's version, "Roskelley began to cry. . . . 'Don't you understand,' [Roskelley] sobbed beseechingly. 'All of us want to go home. Why are you copping out?' " Fisher tries to apologize, but Roskelley won't let him: " 'Don't say it. It won't make any difference. Don't you understand how I hate to go under that glacier too? I'm no different.' " Roskelley continues up the mountain, and when "he was just a blue-and-red spot on the ridge above, Fisher heard an anguished cry echoing down the mountain. *Tell my wife I love her!* "

In Roskelley's book, this encounter has a more uncanny quality, with a suggestion of second sight:

" 'Damn it, Elliot,' [Roskelley] said. 'I wish you hadn't made this decision . . . but at least you made one. I hope you know what you're doing.'

" 'I'm sorry. But I have to do this for me.' . . . We both sat looking into the dirt, tears welling up in our eyes.

" 'You know, I'd like to go out too, Elliot. All of us would. This mountain's dangerous and someone's going to be killed.'

" 'If that's what you believe, then why don't you leave and get off the mountain?'

" 'Because it's not going to be me,' [Roskelley] replied."*

---

*Prophetic feelings, especially those of impending doom, are probably no more common in mountain climbing than they are in ordinary life. If a climber on a mountain like Nanda Devi paid attention to every gloomy intuition that came in the night, he or she would probably spend the expedition cowering in a tent.

Still, sometimes such feelings are uncommonly vivid and ignoring them feels wrong. According to Roskelley, on August 10 a supernatural feeling overcame Jim States, who was disturbed by a disheartening premonition that his father had died. The feeling was unnerv-

August 7: Clear weather gets everyone in gear. Willi, Pete, and Jim States carry to Camp I, then stay there overnight; on the following day they'll push the route higher, taking over from Roskelley and Reichardt. The other members also carry loads up from Advanced Base, and the general feeling is of a skeleton crew grumpily digging itself out from under, yet showing surprising signs of life.

The following morning, Willi and Lev, with States in support, climb above Camp I, making some progress but not fast, according to Roskelley, who watches from below and disapproves of the way they're hauling their extra ropes (dragging them behind in the deep snow rather than carrying them in packs). Reichardt, as climbing leader, attempts to impose a fair-minded regime on all the prima donnas: believing that "[i]t is everyone's expedition," he forces Roskelley to cool his heels while Willi and Lev do their hard, if slower, climbing out front. No one can lead this whole enormous route by himself—switching off and resting are essential. Roskelley knows this better than anyone, but every day when he isn't out front he criticizes the rate of progress, the wasteful way the ropes and hardware are being used. His kick-ass energy gets him through a respiratory infection, one requiring large doses of penicillin, with hardly any downtime; his ambition for this route, his *I am a professional now, and I will make my mark for all the world to see* mind-set drives him on, driving some of the others half-crazy.

Willi, Lev, and States reach a little stance, a tiny ledge-let protected by a thirty-foot rock wall, eight hundred feet above Camp I. They excavate the site as a cache for supplies, then decide to make

---

ing, especially since Jim had had another one a few days before about Lou Reichardt getting hit by an avalanche, and Lou had barely escaped an avalanche shortly thereafter.

Roskelley concludes: "I gave Jim as much reassurance as I could, then quickly changed the subject."

it Camp II because the top of the Northwest Face is still a good three thousand feet away and it looks as if there may not be any intervening spots for camps. Roskelley fumes, considering this decision a pathetic failure; Reichardt also questions the wisdom of putting the second camp so close to the first, using up tents and equipment and manpower better employed up higher.

" 'How many pitches did you get in today?' [Reichardt asks Willi over the radio one afternoon.]

" 'We did quite well . . . the hardest leading to date, a pitch of mixed climbing to avoid a gully . . . Jim ran out a final rope up snow. A dozen sloughs must have hit me in that belay stance. It is really exposed!'

" 'It sounds hairy. How far did you get altogether?'

" 'Two pitches!'

" 'Oh!' [Reichardt's] disappointment was audible. . . .

" 'Reichardt, the strongest should be out in front [someone hisses into Reichardt's other ear while he's on the radio—Reichardt doesn't say who, but this someone is almost certainly Roskelley]! You can't let them do this [put in the second camp so close to the first]. It is crazy!' "*

Despite all the second-guessing, Lev climbs hard, putting up some of the toughest pitches on the face. These arduous, scary leads are what he will later recall as "some of my best days ever in the mountains," days made enjoyable by Willi's company. For Willi, the climbing is an instant immersion in the fixed-rope-and-jumar style of ascent, which he doesn't like for philosophical reasons but quickly masters. On a typical day, Lev and Willi awaken

---

*Louis F. Reichardt and William F. Unsoeld, "Nanda Devi from the North," *American Alpine Journal*, 1977, pp. 12–13.

at 1 or 2 A.M.; they fire up the stove inside their freezing tent, eat a bite, dress in the cramped, dark quarters, then lumber out into the spine-cracking cold. The early start, with only starlight and headlamps to see by, is required because in a few hours the face where they could so easily freeze to death will be melting under a maddening sun, and now they can at least flounder through sugar snow and attach mechanical ascenders and jug up the fixed ropes to the high point of the previous day's climbing. "When you'd led out one rope [above the high point]," Willi told his lecture audiences, "you'd anchor it and then your second would jumar up to you. Then, you'd lead up another pitch. . . . The snow was never exactly what you wanted, either you floundered through or if there'd been serious avalanche action, that part of the face would be bare, hard ice.

"We put a lot of ice screws in. We had a whole box of GI pitons somebody gave us . . . the technically minded members dumped on 'em, because they'd cut their teeth on chromolys [hard chrome-molybdenum-alloy pitons], but for me it was very nostalgic to gear up with a rack of soft-iron 'ringed wafers' again. And a limited number of the priceless 'GI angles.'

"The rope management was hard . . . on these leads; you might have two coiled ropes stuffed in your pack, plus dragging another three hundred feet behind you. Some of us weren't used to doing hard, long leads with those sort of big packs on. . . . I know that Pete Lev, as a for-real Teton guide, had brought along a tiny Carman pack, sort of a bookbag really, and he *insisted* on leading only with his Carman on, because that was a proper leader's bag, he said. You could carry maybe about six pitons in it."

They're slow, but they do inch upward, and Willi keeps up with Lev. At almost fifty years of age he has a surprising amount of leg power left, and those soft-metal pitons in his hands are talismans of a golden age of mountaineering that he himself helped create. On Masherbrum, on Makalu, on the West Ridge, he amazed others with his preternatural strength and drive, and he's still doing it: "[Willi] slowly made his way up to me in an incredible display of determination," Roskelley, the critic, writes about a hard carry Willi makes pulling four tangled ropes. "His stamina was astounding. . . . No wonder he had climbed Everest and Masherbrum."

August 13: Willi and Lev can't make it to the top of the ridge, though (top of the Northwest Face). Exhausted by hard days of climbing and nights at cramped Camp II, they surrender the lead to States and Roskelley, who jumar up to the highest previous point and then go beyond, but who also can't quite make the ridgetop. Then, in the night of August 14, powerful winds start blowing, it starts snowing again, and all bets are off. The team that was to have taken over from Roskelley and States—Reichardt and Devi, with Kumar and Singh in support—can hardly get out of their tents the next morning. The snow keeps falling, off and on, all day, and then the next day, and into the next. "The foul weather continued for six more days," Reichardt reports tersely in his article, "and the mood became black. [We asked ourselves,] 'Why did we come at this time of year?'

"[And the answer was], 'I don't know. Never again, though.'"

SEVENTEEN

Devi has a sore throat, as does Roskelley. She also has a racking cough—again, just like Roskelley, who got his from "running to avoid [an] avalanche . . . at seventeen thousand feet with a load." Infections and coughs are epidemic on expeditions, and they tend to linger as long as climbers stay up high, breathing frigid air and sleeping poorly. Devi also has a hernia, which she dismisses as no hindrance; to this point on the expedition, she's proved herself able to climb and carry with any of the men, even the strongest. Roskelley writes in his book that Devi "perform[ed] above the standards of some of the healthier sahibs," and the proof of her status, also of her generally adequate conditioning, is that she's set to team with Reichardt on the next go-round, pushing the route to the top of the ridge (22,800 feet).

Then the storm blows away these hopes. On August 16, Devi goes down to Advanced Base to rest up, get over her sore throat quicker because of the lower altitude. (Roskelley also benefits from the days of enforced rest: "The storm was the break I had needed . . . my ear and sore throat improved considerably with the warm air of the tent and heavy doses of drugs.") Andy Harvard has also been sick, and to this point he hasn't quite pulled his oar. A tall, dark-eyed young man with a good mind and an air of substance, he's been acclimating slowly, and from now on he'll be increasingly strong. Among these big egos, these Unsoelds, Roskelleys, and Reichardts, Harvard appears tentative, but in fact he has an impressive mountaineering résumé and is the coauthor of one of the best climbing books of the seventies, *Mountain of Storms*, about the '73 Dhaulagiri expedition. He belongs solidly to the Willi camp. "Willi was a complex braid," Harvard said later, "one of the strands being his Bergsonian thought, another being Christian ethics as he interpreted them . . . just a transcendently positive guy. You could see his charisma without necessarily being susceptible to it, and that was okay with him. He was interested in how people learn and think, in how persuasion works, including his own . . . one of his techniques was to reveal a little something personal, getting you to reveal your own interior a bit. Days later you'd realize he'd shown you very little, but the purpose wasn't manipulation, it was just for the joy of argument, to further the discourse."

Andy sets out to carry a load to Camp I, but the sheer abundance of new snow makes it a bad idea. He retreats to Advanced Base. When Devi comes down a day later to rest, they renew the companionship they've been enjoying for some time now. "The other climbers knew what was going on between [them] nearly as soon as they did," Leamer says in his book, and according to Roskelley, "They were becoming inseparable . . . Devi and Andy shared more than an interest in climbing." In fact, they're smitten with each other. They share a tent whenever they can manage it. Whenever the weather and logistics allow, they carry loads together, moving up the ropes at a relaxed pace that permits enjoyment of the astonishing place where they find themselves. "We very much wanted to climb the mountain on account of its beauty," Andy recalls, "and while it was an extremely frustrating expedition, with a mechanistic group separate from a happier one, it was also a fabulous time. Some of my best days ever in the mountains were on Nanda Devi . . . not everyone was capable of summiting, our Indian teammates for example, but there was an opportunity for a splendid effort."

Andy has climbed with Roskelley before. (Also with Reichardt, also Lev.) On Dhaulagiri, Roskelley impressed everyone with his hard work, and according to Andy, "John proved himself one of the great acclimatizers . . . some have it and some don't. Also his baseline personality is good, and this contributed to his success. He's bright, has a good sense of humor, and this promoted a feeling on the part of the rest of us that he'd be an appropriate beneficiary of the collective effort—that he was one of the ones who deserved a summit shot."

But within a year of Dhaulagiri, "There'd been a deep change in him. The evolution of climbing in the early seventies favored this change, whereby he started thinking he could make a living at it, as Bonington and others in England seemed to be doing. The European marketing nexus around climbing didn't exist yet in the U.S., but by [the time of Nanda Devi] John's idea of the stake he had in the outcome of the event was very different."

Willi approves of Harvard: the guy's solid, interesting, almost good enough for his daughter. Before the expedition, Willi had in fact been wondering whether Devi might find someone important on this climb, a life companion. For many years now Willi has basked in the deep, Cordelia-like love of his remarkable eldest daughter, returning that affection with a full heart, exuberantly. They give evidence of being two of the most fortunate types of human: a daughter who knows the bottomless love of a respectful father, and a father whose daughter grows up only to delight him.

Willi grants Devi wide latitude because she's earned it, and because his personal philosophy is to guide by giving way, ceding freedom wherever possible. In practical terms this means understanding another person's capacities unsentimentally, then facilitating that person's stepping forth onto meaningful personal ground. With his children, as with his students and his guiding clients and everyone else who's ever asked him to show the way, Willi operates from a straightforward philosophy, one founded in the belief that life is an ongoing search, one that concludes when life does. He believes further that in our denatured, technologized world the challenges presented by wilderness are uniquely valuable. After his Peace Corps service, Willi accepted a position with the national leadership of Outward Bound, and among his duties was traveling and lecturing on behalf of the newly created American version of the British organization.* Along with Paul Petzoldt, another American mountaineer and outsize personality, Willi proselytized on behalf of the group and its philosophy, which he found entirely congenial. Of *course* young people could be shaped—strengthened, deepened as personalities—by encounters with wilderness. These encounters, carefully designed as they must always be, would nevertheless contain an element of risk: as Willi liked to say, "It has to be real enough to kill you."

Or maybe that should read, "Real enough to make you *think* it can kill you." Outward Bounders were not immediately thrown into raging torrents or sent up huge rockfaces. Rope courses and moun-

---

*Outward Bound was started by Kurt Hahn (1886–1974), a German educator who became an apostle of adventure-based learning after being driven out of his homeland by the Nazis. The Outward Bound schools developed from a training program Hahn designed to increase the survival rate of British sailors shipwrecked in the North Atlantic. Hahn, also associated with Berlin's Salem School, put young sailors through arduous cold-water exercises, teaching them the fundamentals of small-boat navigation and rescue. After the war, his programs won a following as a way to instill character in slack modern youth.

tain hikes were more the order of the day, with situations of real risk introduced only at appropriate levels. But Willi, in whose life risk had functioned as a philosophers' stone, turning base metal (mundane existence) into gold (adventure and revelation), was serious about the idea. His lectures, seemingly thrown together on the walk up to the podium, full of mockery and humor, were consistent over the years and always served the same few core beliefs.

Willi looked upon Devi fondly, but he was also able to look at her as a professional educator, one trained in assessing outdoor-adventure candidates. And the verdict had to be that here was someone skilled enough, motivated enough, to have an excellent chance of climbing a great mountain. In the last few years Devi had traveled on her own under harsh conditions, done hard physical labor, wrestled rhinoceroses to the ground. Summer of '74, she had joined Willi and her younger brother on a commercial trek in Pakistan, during which the Unsoelds led some clients to the top of an unclimbed peak. Devi, in Willi's experience of her, was a mature, capable person with a bold temperament, "a moderate fanatic and also something of a stoic," as he later described her. She was exactly the kind of woman to make a mockery of the idea that women don't belong up high. If not Devi, who? Even Roskelley judged her a bear for carrying loads, someone who performed "above the standards" of some of the fittest males.

Still, Roskelley tut-tuts in his book, "Since any teammate's action affects all the other climbers, Andy and Devi's relationship became a concern of ours. As their relationship grew, so did the talk about it. I thought it was a potentially damaging relationship." He declares that "neither would carry a load without the other," and that "on rest days or sick days the expedition lost two climbers rather than one." The examples Roskelley offers of days when this actually happened, when the expedition suffered on account of the lazy lovebirds, are nil. A reader of his book gets the feeling, instead, that having made a big noise all along about men and women on expeditions, Roskelley must now condemn any pleasurable joining of the sexes. If the climb is not so intensely under the gun that any distraction threatens catastrophe, then many things are thrown into question. Not least would be the structure of A-teams and B-teams, the tight hierarchy that alone offers a chance at success, according to Roskelley's way of thinking. Romance is an enemy not because it leads to a dangerous loss of focus, but because it implies a different way of being on the heights. Maybe even a richer, more memorable way—and one not necessarily condemned to failure.

EIGHTEEN

On these same days in August '76, in other parts of the Garhwal Himalaya, religious observances were under way that offered a strange commentary on the expedition. These were religious pilgrimages, or *jats,* that started in lowland villages, just as the expedition had done, then ascended by stages into the snowy heights, as the expedition was trying to do.

The goddess Nanda was the focus of these celebrations. If the Garhwal is the holiest, most godly region in the Himalaya, then Nanda herself is the most fervently adored among Hindu deities, by virtue of her preeminence in the area. "We tend to be impressed," writes Johan Reinhard, anthropologist of the world's high-mountain zones, "when we hear that a religious cult has over a million followers. Imagine, then, that close to a *billion* people believe the Himalaya to be sacred, and these include followers of two of the world's major religions: Buddhism and Hinduism. Nowhere in the world does a mountain range figure so prominently in the religious beliefs of such a large and diverse population. For these people mountains are the dwelling places of deities and saints, and for some they are the very embodiments of the gods themselves."

The *jats* of the holy goddess, colorful processions centuries old, bring together communities in ceremonies drenched in mystical significance. They are enactments of the people's deep beliefs about their gods, about human fate, about social relations (especially sex roles). The Garhwal is a magnet for pilgrims of all types, but the *jats* of Nanda Devi are intensely local. The genius of the Garhwali people, their unique spirituality and identity as denizens of *this* magical land and none other, shows forth in the *jats*.

The goddess, by legend a village girl of divine origin, must fulfill her karma by marrying a god on a mountain. She becomes a *dhiyani*—an outmarried village daughter—by becoming the bride of Shiva, the great male divinity of the Hindu pantheon. "Shiva comes to the wedding in his customary attire," writes William Sax, an authority on the goddess cult, "nearly naked, smeared with ash, garlanded with snakes and skulls. Nandadevi's parents are horrified."

A terrifying son-in-law, Shiva is nonetheless the only proper consort for Nanda, on account of her holiness. But life on an icy mountaintop with an ascetic god is hard. "Ice burns my flesh, in the air we breathe poison," Nanda tells her mother in one of the ritual songs of the cult. ". . . I wear scratchy clothes made of wool, my poor stomach aches from a second-rate grain . . . Mother, our clothes are of snow."

By outmarrying—leaving for another place—Nanda repeats the unhappy pattern of most brides of the Garhwal. Forsaking all she holds dear, she becomes the chattel of her husband. Village life, in the Garhwal as elsewhere, is "virilocal," meaning that couples live where the husband is from; the bride must make a new life among people not of her own blood. In the case of the goddess Nanda, suffering in an icy, faraway place married to an ascetic yogi leads to resentment. She begs to return to her native village for a ritual, but Shiva opposes her. Finally, she puts a curse on her village, which is then compelled to invite her home and feed her well for a change ("Today, O my mother, I'll eat my fill of rice pudding, and butter").

If Devi Unsoeld knew of the *jats,* knew of their odd timing—late monsoon, exactly when the Americans were climbing—she left no record. Nor did any of her surviving teammates recall being aware or remember anyone else being aware, other than in the sense of knowing that the mountain they were ascending was considered holy. Even the most culturally sensitive of Westerners—and Willi would have to be included in such a group, along with Lev, Harvard, Carter—are like non-Christians attending the first communion of a friend's child. If they show a basic respect, avoid spectacular gaffes, they can be said to be performing well enough. To be aware of *all* the implications of each gesture and murmured prayer is more than anyone could ask.

Even when a climber returns from Nepal or some other exotic place and declares, "Meeting the local people was much more important than the climb," then shows off his collection of prayer flags and lights incense in the shrine he now keeps in his living room, he isn't being really serious. He may have learned a few things, broadened his perspective, but at no time has he become sensitive to the totality of impressions that a native believer, on his native ground, routinely processes. One of the most signal differences between Western and South Asian cultures is a different conception of personhood. In remote places like the Garhwal, identity is said to vary with location, because "the soil substance is mixed with the bodily substance," as William Sax puts it. We of the West tend to believe our identities persist no matter where located, in London, Santa Monica, or the Amazon. If we say something that sounds different—for example, "I was profoundly changed by my trip to the Taj Mahal"—we mean it in a poetic way, certainly not as someone from high-village Uttarakhand would. This is why pilgrimages to *particular* places, at *particular* times of the year, during which *specific* actions are undertaken, are highly important in the tradition. The self is altered in the same way that a mountain is changed when a god comes to dwell on it.

Devi was steeped in Himalayan cultures to an unusual extent, and from her interest in the living goddess, Kumari, we know that she was intrigued by the process whereby one thing becomes another, a young girl turns into an incarnation, an aspect of the godhead. As she told the students she coached at Evergreen, you had to stand in the Temple Square in Kathmandu on the day of the holy festival to know. You had to look the goddess in the face, maybe (if you were lucky) touch her. By the same token, as she told the *Times of India,* "I can't describe it but there is something within me about this mountain ever since I was born." This "something" no doubt refers to her having the same name, her beloved father having seen the mountain in a vision and then set her on a path to want to climb it. Her childhood had been spent in mountains, including many mountain outings under his tutelage; she had lived as a young woman in such a way as to prepare for this adventure, and potentially for many others. Whatever else the trip was about, certainly it had a spiritual dimension, regardless of whether anyone was prepared to admit this directly. If it meant anything to be Willi Unsoeld's daughter, it meant noting the possibility of spiritual influences, engaging actively in the search for a unique destiny. Just for the sake of argument: If someone actually *was* an incarnation of the goddess, what would that feel like? What would it look like? Would there not be odd coincidences, unmistakable signs? Premonitions and remarkable revelations? All of this was nonsense, of course, not to be spoken out loud, for fear of sounding grandiose, but really: What would that be like?

· · · ·

The *jats* of the goddess are of three types. The Royal Pilgrimage *(raj jat)* is staged every dozen years or so (four times in the twentieth century); the Small Pilgrimage *(choti jat)* is held each year and wanders from village to village; and the lesser pilgrimages are staged late in the rainy season, each procession identified with a particular village.

All of these ceremonies are said to be the journeys of a divine bride, one traveling from her birthplace to her husband's remote abode. The ritual songs of Nanda Devi lament this unhappy trip— village women sing them over a series of nights, always referring to Nanda by her other name, Gauri, which suggests her fair beauty. The songs offer a female perspective on many topics, from the origins of the gods to the bitterness of woman's lot. Brahmanic priests—males—consider the songs less significant than the Sanskrit texts that they traditionally study; in those texts, the goddess is not as central a figure, and the world is said to come into existence mainly through the efforts of male divinities.

According to Sax, women singers learn the songs from their mothers. (Men also sing goddess songs, but different versions.) The women's songs show Gauri to have been born of Maya, the primordial figure who creates Gauri by splitting her own body in two. Maya's menstrual blood, according to the songs, is the birth medium of other great gods as well. For instance, as it says in one of the songs:

> *Maya enveloped the ocean.*
> *The blood began to flow from her womb.*
> *Maya's blood began to flow,*

and from it the god Brahma was born.
Now Maya was very happy:
"I created my man from my own body!"

The pilgrimages of the goddess are lively, extravagant affairs.
The Royal Pilgrimage is "among the longest and most difficult pilgrimages in the world," according to Sax, "a three-week, barefoot
journey of 164 miles led by a four-horned-ram. . . . After traversing
rain-swollen rivers, dangerous windswept passes, and terrifying ice
fields, pilgrims reach the lake of Rupkund, located at fifteen thousand feet and surrounded by hundreds of human skeletons. Then
they cross a narrow vertical spot called 'the Path of Death' and
proceed to . . . 'the lake of the fire sacrifice' where, according to the
faithful, the four-horned ram leaves the procession" and ascends to
the top of a mountain.

In '87, when Sax participated, "Everyone came for the Royal
Pilgrimage. . . . A cabinet minister arrived by helicopter, and the
four-horned ram showed up in a chartered taxi. Two men in their
nineties walked all those icy miles barefoot, and young hiking-
club members [were] festooned with the latest high-altitude equipment. A private filmmaker from Bombay followed the four-horned
ram. . . . High and low, rich and poor, politicians and pilgrims, goddesses and demons, they were all there."

As if in imitation of a climbing trip, the "priests and pilgrims
were [not] to shave, wash their clothes, eat rice, wear shoes . . . or
sleep anywhere but on the ground." Day after day the procession,
sometimes watched by as many as fifteen thousand believers, makes
its way up from the steamy lowlands, following a complex itinerary
dictated by political as well as religious considerations. Devi, trekking from Lata with her unruly team, was called *didi* (sister) by the

porters, all men of the Garhwal; in the same way, the goddess is greeted at each village with cries of "O my sister, you've come at last," "Hey, little sister, to you be glory," and so forth.

A second myth connected to the pilgrimages, one of almost equal antiquity, concerns Devi and the Buffalo Demon. In the Garhwal, male buffalo are considered worse than useless: unsuitable as food and too clumsy for work in the small, terraced fields of mountain-side farms. Male buffalo are believed to have a monstrous quality, a reflection of their enormous strength and legendary stupidity. In the myth of the Buffalo Demon, Devi brings a baby bull home to raise as her son. Shiva warns her that the low-caste animal will turn against her, but she rejects his advice. The animal soon grows into a horrifying presence. It even tries to "marry" Devi, an especially repulsive idea, with suggestions of intimate contact between animal and god. Like a figure in a nightmare, the Buffalo Demon keeps coming back no matter what (when Devi knocks off one of its horns, for example, new demons sprout out of it).

The Buffalo Demon symbolizes brutishness, and in its selfish stu-pidity, it threatens everything humane. To subdue it the goddess transforms herself into blood-drenched Kali, the terrifying spirit whose images feature a bloody tongue, multiple arms, a girdle of snakes, and garlands of skulls. Devi does battle with the Buffalo Demon and slays it; in some versions of the myth, she then drinks its blood. This titanic battle, restoring peace and divine order, is celebrated during the *jats* by sacrifices of actual buffalo in a number of villages. The animals must be full grown and uncastrated, and in the manner of biblical scapegoats they are said to take on the curses of the local people. After a ritual walk around the village, the living Buffalo Demon is beheaded in the presence of mystic symbols of Devi/Kali.

. . . .

August 16: In camp with Andy, Devi recuperates and fields a potentially ticklish problem. Lev has become close with the few porters who remain with the expedition, and in the course of frying up a few chapatis he's asked them why the climb is having such bad luck. One of the Garhwalis—maybe the same one who told Pete that they'd *known* Devi was coming, that the goddess was fated to return—declares that the weather is terrible and the climb has ground to a halt because the sahibs are eating beef on the mountain, which is taboo.

Devi finds this laughable. That this whole enterprise, extending over years and requiring the shipment of tons of equipment and supplies, not to mention the efforts of a dozen climbers and eighty hardworking porters, plus *bhakriwallahs,* should falter because of a few chews of jerky strikes her as absurd, no matter how sensitive she is to the local folkways. When she gets on the radio that night to talk to the higher camp, she can barely restrain her hilarity. Kumar, the Indian officer, likewise isn't impressed with what the porters think and rants via the radio: "What bloody insolence! I am eating it and I am the highest caste of Brahman. In adversity you can eat anything—even human flesh!"

According to Andy, "Devi found the Himalaya fascinating, but this wasn't what she was. She didn't say, 'I'm a Hindu now.' The cultures were deeply attractive to her, and she recognized what she'd fallen into . . . still, she kept a distance. She was less like someone trying to become 'Eastern' than like an archetype of a kind I've met on every continent, in every part of the world. Not a simple influence-construct. She was different from Willi, too, although they shared a lot of beliefs. Willi was primarily an intellectual and a

seeker, someone who thought hard about how to define moral behavior . . . he arrived at a combination of Christian ethics and
Hindu metaphysics and other influences, and this gave him a frame-
work for his thought. But Devi arrived at things not so much by
study or cultural comparison—she wasn't 'about' that sort of effort,
she was more about living her life, having being. It was a life that
would've made sense within many cultural forms."

A few days before, the missing thirteenth climber, John Evans,
arrived on the mountain. Roskelley has been calling Evans "the
Messiah" because everyone has been awaiting him so breathlessly,
hoping for deliverance from their dark state of mind, and Evans
himself is a sort of Spencer Tracy–type figure, strong and utterly
dependable. On earlier climbs—including the Pamirs expedition of
'74, with Roskelley and Lev—he distinguished himself by his solid
work and good temperament. When he shows up at Base Camp,
he's got the rope they need plus a big load of mail from home. The
letters cheer everyone up, and the rope makes things look more
doable technically, should the weather ever cut them a break.

More snow, hundreds of inches. "[I]t took Lou and me four
diggings a day to keep even with the snowfall," Roskelley says of
their labors at Camp I, where the tents become smaller and smaller
inside as more snow falls without, and a climber trying to sleep
through the night is pushed away from the walls into a diminishing
central space. "We read everything we could find, right down to
the instructions on our film canisters," Roskelley says, and the
books and magazines being passed from hand to hand are precious
means of entering a nondiminishing interior, one free from fear of
suffocation. Lev is a great reader, and with Marty Hoey gone and
the social breaks falling the way they do, he finds himself without
a special companion, a particular friend to share a tent with. He
reads for long hours and days at a time. Evans has brought in recent

issues of *Time,* and the news of the first post-Watergate, post-Vietnam presidential campaign is both immensely remote and movingly intimate in its flavor of Americanness. For many climbers, removing themselves from their homeland and the people who love them results in the kind of emotional simplicity that puts a life in order: nine thousand miles away, it's possible to see what *really* matters, feel things directly. To shed tears. To think, "Why didn't I tell her I *love* her, I *need* her, I *can't live without her*?!" The letters that climbers write home are therefore often among the most heartfelt of their life. The suspicion arises that one reason certain people climb—especially the more indomitable males—is precisely to arrive at this state of emotional transparency. As Jim Wickwire, author of *Addicted to Danger,* a remarkably frank climber's autobiography, wrote, "In the mountains . . . my heart opens," and what it often opens to is people half a world away.

Certainly Roskelley, a Buffalo Demon if ever there was one, doesn't hide his tender side as regards his family back in Spokane. His books are full of affecting expressions of love and longing for a treasured wife. Once a climb is over—once Roskelley has touched the summit himself—he wants to be back with that wife, back with those kids who depend on him. This often leads to an unseemly tear down the mountain. On Dhaulagiri, his first Himalayan summit, Roskelley got out of there so fast that Lev felt his own summit chances had been compromised. The higher camps were emptied of supplies, and the idea of being supported in turn by the A-team summiteers was barely acknowledged.

August 19: The snow still coming down, Reichardt becomes "acutely aware that only seventeen days of high-altitude food [are] left, with the highest occupied camp at only 19,900 feet. The lead ropes had reached 21,500 feet, but were so deeply buried that they seemed divorced from our current prospects." In fact, the snow is now falling more heavily than ever. They haven't reached the top of the ridge, and above that are three thousand more feet of vertical rise. The whole thing begins to look *truly* impossible, rather than just probably so. A few more days stuck in tents reading *Doctor Dogbody's Leg, Oliver Twist, Demian, Moby-Dick, All the President's Men,* or *Tinker, Tailor, Soldier, Spy*—to name just a few of the titles being passed around—and they'll have eaten their way out of contention.

That would be a disappointment, but also a relief. It appears that the mountain simply does not want to be climbed this year, not by them. Maybe they'll be saving themselves a catastrophe by bowing out. After the morning's snowfall, though, the skies suddenly clear, the sun comes out, and the climbers emerge from their tents looking amazed. It's hard to believe so complete a change, and the timeliness of it. Why has the mountain chosen *this* moment, with their supplies almost at the turnback point, to lighten up? Is there a "meaning" in it all? The odd coincidence suggests, again, some kind of trickery on high.

Roskelley, not one for such speculation, notes simply in his book, "Talk of quitting the mountain ended as suddenly as it had started. The sun, with its warmth and light, sparked our desire to climb again."

NINETEEN

August 20: The next day is ringingly clear. The great peaks west of the mountain—Devistan, Trisul, Nanda Ghunti—appear mantled in new cream. While Roskelley and Reichardt go up to Camp II, preparing to push the route the following day, Willi and several others carry loads to Camp I, where Devi and Andy will be sleeping over. Willi is ecstatic to be out in all this freshness again. He knows how to be patient, wait out storms, but can also sense a moment to be seized. On Everest in '63, there were blows so fierce they literally tore tents from their moorings and hurled them hundreds of feet through the air, with people inside, and then there came a spell of good weather, miraculous temperate weather, a window in which to accomplish amazing things. This idea of "miraculous" breaks in the weather, though, must be taken with a grain of salt. An experienced mountaineer is experienced exactly in the sense that he knows how to put himself in position for a break, should one happen along. Willi's night out with Hornbein, for instance—the "one night in fifty" when murderous winds did not blow—was an anomaly, but Willi and Tom had chosen to go for the summit in a spell of settled weather, a break that felt as if it might last awhile.

How anomalous, then, was it for a temperate night to happen pre-monsoon, late in the warming month of May, after two or three clear days?

People without any experience on high mountains, hearing how thin the air is and how cold it can get, imagine that every climb is a deranged bid for suicide, but someone with Old Guide tendencies can make a lot of his own luck. You must always be humble, of course, ready to back down (if you still can), but the sensing of "miraculous" openings is less a question of black magic than of having learned a thing or two. On his way between Advanced Base and Camp I, Willi wades through fresh snow, clearing the ropes hidden under several feet of it. At about the same time, a thousand feet above, Roskelley and Reichardt are doing roughly the same thing, wallowing through powder up to their thighs and struggling for every foot of vertical gain. At Camp II they discover the single tent still intact, though covered and partly squashed by snow. "Willi and Peter had kept [it] perfectly clean during their previous stay," Roskelley notes approvingly, and he and Lou move in for the first of several nights.

August 21: Another brilliant day. They free the ropes up to the previous high point, then push on, not quite gaining the ridge despite Reichardt's breaking "lead after lead [through] a hard, inch-thick crust" over powder snow. But on the twenty-second, after an early start, they reach the broad crest of the North Ridge. "[T]he ridgetop was flat, a comfortable balcony from which we could see the long brown hills of Tibet to the north," Reichardt says, "the Indian plains to the south, row after row of ice-clad peaks of our height in the near distance." Just a half mile away, up the gentle rise of the snowy ridge, is the foot of the great Buttress. "Just getting this far was a true accomplishment," Roskelley writes, and the two lounge about for hours, enjoying the feast of clarity. When they turn their eyes to the Buttress, looking for possible routes up its snow-splattered steepness, Roskelley thinks he sees possibilities.

"Lou thought it similar to the South Face of . . . Washington Column," Roskelley notes, naming a cliff in Yosemite Valley just west of Half Dome. The South Face of Washington Column is dauntingly big, but not as big as some of its near neighbors. Full of vertical cracks, flakes, roofs, and other local features interesting to rock climbers, it presents a polished aspect when seen from a distance of a few hundred yards away. The Buttress of Nanda Devi, to judge from photos taken by Evans and others, presents a much more corrugated surface, suggesting a greater number of weaknesses (potentially useful for climbing). On the other hand, the rock of the Buttress is part quartzite, sharp-edged and of a junky quality, and covered with ice; moreover, the cliff starts at twenty-three thousand feet, an elevation where hard rock-climbing moves may be impossible.

They descend from the ridge on fixed ropes, and maybe the thought of what he's just seen is what gets Roskelley all on edge, because he blows his stack when he encounters his friend Dr. States a couple thousand feet down. "Without thinking, I yelled at Jim for dumping his load so low," Roskelley confesses—all the other carriers that day, he discovers, have also dropped their loads too low (in his opinion), at an elevation where fetching them up to the ridge will be hard work. "Though not pointed at Jim specifically," Roskelley says about his outburst, "the incident caused more ill feelings."

Roskelley can perhaps be forgiven this show of nerves: the Buttress is very much on his mind and will continue to be for the next few dangerous days. He has to climb it, for 150 urgent reasons, and to do so he has to have a solid Camp III on the Ridge, stocked with tents and gear and food. Meanwhile, these other people just aren't pulling their weight, they're not hauling the way they should—it's as if they're against him, wanting to trip him up! He has problems with almost everyone: according to Andy, "John regularly had tirades, and not just at the hard parts of the climb. He attacked all of us at one time or another . . . Devi especially . . . Willi, too. . . . John's transparent and always says the first uncensored thing that's on his mind."

They're all failing him, but the particular focus of Roskelley's rage is Lev. The differences between the two go back at least to Dhaulagiri, and then there's a more fundamental problem, growing out of their temperaments, Roskelley being a high-strung, lightning-reaction sort of guy, Lev more of a loping, drag-the-heels, I-won't-move-till-I'm-persuaded type. Roskelley is also the coming thing in climbing, an extreme-route specialist and barn burner, while Lev stands astride the split between Willi's generation and the newer one, being both humanistic and technically minded as a climber. He keeps talking up other routes, other ways to go even now, at the eleventh hour; signing on to the Roskelley program in a whole-hearted way he just can't do. The struggle over Marty has not been forgotten, either—if another woman were on the mountain, if Pete had a partner of his own and a particular tentmate, things might be different.

They argue over an escape route—a set of ropes set up parallel to the main ones—that Lev installed ten days ago. Roskelley dislikes it because it's a waste of equipment, he thinks; Lev insists it'll prove useful if the main route gets wiped out by avalanches. "Peter exploded at Lou and me at Camp II," Roskelley writes about an encounter on August 23. "We apologized for yelling about the loads being dumped at the wrong site, but insisted his [escape] route had wasted too much equipment and was not safe. Again we could not agree and the issue remained unresolved."

Roskelley senses, just when he's summoning all his resources for this impossible try, that some of these people just flat-out don't like him. Amazing. He doesn't care, but their resentment may turn into active sabotage, and he just won't have that, by God. "The bad weather, cold, crowded tents, wet clothing, and constant danger gave us all a persistent empty, nervous feeling," he writes, perhaps saying something about the others but certainly saying something about himself. "Kiran summed it up when he said our emotions were extremes. . . . The conditions contributed to our frequent outbursts. . . . Anyone could be a target."

August 24: Reichardt, Roskelley, and States climb to the ridge and pitch a tent for Camp III. Kiran, also carrying up to the ridge, arrives hours behind the others in rising winds and swirling snow. Exhausted and not used to the altitude (almost twenty-three thousand feet), he rests an hour before setting off back down the ropes. By 5 P.M., people in Camps II and III are worried about him, because no one's seen him for a long time, and it's quite possible he's gotten fouled up with his jumaring, which he's never quite mastered. Somewhere between Camps II and III are Willi and Devi. They've also carried loads this day, all the way up to the dump that Roskelley insists on, and hearing that Kiran may be in trouble, they find a spot on the face to wait for him.

Snow falls, then the sky clears. Then more falls. According to Willi, who wrote an account of the events of this afternoon, the worsening weather only adds to a special mood he finds himself in: he's not put out, in fact he's pleased to be here, on this monumental, avalanching face, alone with Devi for once. Free to talk or not to talk as the spirit moves them. Free to feel it all. "She was absolutely euphoric to be on the mountain," he told audiences, "the mountain after which she was named. She would burst out at me, 'Dad, have you ever felt your body more *alive*? Do you feel the cunningness of your boot-sole edges, doing what they were meant to do?' "— meaning, apparently, finding a way to stand without pitching off.

"I hadn't thought about that recently," Willi said. "Except for the sharp pain in my ankles, where I'd been hanging too long on the steep ice. But she dug this thing, I saw, she really dug it. And so there we were, finally . . . where we were."

Kiran keeps on not appearing. Willi yodels up the face for him, reflecting that this situation is typical of fixed-rope climbing, with people passing up and down alone, the whole idea of *partnering* abandoned, everyone having traded companionship for a specious idea of efficiency. Devi tells him of her biggest disappointment on the climb so far: "I wish the group could've been together. I wanted that so much." Willi understands, but in his programmatically positive way he lists all the things that're *good* about the climb, and she has to agree. Trained at his knee in the rituals of American-style optimism, Devi can match him note for cheery note. What saves them from being a pair of insufferable Pollyannas is their Unsoeld frankness and earthiness. There's also a kind of bottom-line mental rigor, whereby they only feel comfortable discussing a topic if they examine it from the underside, too. The black humor of things does not escape them. Devi wants everyone to be together, and Willi is a kind of rocket scientist of the higher group-spirit, yet here they are in this absolutely screwed situation. Pushing on somehow.

Leamer, Willi's biographer, met Devi when she was a young girl, and his strongest impression of her was of "this feminine, beautiful thing in this masculine environment . . . her mother was rather masculine, too . . . mountaineering is so essentially the masculine element, with all that sturdy striving, and she seemed out of place." Willi's few public descriptions of Devi make implicit reference to this defining element: "Devi . . . was always ready with a raucous outburst. A sheer enjoyer of life. I've never forgotten the time she tackled Rascal [Roskelley], literally tackled him like in football. . . . John tends to be a little stuffy around impressionable young ladies, he's even been known to bear the 'chauvinist' label, and Devi took it upon herself to remove that scarlet tag. She did so with a flying tackle, after which, in his amazement, he found himself flat on his back, because she hits *hard*."

And furthermore, "Devi just got a *charge* out of outraging people. She was tender when required, and on this expedition she was the main go-between for those who were hurting the most. But in her friendly manner, what she was like more than anything else was a young *bull*."

This is intended as praise, coming at a time in social history when it may have seemed generous to liken a twenty-two-year-old daughter to a farm animal. But these statements about his daughter also suggest how oddly narrow was Willi's conception of the worldly flux. He had succeeded in his long-term goal of making "a life entirely in the mountains," and the force of his example had brought thousands of young people into his orbit. He may have been largely unaware of the power he had to foreclose alternative views; in his company, the game of mountaineering seemed mountainous itself, larger and more packed with meaning than almost any other conceivable endeavor. The extent to which his own daughter, to whom he granted so much practical freedom, was restricted in her choices in life may therefore have escaped him. Devi wasn't climbing a mountain to please him, nothing so simple or unhealthy as that; but she was, in fact, doing the sort of thing that he had taught her to respect, having a spiritual adventure that was also an arduous physical test, proving herself among the men.

In her interview with the *Times of India*, Devi took pains to distinguish herself from a real mountaineer: "I have been brought up in the mountains. I have lived a third of my life in Nepal and am familiar with the Himalayas. . . . The mountains will always be part of my life [but] I may not take up mountaineering as a career . . . I feel it is a form of escapism. It is easy to turn your eyes away from the social problems of the world. . . . If you feel involved with the social problems, you cannot like that sort of thing for long." We hear the sound of seventies-style youth rebellion in that, getting one up on the older generation. But the influence of a father as mythic and forceful as Devi's own is not to be escaped so easily. In a way, a daughter's emergence from this kind of situation is even harder to devise than a son's. Devi's older brother, Regon, had been giving Willi a hard time for years, resisting him wherever he saw an advantage. For the son of a vital, larger-than-life father, the battle is often joined early and can seem to have a life-and-death quality; we don't see Regon going to the Himalaya with his father, after all. (Krag, Devi's other brother, also backed away from the trip: he didn't like what he knew of Roskelley.)

A daughter, though, sometimes basks much longer and more comfortably in the glow of a father as large as the sun. In the nineteenth century, the daughters of famous men—people like Twain, Tolstoy, Darwin—often devoted themselves entirely to their father, declining to make what we would now call lives of their own. This was clearly not going to be Devi's path, but at twenty-two she was still a student at the college where Willi was the star, still lived in his house when not traveling, and her search for an intellectual space of her own was only beginning.

Kiran still not in sight, Devi and Willi get casually on to another topic, the thing with Andy. Willi likes him, likes them together, so it's not really disturbing to hear her announce, "I'm not going back to school in the fall, Dad. I'm going to travel with Andy, see what we have to build on. See if there's enough." Willi indicates cautious approval: "It has potential. It's worth the risk." Willi's own marital experience, twenty-five years with the same woman, has perhaps had an instructive effect on Devi. A *suitable* match hardly begins to describe what she's after: she wants a lifetime attachment, a permanent connection working on all levels. Anything less isn't of much interest to her.

Of this relaxed encounter on the snowy face, during which they deal offhandedly with matters of much significance, Willi will later say that it was "one of the most precious memories of my life." After a while they begin climbing again, hoping to find Kiran before he freezes to death; at an altitude of about 21,500 feet, there he suddenly is, in the blowing snow, laboriously making his way down the ropes. Willi yodels and they join up, and then the three of them descend to the lower camps.

August 25: Dr. States moves up to III, joining Reichardt and Roskelley. This is a bitterly controversial move: like a simple pawn advance signaling checkmate, it puts the A-team squarely out ahead, the B-team morosely in its place. "Peter and Kiran . . . were furious at this development," Roskelley notes. "They felt they had earned the right to move up, that Jim was being given the chance because I insisted." Roskelley has, indeed, insisted: he intends to climb the Buttress with his old pal and nobody else. "Jim and I were by far the fastest, most proficient team on the mountain," he argues. "[We] had climbed some of the most difficult routes in the Canadian Rockies . . . as well as a major first ascent of a technical rock-and-ice face . . . in Bolivia."

As climbing leader, Reichardt calls the shots on this sort of thing. Thus, when Lev demands to be allowed to move up to Camp III, too, Lou must tell him no. Lev has been advocating an alternate route, one that skirts the Buttress, going out left on the Northeast Face of the mountain, the side that faces Tibet. Lou doesn't like this idea at all: they know next to nothing about the northeast side, which is just around the corner, but completely invisible, from their position on the ridge. According to Roskelley, "If we couldn't climb the Buttress, there would be no summit." Reichardt concurs, although, as he confides to his journal of the time, "You can pick out a possible [Buttress] route, so all is not lost, but the whole thing is plastered with snow and ice. Frankly, it is pretty horrendous. . . . Considering the difficulty, time and weather, we will be very lucky to make it."

Roskelley has most of his ducks in a row now. Camp III has been established, States has moved up to join him, and Reichardt's in charge; plus, there's gear and food aplenty, enough to make a solid try. But the rumblings from below do not die out. After a face-to-face argument with Lev earlier in the day, the hassle over routes and berths at III continues over the radio, with the most annoying news coming at the 7 P.M. transmission, when Devi calls to say that Kiran and she will be carrying loads tomorrow, but that Lev and Nirmal will not. "Peter said he would take a rest day unless he could move up," Devi says as cheerily as she can. But this is insubordination, rebellion: Lou has ordered everyone to carry loads, to bring up more supplies so that others can move up later.

"[We] knew if we didn't make good progress," Roskelley says, "the team would demand we turn our effort to the [Tibetan face]. We . . . needed results fast to keep the expedition from stalling."

Northwest Face ascent route, Nanda Devi. *Photo by John Evans*

Devi Unsoeld at Camp I, Nanda Devi, 1976. *Photo by Peter Lev*

TOP: Peter Lev.
Photo by John Evans

BOTTOM: Willi, Devi,
and other climbers,
Northwest Face.
Photo by John Evans

John Roskelly and Lou Reichardt, approach to Nanda Devi, 1976.
Photo by Peter Lev

Devi Unsoeld, Ridge Camp. *Photo by John Evans*

LEFT: Andy Harvard, High Camp, below the summit of Nanda Devi. *Photo by Peter Lev*

BOTTOM: Climbers on the Buttress, Nanda Devi. *Photo by John Evans*

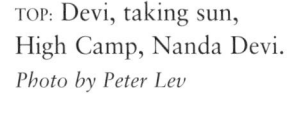

TOP: Devi, taking sun,
High Camp, Nanda Devi.
Photo by Peter Lev

BOTTOM: Willi, Nanda Devi
Expedition, 1976.
Photo by Peter Lev

LEFT: Willi, Camp II,
Nanda Devi.
Photo by Peter Lev

BELOW: High Camp,
Nanda Devi, at
the precipice.
Photo by Peter Lev

Willi and Andy Harvard—retreat from Nanda Devi. *Photo by John Evans*

This is a curious line of argument, which boils down to saying that only Roskelley and States can climb because they're the fastest, and the reason they have to climb fast is because they're the ones who have been chosen. At any rate, in all the arguing and accusation-trading over the next few days, no one stoops to invoking "tradition," recalling the heroic mountaineering past, when comrades carried gamely for each other, and everyone rejoiced if anyone got to the top. Roskelley comes closest to striking a pose of offended traditionalism—he hates the rebels, can't believe their backstabbing, yet he stops short of an argument in terms of the great ideals. Climbing idealism is now, at this moment, officially dead. The death has occurred on an American expedition, one led by the most idealistic, most honored American Himalayan climber of the post–World War II era. Like most such moments, it passes without acknowledgment.

August 26: Roskelley and States tramp to the base of the Buttress. Whether or not the expedition's running out of time, they've *told* themselves it is, and Roskelley climbs the first few pitches at a furious pace. The weather's cold. Clear skies start clouding up early, and spindrift avalanches mix with falling snow. Roskelley takes all the leads himself, so there can be no doubt whose route this is. For his part, Jim States is a noble, rock-solid belayer, willing to perch for hours on tiny stances in the cold. At the end of the day, as Roskelley notes, "Jim was ghostly white. His beard and mustache were solid ice and he must have frozen waiting for me."

Part of climbing well is climbing fast. The crux of the effort that Roskelley has been planning for over a year now is superrapid progress up the unknown Buttress—if just any duffer could climb it, what would be the point? Happily, the cliff does present challenges, and the added intensity of climbing under the gun, under self-imposed time constraints, makes it a problem worthy of serious mountaineers. There can be no doubting Roskelley's heart: "I began jamming the overhanging fist crack," he writes about one early pitch. "I was not wearing gloves and my hands froze instantly. . . . I could find no more toeholds for the front points of my crampons. The crack was choked with ice."

He continues, "Hanging on one jammed fist, I reached for a two-and-a-half-inch bong piton and placed it in the crack. . . . Finally I drove the bong deep, clipped in a carabiner and an étrier, and somehow got my cramponed boot into the lower step [of the étrier, a portable fabric ladder]. I was almost done in." Describing this pitch to Reichardt later, Roskelley recalled the "[u]nrelentingly steep, holdless slabs [leading] upwards. Every sloping stance had to be carefully cleared of snow. . . . I led on a 9-mm rope, praying that if I fell, it wouldn't hit any of the sharp rocks present in such profusion. . . . It was cold, exhausting work."

Willi, who jumared up and down the Buttress, getting to know it fairly well, remembered this pitch as the one Roskelley said was the hardest. In lectures he gave after the expedition, Willi went out of his way to praise John's effort; at an American Alpine Club dinner, December of '76, he called Roskelley "one of the premier Himalayan climbers that this country has produced. For sheer raw speed under impossible conditions, I'd give him my vote." Speaking to an earlier audience, Willi called Roskelley's climb an "absolutely superb job. . . . He and Jim States in three days blasted through fifteen hundred feet of the most difficult high-angle climbing that I've ever heard of being done in the Himalaya. I would rate it on a par with the South Face of Annapurna."

Roskelley himself is more careful of his comparisons. About another hard pitch, he says it "could have been the 'exit cracks' on the Eiger North Wall," referring to the famous Alpine face on which the best climbers of the past century tested themselves. But for the most part, he describes the climbing in concrete terms, making it sound thrilling and adventurous in the way of a lion hunt in a magazine like *Sports Afield,* but not like the greatest thing since sliced bread. The risk is substantial, because he's leading on unknown ground at altitude, but the rock was "a blocky type of quartzite at the start," as he said to the Alpine Club; "there were cracks that we could work on. Everything had to be cleared off to lead it . . . [it was] a time-consuming process." In his book, Roskelley gives the reader an exciting, move-for-move account—just the sort of thing that adventure-book readers supposedly like—but in his speech to the club's mountaineers, he draws back from extravagant claims ("There was some fairly difficult climbing in there . . . I rated it maybe 5.8 . . . kind of hard to rate, though, there's so much snow and ice . . . kind of ridiculous").

As an author, Roskelley recognizes the need to be writing about *something*—a victory, a notable accomplishment. If he were to say, "Yeah, it was pretty hard, and I'm sort of proud of what I did, but let's not get carried away, okay?" he would be working against himself. Nor was he the only one to have an investment in an epochal outcome. Willi, with his talk of the South Face of Annapurna, was playing the time-honored role of the leader of an international expedition, one who writes an article or gives a speech afterward and quite understandably finds what his comrades have accomplished outstandingly impressive. Grade inflation is more or less built into the process; no one likes to think he's just participated in a middling effort, especially when *real* risks have been faced daily, *real* heroism has been displayed, money has been spent and time taken off from ongoing careers and lives.

The climb of the Buttress was an accomplishment, certainly, but different views of the stature of that accomplishment can be defended. These were not fifteen hundred feet of unrelenting vertical rock, either; after some hard pitches at the start, Roskelley reached a sixty-degree snow slope, with intervening rock ramps, that allowed for nontechnical progress upward. On his second day on the Buttress, he dealt with spindrift avalanches that engulfed him for minutes at a time; his skills at aid and free climbing were fully tested, and he encountered mixed climbing as hard as any he'd faced. But again, the technical pitches led to a generous break in the verticality, an area that he named Sugar Delight Snowfield, on account of the quality of its deep powder. From this point on, a large gully angled toward the top of the Buttress, maybe four hundred feet away. Reichardt joined Roskelley and States for the third day, and he wrote afterward that it was "mercifully easier. . . . From 'Sugar Delight' . . . [the gully] bypassed the severe difficulties that would otherwise have been our fare."

Following later on the Buttress, Andy remembered things differently both from Roskelley's vivid, boy's-own-adventure account and from Willi's talk of "the most difficult high-angle climbing ever." "Would we have made an attempt without him, if John hadn't been there to lead the Buttress? *Sure* we would," Andy says, "*sure*. We all chose the route . . . and we'd all been thinking about it for a long time. The Buttress had everything on it in the way of terrain, from third class [steep hiking] to hard-but-not-overhanging pitches to one hard pitch of overhanging. And—*that was it*. It didn't really seem all that long. I would say less than fifteen hundred feet . . . maybe less than a thousand. It was at twenty-three to twenty-four thousand [in elevation], which is high but not all that high by Himalayan standards. Plus, the weather was generally okay. No storms and pretty clear at times."

Andy's memories may be faulty. Or perhaps he's resentful of Roskelley and wants to belittle his accomplishment, for reasons having to do with Roskelley's hard-nosed behavior. Following pitches that have been led by someone else—not even climbing them, just jumaring up fixed ropes—is a very different experience, from which most of the fear and uncertainty have been removed. Andy never had to jam his way up an icy crack, with bare hands, wearing a fifty-pound pack and dragging hundreds of feet of rope, but by the same token, Andy had been on Dhaulagiri, he had climbed widely in Alaska and South America, at elevations roughly the same as the elevation of the Buttress; he had earned a reputation for solid, sober performance and for keenness of mind. His book about Dhaulagiri, *Mountain of Storms,* is above all generous-spirited, full of amusing and well-tempered portraits of his fellow climbers (including Roskelley and Reichardt).

Difficult or not, the Buttress did have to be surmounted; and on August 29, Roskelley swims up through many yards of powder to the top. He hammers in several pitons for a secure anchor, then surveys the gently angled snowfield where he finds himself, a promising site for Camp IV. Back at III that night, he reenters the ugly human reality of it all. Devi, Andy, Pete, and the Indians have moved up to Camp III despite Lou's commands. Here they've lain about all day, acclimatizing. "Their move to Camp III . . . had only wasted food, and had not produced any loads," Roskelley writes. "The situation was becoming critical."

Two days before, Willi had warned that Lev was on the verge of quitting the team; that one of the Indians was, too, and that "you've made it hard for me just to keep people here on the mountain," as he told Reichardt over the radio. As a last-ditch attempt to derail the A-squad, the B-squad took a vote and decided that the first summit team should consist of Lou and Devi, not Roskelley and States; Reichardt replied that he felt "very honored," but that he couldn't think of depriving Roskelley and States of a summit shot. The morning after this exchange, Lev came roaring up to

Camp III, all the way from Camp I (almost four thousand feet) in a couple hours; instead of quitting the mountain, he'd decided to have it out with Roskelley once and for all. With Reichardt and States looking on, the two aired their suspicions and distaste for each other, resolving nothing beyond the fact that Roskelley was pretty much calling the shots at this point, having gained so much ground on the Buttress. Lev's only option was, indeed, to leave the mountain in protest; but that wasn't his style, in the end. He was a mountaineer and a mountain guide. He had carried a lot of loads, no matter what Roskelley said, and he'd continue to carry, even if it helped someone who got up in his face. And then maybe he'd have a summit shot of his own, if things broke the right way—he and the other B-teamers.

Reichardt's account of this period of stress and struggle, indited for the permanent record of the *AAJ,* is airbrushed to an almost comical extent. Where Roskelley talks about Lou feeling "disgusted," being engaged in "heated" exchanges, "snapping" at opponents, and feeling full of rage at the supposed poor load-carrying of Lev and others, Lou's own article refers to Lev as a "stalwart" among the carriers, one who brought loads all the way to the ridge rather than leave them at the lower dumpsite. "Below, Evans and the two Unsoelds made their sixth consecutive carry on the face," Lou writes, referring to events of August 27, a day about which Roskelley records, "Again, no one had carried from Camp II and Lou was disgusted." Lou speaks of feeling "exhilarated" as Roskelley and States make rapid progress, since this means "the Buttress could be climbed quickly!" But then, in a little miracle of whitewashing disinformation, he says: "The others below, particularly Pete Lev, were also excited and wanted to share the leading, but I told them it would be a mistake to change teams at this critical point."

August 31: The A-team marches to the foot of the Buttress. They will ascend it on the ropes that have now been fixed. The day before was a day of rest and bitterness, with A-teamers and B-teamers both occupying Camp III and sniping at each other. "There was no love lost between our two tents," Roskelley says, after once again castigating the others for not carrying the way they should.

But at this important moment—with the move up to Camp IV imminent—the shirkers become helpful, above and beyond the call of duty. Andy and Devi break trail to the foot of the Buttress for the others. Kiran carries Reichardt's seventy-five-pound pack for him, and Lev comes along and ascends the Buttress partway, carrying a load and replacing the 9-mm ropes with stronger, more fray-resistant 11-mm. In fact, Lev climbs up to Sugar Delight Snowfield, two-thirds of the way up the cliff, where he waits with Roskelley for over an hour. Rougher weather is blowing in, and States and Reichardt are slower ascending the ropes. According to Reichardt, "Peter was already at the ledge [of Sugar Delight]. He gave us food and wished us the best. He had every right to be continuing with us!" This may be more of Lou's diplomacy, making things smooth for the record, but the actions of the B-teamers on this day have spoken louder than their complaints, their foot-dragging and their few acts of rebellion. The amazing reality is that the fractured Nanda Devi expedition has somehow brought enough gear to this critical point, that an advance party, adequately supported, is moving up and positioning itself for a realistic assault on the summit. Some shred of the old ideology—the teamwork thing—still remains.

Down below, meanwhile, Willi and John Evans continue stocking the other camps, setting a quiet example of dutiful service far from the glamorous high-point. According to Leamer, "[Willi] had set out to make this the right sort of climb, setting a new standard here as he had set one on Everest. But this was not group climbing here. This was no moral equivalent to the expedition thirteen years before. This was a pack of isolated individualists, the very anathema of what he thought the world should come to."

And Leamer concludes, "Title or not, [Willi] was not the leader of this expedition. It was being led by pride, machismo, guts, and sheer drive. . . . For the first time in his life, Willi had met a group of people he couldn't work with well or, more accurately, lead."

That may be the case, but *something* is holding the group together—just together enough—and allowing upward movement, progress that's hard to distinguish from the classic lead-camp-lead movement of scores of other expeditions. On the best of those other expeditions, a comradely feeling seemed to be at the heart of everything, driving everything, making sense of it all, and clearly this has been lost on Nanda Devi. But maybe not *all* has been lost.

TWENTY

September 1: The summit climb, though not without difficulties, is a romp. The A-teamers awaken at 6:00 A.M., thinking to have a rest day but enticed outdoors by the lovely weather. "It was warm and windless," according to Reichardt, "the first time we could remember not seeing a [snow] plume on the summit. This was too good a chance to miss." They hasten to dress and pack packs, and by eight-thirty Roskelley is "[breaking] trail through the knee-deep sugar snow to a saddle several hundred yards above camp," according to his own account.

"Snow conditions were abysmal," Reichardt says. There's a crust formed by the wind of other days, then powder underneath that seems not to have a bottom. They swim upward. "Roskelley did his bit; then I; then Jim," says Reichardt, but Roskelley describes leading a short but stiff rock-pitch by himself, after which he has to half-pull up Reichardt and States. Twice, Reichardt threatens to turn back and even goes so far as to untie from the rope. Roskelley, unable to move at less than top speed, keeps tugging on his slower companions, and this drives Reichardt crazy.

An avalanching slope; fluted gendarmes (ice towers); cornices to flounder through; and at last Jim States, in the lead at that moment, hurls himself onto the snowy top. At 25,645 feet (7,816 meters), on this blessedly calm day, it's warm enough for them to lounge about for over an hour, hats and gloves off, chatting about this and that. Though Reichardt makes no claims about the climb in his *AAJ* article, "Lou said he thought this was the best American climb since the West Ridge of Everest," according to Roskelley's version. To have barged on through so easily, after all those weeks of miserable monsoon weather, the whole hateful interpersonal struggle, everything they've endured, is a little disorienting. As on the day, more than a month ago, when they miraculously found a way up through the "impossible" Rishi cliffs, the summit has come to them on a platter, like a gift from the Bliss-Giving Goddess.

Climbing that short rock-pitch, "I needed to attack the [section] quickly to eliminate any second thoughts," Roskelley says in his account. The three climbers had failed to bring along the kind of hardware needed to protect the pitch; not about to be turned back, Roskelley relied once more on his speed, that special quality that both proved his superiority as a mountaineer and sometimes irritated even his close companions. Part of climbing well is climbing fast, but not all situations yield to it or require it. Two years before Nanda Devi, on his way back from climbing in the Pamirs, Roskelley climbed the North Face of the Eiger with a friend, and on that famous wall with its almost constant rockfall, it was a good idea to move as fast as possible. Climbers like Roskelley or the late Alex Lowe or the current Himalayan record-breaker, the Slovenian Tomaz Humar, tend to seek out challenges that require speed as well as strength and skill, but sometimes they find themselves in situations where remarkable speed is simply inappropriate. Then they need to damp things down a bit—if they can.

Willi was once capable of moving as fast as anyone, but now

he's older and no longer in the running, and on Nanda Devi he configures his role in a way to offer a quiet rebuke to the other approach. Before he came over to India, he was telling an interviewer in Seattle, "This will be the logical expedition for me not to reach the top. I . . . look upon it as my greatest challenge not to reach the summit," since expedition leaders almost never do, and living gracefully with such an outcome would be a kind of moral test. Maybe even that overstates it: Willi simply wants to do the best job he can, help as many others as possible get as high as they're able, then call it a day. Retire from Himalayan climbing as a solid citizen. And as the climb has taken shape, he's remained true to these modest aspirations—it might even be said, increasingly true. Roskelley races out in the lead, defining excellence as breakneck speed and summit fever, and meanwhile Willi does the grunt work down lower, humping it between camps, dealing with the Indians and taking time to instruct them in technique, since none of them, not even Kiran, is really adept. "It flashed through my mind," Willi told his lecture audiences, "that some members of the expedition had claimed that 'Nanda Devi is no practice ground!' Well, it was obvious that that's what we were offering. Sort of advanced jumar practice. And the question was whether this was legitimate in light of the seriousness of the terrain."

Willi could never resolve that question, but all his years as a guide and his hands-across-the-sea-type personality argue for taking a minute, imparting wisdom to those in need. Roskelley doesn't much hold with this. His mind-set is suggested by that statement about the rock pitch on the summit day, about "needing to attack it quickly to eliminate second thoughts." Sometimes it seems that slowing down, taking a good look around, might bring a *lot* of second thoughts as well as fears. Defining the mountainscape as a soulless realm of impersonal forces ready to crush you—a partly accurate but incomplete description—might yield a brilliant climber ready to test himself to the utmost, but that definition is less likely to yield someone who's profoundly at home in the mountains, who loves them in an exemplary way. Knowing climbers as well as he does, Willi thinks he knows Roskelley's perspective, and he offers himself as a quiet counterexample. Unfortunately, the young Buffalo Demon's immune to instruction. His need to get to the summit fast, to shape this climb as *his* mountain masterwork, precludes alternative views.

Back in the United States, Willi will be able to mold this wonderful material, turn it into inspiring stories for his friends and audiences. Like Roskelley, he's been taking notes and sending detailed letters out, and he responds to all the troubles of the climb in a complicated way, as an active participant but also as that morally ambiguous figure, a potential *writer,* one who can't help but find intriguing exactly those elements of the climb that make it problematic. While Roskelley and the others move up to Camp IV, Willi moves on to III with Evans, and now he's well situated to see the whole drama as it unfolds. On September 2, the summiteers descend the Buttress; they've left some sleeping bags at IV, for the next party to use, and they expect to meet that party on its way up. But no one greets them at the base of the cliff. Earlier that morning, Willi had broken trail for Andy and Devi and Peter, but Devi's hernia had popped out. Not a problem in itself, the hernia was perplexing, disheartening. The upper slopes of the mountain were at that moment engulfed in cloud; as a day for tackling the Buttress, carrying heavy packs, it suddenly seemed ill-omened.

Having returned to Camp III, the second party fails to greet the conquering A-teamers with much enthusiasm. "Kiran and Nirmal ran out of their tent to greet us," Roskelley records, "[and] John Evans and Peter came over . . . [but] the others were . . . very cool."

When he spoke to Leamer after the expedition, Roskelley recalled that "the other . . . members were acting as if it took an enormous effort to get off their dead rears," and the enthusiasm of the Indian climbers could perhaps be explained by what now lay before them: fixed ropes all the way up the Buttress, a proven summit route to follow.

On the radio the night before, Willi and Devi had been effusive in their congratulations. But now the reality of the situation asserts itself, the knotty human reality, which is that for over a year John has been shaping this effort in a way to suit *his* skills and preferences; now, sure enough, he's pulled off just what he wanted, a rapid ascent by an elite unit, a unit that defined itself as better and stronger and more *deserving* than the rest of them, and no surprise, the rest of them are not overjoyed. Willi appreciates the skill of the ascent, but he's disappointed, as Devi also is, that the group couldn't be more together. Haven't they lost some kind of lovely opportunity here? Have they really been so pressed for time that the first team could not have included Devi or Lev or Andy? They're not out of food, after all; and it appears that they're not out of time, either. It's not as if they've been racing the monsoon, desperately trying to get up the mountain before the storm breaks; no, they've been *wallowing* in the monsoon the whole way.

It's a difference of philosophies, that's all you can finally say about it. Roskelley wants the mountain as a place to prove his supremacy, and they want it for something messier, less conclusive, less useful. Roskelley can't understand why he hasn't been embraced for pioneering this great route. He seems to expect they'll like him better for what he's done—which is exactly what they can't, or won't, do. This emotional impasse forms the background for a fierce discussion later that morning. Reichardt and States, also disappointed at their tepid welcome, stay out of it, but Roskelley lights into the others on the grounds that they don't deserve to go higher, that they're not strong enough for the Buttress. Oh, Lev can probably handle it, and maybe Willi and Nirmal, too; but, "You're not gonna make it, Devi," he says to her pointedly, "you're in no condition physically to go up there now." He knows about her hernia, which could cause trouble, and he reminds her of the cough she's had from the start of the trip, plus her intestinal problems. Then, turning on Andy, he says, "You've never even carried above this camp. Neither you nor [Devi] have acclimatized. You've got no business [up there] either."

According to Leamer, Devi at this point goes for the communal peanut butter can. Ever since Delhi she's been mocking John's obsession with hygiene, his excessive fear of third-world microbes, which to her is symptomatic of a larger discomfort with all things exotic and non-American. She plunges her fingers into the tub and slowly licks them off. In the context of the moment, this is a shocking gesture—it violates the rule that John has insisted on, and that Jim States, the resident medical authority, has endorsed, to keep everyone's dirty hands and germs out of the communal food. "I've told you a thousand times about that!" Roskelley roars, and then he adds, more in sorrow than rage, "You're just hurting yourself, Devi." To which she says nothing, merely stares at him with unmitigated distaste.

Roskelley later has some words with Willi, in private:

"I just don't think she should go up."

To which Willi replies, "Well, John, what can a father do?"

"I don't know."

"What would you do if she were your daughter?"

"I don't know, Willi . . . she's not."

She should not be allowed to go on the Buttress: this is absolutely clear to Roskelley, and he speaks with the authority of one who really *knows*, who's just risked his neck on it. That his words might be discounted because of things he's done previously on the climb doesn't seem to occur to him. Though he declines to comment directly on what Willi says, Roskelley implies in his account that Willi's statements are a pathetic abdication—by this point, Devi has been given her head so long, has been encouraged in so many delusional ideas, that no one can control her.

We might well ask: Why was it so obvious to Roskelley, but not to Reichardt or to Dr. States, that Devi was out of her depth, needed to be warned off the summit? That afternoon Dr. States examines Devi in a tent; he declares that her hernia is okay, but that it needs to be watched, that it could act up and become a problem. He describes what will happen if the hernia strangulates: "[I]t will take about two hours to kill the bowel and . . . two days to kill the patient." Devi listens to this warning, as does Willi, but in the end she's undeterred.

Devi had carried no loads beyond Camp III, but then no one had except for the summiteers (and Lev, who had carried some food up the Buttress). She had now been at twenty-three thousand feet for a number of days; she was acclimating successfully, had no headaches or other signs of distress, and down below she'd carried like a trouper. Andy, sharing a tent with her and sharing summit plans, disagrees with the idea that Devi had been sick all along:

"That's simply not true. . . . I knew her condition at that time, every day and every hour, and she had about the same level of gut problems and respiratory problems as the others. The hernia was a preexisting condition and it simply never became a problem on the mountain. . . . Saying that she was sick from the start is like saying that only a few people actually belonged on the mountain in the first place, or maybe we should say, one particular person."

Willi's "What can a father do?" according to Andy was "just something that a father might say to an angry guy who didn't have a basis for sticking his nose into things in the first place . . . it wasn't an abdication of responsibility, an admission on the order of 'I lack resolve' or 'I'm too weak.' It was just a recognition that she was determined and reasonably fit and had fastened her hopes on the summit, as I had . . . and not in a summit-or-death kind of way, either. Neither of us was that type of climber. Of course, there's always the voice that says keep your child from all harm, from going up on a mountain or out on a river or to a foreign country, but we were well beyond that point, weren't we."

Roskelley's opinion can be explained in terms of a lack of tact or hurt feelings of his own or old-fashioned chauvinism ("It was going to be hard for him to swallow if a woman did finally reach the top," Andy says). Or perhaps it was what he felt in his heart and felt compelled to say, regardless of consequences. He was only recently down from the summit, profoundly exhausted (he would soon become symptomatic with spinal meningitis), grumpy because nobody was appreciating him the way they should. Yet despite, or maybe because of, everything that was clouding his judgment at that moment, he spoke with force and frankness. He'd spoken in the same way to Elliot Fisher when Elliot was retreating off the mountain, three weeks before; then he'd needed to assert that *he* would not be the member of their expedition to die on Nanda Devi, that his skill and spirit would protect him. Now, having gotten the summit, facing only a routine descent and the longed-for voyage home, he speaks again in the same prophetic tones, no doubt to contrary effect: someone as proud and inspired as Devi could only be stiffened in her resolve.

September 3: In fair weather, the second party approaches the Buttress for a second time. John Evans breaks trail for everyone, and Lev begins ascending the ropes ahead of Devi and Andy, all three of them under vast packs. Evans will spend a lot of hours out in the wet and cold this day. The plan is to give aid and training to the Indian climbers, and for the members of a third party (Willi, Evans, the Indians) to ascend as high as possible, carrying an extra tent and other supplies in support of their own future summit try.

Evans, the brick, a man about whom Lynn Hammond, Willi's colleague at Evergreen, once remarked, "As soon as I saw his forearms, I knew I wanted him on *my* expedition," is generous and hardworking; in the next few days, though, he'll start feeling increasingly cranky and lethargic, and he'll never climb higher than partway up the Buttress. (As Roskelley is on his way to spinal meningitis, Evans is already ill with hepatitis.) The Indians, not skilled on the ropes, even after receiving instruction, set a slow pace. Yet after only three pitches of ascending they come in sight of Andy, who's above them and going even more slowly; he has that big pack to handle, but what's really slowing him down is Devi, just ahead of him and moving *really* slowly.

Willi might well have been far out in front by now, on his way to Camp IV with Lev and on to another summit. But his chosen role is this modest, self-effacing one, laying back with the slowpokes, and he doesn't mind. But seeing Devi moving this way gives him pause. He'd expected something different from her. His account of this part of the climb, published in the *AAJ*, like Reichardt's puts a sometimes amazingly false face on all the troubles and resentments. For example, about the intense argument over Devi's condition, he records, "[John] and Jim both expressed worry about . . . Devi's current diarrhea and flare-up of an inguinal hernia. . . . However . . . Devi had never been slowed by either diarrhea or hernia while carrying [loads]." Then he adds, in the face of Roskelley's unequivocal forecast of doom: "Our situation seemed so ideal that within the next three days both [Roskelley] and Lou headed for Base Camp—Rascal intending to await our [successful] return from the summit."

Perhaps it's unfair to quote climbers' official accounts back at them. But if a truthful account cannot be written for a specialized mountaineering journal, to be read by other mountaineers, many of them Himalayan veterans, then where can it? About the slow going on the ropes of the Buttress, Willi notes, "With seven climbers trying to use [them] at once, the waits were too long and so we four turned back from the top of the third pitch." The problem was not the number of people, but Devi's snail-like progress. She was skilled on mechanical ascenders, had handled heavy packs easily before, yet now she's climbing at a rate to bring into question whether she can surmount the Buttress at all, let alone in the remaining daylight hours. Snow begins to fall. At Camp III, Roskelley and the others watch the progress of Team 2 on the Buttress, and all day they can hear voices calling back and forth. Roskelley knows that some of the fixed lines have been fraying—in places, the outer rope-sheath is completely gone, with the nylon core showing through, and all this jumaring can only be making matters worse. His account is full of a sense of impending catastrophe, for example: "I was concerned . . . knowing the difficulties they faced. . . . Even the idea of [the Indians] practicing on the lower ropes made me nervous."*

Willi commented in his lectures, "I watched Devi doing [the

---

*Lev recalls, contra Roskelley, that by this date he had replaced the lower ropes—"They were just fine."

fourth pitch], taking about one hour on that three-hundred-foot section. . . . I remember Jim States turning to me and saying seriously, 'Willi, if they have to bivouac tonight [midway up the Buttress], I'm going to order Devi to come down.' And I remember my answer to him: 'Yeah, Jim, she'll probably tell you to stick it in your left ear.' This was the kind of [young woman] that Devi was always known to be. . . . She'd call the shots as she saw them, and if she was up high on the Buttress, she'd feel much more capable of calling those shots than any doctor a thousand feet below."

Mixed with Willi's pride is simple fatherly fear. "So they ground their way up into the darkness," he recalled, "and we postponed making radio contact, kept postponing it, and then at seven o'clock we finally got an answer from Pete Lev." (Roskelley puts the hour at 8:30 P.M.) "[Pete had] bombed on ahead toward Camp IV, feeling he could help his partners best by going ahead and getting the camp ready, preparing warm drinks and so forth. And he said that he hadn't seen Devi and Andy since about four o'clock, when he'd left them on Sugar Delight Snowfield."

Willi orders Lev to call on the radio every half hour. Lev enjoys a beautiful sunset at IV, fixes himself a good dinner, and his half-hourly calls are all in the negative. The camp on top of the Buttress is close to the edge: "The site, sloping at twenty degrees, was only one yard away from the Northwest Face," Roskelley writes, yet despite this immediate proximity to the cliff, climbers on the Buttress can't make themselves heard at IV. The wind generally blows from the wrong direction—from the northeast—carrying their voices back, and the top of the wall is a cornice of unconsolidated snow, into which the ropes have cut a deep trench. Surmounting these last few yards is "a bitch," Lev recalled, since a climber's jumars can't be slid up the in-cut ropes. "Fighting for every inch," Roskelley says of his own ascent on August 31, "cutting deeper into the crest with each struggle, I finally [had to release] my jumars, throwing my body . . . onto the flat slope above."

This is what awaits Devi and Andy, and for all Lev knows, they've been stuck just below the top, in sight of safety, unable to make the exit moves. Shortly after nine, Willi gets out of his tent at Camp III and yodels piercingly up into the starry dark. For a long while he hears nothing. Then, "we heard Devi's faint, high-pitched reply," Roskelley records. "Her voice had cracked slightly . . . she was still alive."

According to Willi: "We got our next word at eleven, when Peter called and said that [Andy] had arrived." Andy had climbed behind Devi all day; then at Sugar Delight, he switched positions with her and continued in front, staying just above her and monitoring her progress all along, which was constant if slow. At the top of the snow gully, where the ropes cut into the cornice, he flounders through by main strength, with Devi not far below him. He joins Lev in the tent pitched at the edge of the precipice. At around midnight, people down in Camp III can hear a voice calling way up the Buttress. It's Devi, apparently, crying for Andy and Peter, who are only thirty feet away but unable to hear her because of the configuration of the wall. After what feels to him like too long an interval, Andy goes back out into the blowing night. He makes his way to the cornice edge; there he finds Devi struggling at "the place we all had had trouble," as Roskelley later described it. Andy grabs her and pulls her over the crest, to safety.

Willi gets the news around midnight. "Devi had mastered the final pitch," he told his lecture audiences, "but [it] was a terribly, terribly slow trip up there . . . understandably the next day they were quite exhausted." He himself sleeps poorly that night, and the next day, despite continued good weather, remains in III, resting up for his own last push on the Buttress.

TWENTY-ONE

So near the summit. Only about one thousand six hundred vertical feet away. Roskelley's group, on their own summit day, got going at a ridiculously late hour and still made the top with plenty of time to spare. The nearness of their objective must have worked an influence in the next few days, although no one afterward spoke of it in those terms; but for Devi, Andy, and Pete a memorable accomplishment was almost at hand.

The summit of Nanda Devi has now, twenty-five years later, been visited by fewer than thirty people. This compares remarkably with Everest, where to date over eleven hundred people have summited, including many plodding upward led by guides. Shortly after the expedition of '76, Nanda Devi and its Sanctuary were declared off-limits to climbers, trekkers, native shepherds, native plant-gatherers, and just about everybody else.* The Sanctuary had been closed to foreigners between 1952 and 1974, for political reasons, but after

---

*The last ascent of the peak occurred June 13, 1993. The expedition, organized by a unit of the Indian army, accompanied scientists from six research institutions and served the management requirements of the Nanda Devi Biosphere Reserve.

'82 the closure was motivated by alarm over the savage ecological degradation that attended the brief open period. Between '74 and '81, this holy terrain was transformed almost beyond recovery by expeditions and the local people who served them, and even more by herdsmen following the trekking paths. "In earlier times," according to Deepak Sanan, author of *Nanda Devi: Restoring Glory*, a thorough account of the threatened ecology of the Sanctuary, "only a few flocks had gone over the Dharansi col [a pass near Lata], and Shipton recorded in 1934 that the meadow at Dibrugheta was seldom used. [But] in 1977, over four thousand head were recorded grazing [in nearby meadows]. Each year the flocks reached out to new pastures in the outer sanctuary and... justifying the worst fears of environmentalists, [local herdsmen] the following year led their flocks . . . onto the very meadows of the inner sanctuary."

Climbers and other Westerners left "[l]itter at the regular camp sites, polythene clogged springs and all manner of [other destruction]. . . . With each successive year the ugly gashes of damaged soil where both man and animal slithered down steep slopes; the scars of forest fires where careless seekers of warmth left smouldering embers; the raw wounds of birch and conifer lopped [for bridges] over the sanctuary torrents; the stunted remainders of juniper and rhododendron [cut] to supply fuel at higher altitudes; became more noticeable, competing with . . . the sanctuary's enthralling vista of rugged grandeur."

The beauty of the Sanctuary had always been doubly precious, first for itself but second as a symbol of immanence, of the presence of the goddess. Although the causes of the degradation were understandable—for local herdsmen and others, the economic opportunity was a godsend, literally a lifesaver—the changes were so massive and happened over such a short time that officials in the

Indian Ministry of Environment and other public agencies were shocked into action. Before all the bharal (blue sheep) could be shot by poachers, before all the musk deer could be hunted for the perfume industry, before the birch stands were entirely gone and the rare plants collected as ayurvedic medicines were made extinct, an activist minister of the environment, Nalini Jayal, declared the region a national protectorate, with the entire catchment of the Rishi Ganga closed indefinitely. A few scientists were allowed to complete baseline surveys, but by '84 they, too, were mostly prohibited from entering the Sanctuary, which in '88 was added to the U.N.'s list of World Heritage sites.

This notable act of preservation, in a developing country with a boisterous democracy, is on a scale with the largest set-asides in American conservation history. It came during the last years of Indira Gandhi's final administration; Gandhi and her governments, which had ruled through an assortment of means, including press censorship and arrest of opponents, were known for bold assertions of national authority. The needs of an impoverished rural populace, especially pressing in the Garhwal, had to be balanced against the bigger picture, and the result was a gesture full of meaning to the hundreds of millions of people with an investment in the idea of Nanda Devi's environmental sanctity. That sanctity, which Nalini Jayal and others hoped to restore by barring shepherds and plant-gatherers, had previously been compromised in a far more momentous way, however.

In October '64, China detonated a nuclear device at Lop Nor, in Sinkiang Province. In '65 the Chinese detonated a second device, dropping it from a plane, and a year later they successfully launched a nuclear-tipped rocket in southern Sinkiang, which borders northern India. The CIA proposed an intelligence-gathering mission, and President Lyndon Johnson gave approval. Spy satellites were unsophisticated at the time, and the few the Americans had in orbit were concentrated over the Soviet Union. Therefore the CIA favored a terrestrial monitoring effort, the goal being to place a listening device high up some Himalayan peak, its sensors trained on the nuclear facilities inside China.

Nanda Devi was considered the best possible candidate—elevated enough and offering excellent line-of-sight access into Sinkiang. From the start, the Americans used the Indian Central Bureau of Investigation (CBI) in a compromising way; fearing that the elected Indian government, which took office just after the project got under way, would quickly terminate it, the CIA required its Indian allies to keep everything hidden from Indira Gandhi and her deputies. According to an article published in *Outside* in '78, written by Howard Kohn and based on interviews and research by Galen Rowell, the CBI was dependent on American expertise at the time, and American undercover agents on the CBI payroll were influential at the highest levels. The Indians contributed four experienced mountaineers to the project. The CIA recruited its own team of climbers from among the strongest members of recent American Himalayan expeditions, including Everest '63. (Willi either declined to participate or was never approached. He was serving with the Peace Corps in Nepal, and the Peace Corps was careful to avoid any appearance of CIA connection.)

As with Everest '63, the team members went first to an American mountain to practice. The National Park Service, at the request of CIA agents directing the team, closed the South Face of Mount McKinley to all other mountaineering, and the spy climbers worked on communication and logistics. (As with the Everest team practicing on Mount Rainier, the weather refused to cooperate, and the spy team failed to summit McKinley.) The climbers also trained at a navy facility in Harvey Point, North Carolina, under a CIA case officer named William McNeff. Here their exercises were "cloaked in immediacy and intrigue," according to Howard Kohn's article. "[A] demolitions expert confided the subtleties of plastic explosives, teaching the climbers how to carve an L-shaped recess in an icy mountainside to use for a platform for the tracking station; and another technician put them through an . . . exercise on how to assemble the apparatus."

In the autumn of '65, the climbers flew to India, where they posed as members of an Air Force High Altitude Test program. Local porters carried, but the climbers themselves flew by helicopter directly to the Inner Sanctuary. One of the Americans, a naturalist as well as mountaineer, was fully aware of the extraordinary beauty and fragile uniqueness of the Inner Sanctuary; he makes no mention in his interview of the religious significance of the lands he and his teammates were visiting, but in '65 the Sanctuary was still utterly intact, its herds of bharal and serow and musk deer, its snow leopards and other predators, living in primordial balance, the vast meadows under towering icy faces as yet untrammeled. According to Kohn, "A pack loaded with a heavy metal contraption makes no sense for an ascent into the . . . thin air of the Himalaya. But [one of the packloads] was special. It radiated a warmth that seemed to cling even after the pack was removed. All the Indian porters wanted to carry it. The Americans . . . were less enthusiastic." The listening device, intended to function for years, was to be powered by a nuclear core. The generator that ran the device—a Space Nuclear Auxiliary Power unit, or SNAP—was loaded with plutonium 238, a nuclear synthetic that produces heat as it decays. Such fuels are harnessed for electricity by being encased in a number of metal sheaths, which produce an electrical charge by heating up at different rates. (Other things being equal, a SNAP generator can be expected to function for about seventy-five years.)

At the end of the monsoon season, the Indian and American climbers started an ascent along Tilman's route from '36. A group of porters carried the disassembled listening device plus nuclear fuel, the plan being to approach the summit of Nanda Devi via its South Face, then traverse onto the Northeast Face and plant the receiver. The mountain did not cooperate. Storms and other obstacles forced a halt at about twenty-three thousand feet, just above the site of Tilman's Camp IV. Unable to advance and without a direct line of sight into Sinkiang, the climbers did not assemble the device, but instead excavated a cache among the rocks. Here they stored the apparatus and fuel, planning to return the next spring for installation.

A team of climbers did return the next April, only to find the cache entirely destroyed, according to Kohn, "swept away under a torrent of mountain rubble. A wall of snow and fragments of cliff had broken loose from above and come surging down, leaving behind a clumsy artistry of resculptured furrows and hollows on the spot where [the climbers] now stood dumbfounded."

A substantial amount of plutonium—perhaps no longer securely encased—had been deposited on the slopes of the mountain consecrated to the Bliss-Giving Goddess, the most hallowed geography in the Himalaya. A more profound defilement is hard to imagine. Even more troubling, "the spring thaw on the southern slope of Nanda Devi is a major source . . . for the Ganges. The Rishi Ganga . . . crashes down the slope into the Dhauli . . . which joins the Alaknanda about [thirty miles] below Nanda Devi Sanctuary. The Alaknanda is one of the largest tributaries [of] the Ganges," a river sacred to half a billion people. "The Alaknanda-Dhauli juncture is a sacred place," according to Kohn. "A temple sits on a rocky ledge dividing the two rivers, and for hundreds of years

Hindu worshipers . . . have paraded down stone steps into waters from Nanda Devi's slopes."

Nonplussed, the American climbers bivouacked. One of them was inclined to return to base for further instructions from the CIA's McNeff, but another saw no reason not to celebrate the unique turn of events that had brought him to within twenty-five hundred feet of a fabled summit. In a single day he climbed to the top by himself, thus achieving, in the face of ethical concerns that might have troubled a lesser man, the highest solo ascent by an American. "He [summited] without trouble," Kohn writes, "but his trip down was more treacherous. As he approached the camp he lost his footing and went sprawling several hundred feet down a snowy incline, miraculously coming to rest, unhurt, just short of a cradle of sharp rocks."

The secret expedition regrouped below. The somber consequences for individual CIA careers, as well as for American diplomacy in Asia, were plain, and the team's CIA handlers puzzled over what to do. The avalanche debris had come to rest three thousand feet above the Sanctuary floor, roughly at the elevation of Willi's team's Advanced Base. The plan was to try to recover the SNAP, but the avalanche cone hiding it was enormous: Kohn likens it to "a Giza pyramid" in size, and Rowell aptly describes the task of locating the SNAP as being "equal to . . . locating a diamond ring dropped at sea." Nevertheless, the Americans helicoptered in lengths of rubber fire hose, attached them to natural water sources on the mountain, and attempted to wash away thousands of tons of mountain. This effort failed. CIA higher-ups in the United States then ordered that the generator be abandoned. As Kohn notes, "Plutonium 238 remains dangerously radioactive for three hundred to five hundred years . . . even if the SNAP generator had survived the avalanche intact, its outer core would eventually corrode. . . . Handling or inhaling plutonium can be fatal, and it would be impossible to retrieve the radioactive material once it escaped into the snow."

The same higher-ups in Langley soon removed McNeff as agent in charge. The next year, "another American from the prestigious 1963 Everest expedition [was] recruited to help replace the climbers who'd left," Kohn says, and a new attempt was launched to plant a listening device—not on enormous, unstable Nanda Devi, but on nearby Nanda Kot, at 22,510 feet a more manageable summit. This attempt succeeded. That device, also nuclear-powered, intercepted radio signals from Sinkiang for the next two years.

This environmental tragedy—a tragedy whose final act has yet to play out—was for many years a story no one dared tell. In the early seventies, the editor of an English magazine learned of it and went some distance toward researching and publishing an account, but in the end he made a difficult, disciplined decision not to do so at a time of delicate relations between India and the United States. The Sanctuary was still closed, and almost certainly restrictions would not have been lifted in '74—making possible the Unsoeld expedition, among others—had all the details become a matter of public record. Foreign mountaineers, Americans in particular, have long been objects of political suspicion, and the details of the American espionage, with flagrant co-option of the Indian CBI, would likely have precipitated a crisis.

The behavior of the Americans can be understood in various ways. Some participants were self-described cold warriors, eager to protect what they saw as American interests and unnerved by the development of Chinese nuclear weaponry. Others simply appreciated the opportunity to climb, the adventure of it, as well as the wages being paid by the CIA ($1,000 per month, a sizable amount in '65). Even the climber who raced to the top of Nanda Devi, having just realized the loss of a nuclear core, can perhaps be forgiven his high spirits: mountaineers far up glorious peaks tend to want to go for the summit regardless. But what the episode mainly reveals is a deep American cluelessness, a cultural naïveté that can countenance outcomes that look truly mad. At such times, the American can-do spirit seems demonic; the release of plutonium at the headwaters of the greatest river in Asia, along with the desecration of a landscape of incomparable value, can be said to rank high on the list of the world's most callous stunts.

Gandhi's government probably remained unaware of events on Nanda Devi for many years. It seems unlikely that the Sanctuary would have been opened otherwise, although the political costs of admitting ignorance might also have been substantial. Almost certainly the Johnson White House never learned of the CIA's blunder: CIA officials were reluctant to broadcast the news, understandably, and they reasoned that with a little luck, no one would ever be the wiser. Meanwhile the device on Nanda Kot was in place and providing some information. The situation had ended up a big win.

In his last days on Nanda Devi, Willi's often in a good mood. He comes to like jumaring, sort of: climbing the Buttress on September 6, as he later said, "I thoroughly enjoyed my solo," even though he continued to be troubled by unpartnered climbing. "Had a very heavy pack," he said in one of his lectures, "[and] since I was the old man on the expedition, I was carefully monitoring my bodily responses. And those responses were just fantastic. No problem with the altitude. Moving over superb rock."

Willi almost always sounds this note, the note of just *loving* it, being at home in the mountains. Despite the hardships, the manifold dangers, the consciousness of nature's austere splendor keeps breaking in on him, and he simply has to give it voice. This is what makes him Willi. It's also what makes him seem young, despite the bad hips and the graying beard. God or the Great Wheel of Being or something has stacked the deck in his favor, throwing the magnificence of the untamed wild world into the bargain. As a thirteen-year-old, cutting capers on the gentle snow-slopes of Middle Sister in the Oregon Cascades, he felt ecstatic just to be alive, and he still feels that way—he still cuts capers in his heart.

Willi's love of nature is similar to Thoreau's and Emerson's, and like the American transcendentalists he stands in a line of direct descent from German Idealism by way of Wordsworth and Coleridge and Carlyle. But the outdoor philosopher he probably most resembles is the physically daring, religiously conflicted Scottish-American John Muir. Muir achieved a nature-is-my-cathedral epiphany fully as sublime as Thoreau's. He did so while pursuing experiences in the mountains that continue to inspire active climbers: the list of his first ascents in California, most of them accomplished solo and with little equipment, is hard to rival in the history of American mountaineering. (Compare his adventures in the Sierra Nevada with Thoreau's gentle walks in the Concord woods.) Muir added a valuable insight to the High Romantic idea of wilderness: he decentered the human, coming to realize that all of nature, not just man, deserves existence. The notion that rattlesnakes were good in themselves, and did not have to be "good for something," drove his work to preserve vast tracts of American wildlands—without these efforts our world looks entirely different.

Like other High Romantics, Muir came alive in the outdoors, and his imagination was especially fired by the rugged vastness of the West. "The clearest way into the Universe is through a forest wilderness," he wrote in *A Thousand-Mile Walk to the Gulf*, and his writings in general are suffused with a feeling of nature's sublimity. Muir, a kind of homegrown pantheist, sensed holiness everywhere, but in the West he rejoiced at the absence of conventional religious influence. The extent of his relief at this absence can best be measured against his family background. His father was a strict Scots Calvinist, an 1840s immigrant to rural Wisconsin, where the young Muir grew up on a farm learning Scripture "by heart and by sore flesh," as he described the process. As a doctrinaire Calvinist, one who exercised dynamic control over his son's life, Daniel Muir was especially vigilant against the sins that arise from the free exercise of natural capacities, for example, the imagination. Even reason was dangerous (maybe especially reason), but imagination untempered by an awareness of man's innate sinfulness was an abomination.

The Romantic idea of imagination—which allows each of us to perceive his or her own higher truth—is "radically discontinuous" with orthodox Christian consciousness, according to H. P. Simonson, a scholar of the American Romantics. Transcendentalism saw imagination as "the very vessel by which divinity passes into humanity," but Calvinism harbored a "serious distrust toward imagination's idolatrous potential." It valued faith over imagination, insisting on unstinting efforts to reform the sinful human heart. An excited imagination at loose in the world, channeling what it believes are "divine truths," is a spiritual disaster waiting to happen. The Romantics also likened human creativeness to God's, whereas the Calvinists insisted on an absolute difference between "man's 'I am' and God's I AM THAT I AM," according to Simonson.

Wordsworth's *The Prelude* is a hymn to the poet's power to imagine whole worlds, that is, to write long poems just like *The Prelude*. By the middle of the twentieth century, Romanticism has lost the tone of awe before its own powers, but the "natural supernaturalism" of Emerson and the others persists, with the wondrous creativity of the imaginer now taken for granted. Muir's father abominated all nature worship, and Muir's rebellion launched him into one of the most fruitful, socially useful encounters with wilderness in our history. But Muir was a spiritually unquiet man. One sign of his dissent from the full Romantic orthodoxy is to be found in his publishing history; unlike Emerson and some others he did not rush into print with his works of personal revelation, but instead waited decades before allowing his personal writings to appear. Muir was conscious of an overweening quality in Romanticism, even when it insisted on the vastness of God's creation and the smallness of the human datum. The subject—the imaginer—might refer to his own insignificance, but the "I" was always central and sovereign, claiming absorption in the divine glory while offering evidence of just the opposite.

Muir was enough of a Calvinist to be uneasy about such reveling in the self. He wrote a number of influential books, many distinguished by original field observation and fully in accord with the most advanced scientific thinking of his day.* Unlike Emerson, he studied botany and geology and had a scientific bent, and unlike the down-to-earth Thoreau he worked hard to introduce a kind of experimental rigor into his writings.

Only in his old age did Muir feel comfortable enough with, or removed enough from, his youthful egoism to reveal his more pan-

---

*Muir spent five semesters at the University of Wisconsin, where one of his professors, Ezra S. Carr, taught the theory of Ice Age glaciation. Muir later argued for the glacial origins of Yosemite's spectacular landscape, a theory that flew in the face of the standard theory of Yosemite's "cataclysmic" origins, advocated by Professor Josiah D. Whitney of Harvard, the state geologist of California.

Muir also encountered Charles Darwin's work at Wisconsin, and his nature writings show a solid understanding of evolution by means of natural selection. He had no trouble reconciling Darwin's ideas with his personal religious faith, nor was he scared off Christianity by his father's biblical fundamentalism: the Bible for Muir was both the Word and a document shaped by historical conditions.

theistic responses to nature. At age seventy-three, he collected some journals written forty years before and published them as *My First Summer in the Sierra,* a book that combines vivid descriptions of Yosemite Valley with an equally vivid account of a nature-based spiritual awakening. *My First Summer* is nothing if not transcendentalist, but it's also informed on almost every page by Christian consciousness, with images of Communion, baptism, and resurrection plentiful among the references to granite outcrops as "altars," visitors to Yosemite as "pilgrims," and Yosemite itself as a sacred "temple." Before *My First Summer,* Muir had been known to his public mainly as a naturalist arguing for wildlands, but the ecstatic transfigurations of *My First Summer* spoke to them in an electrifying new key.

In the journals he kept in his last years, however, Muir seems less of a nature-inspired Romantic. "There is a Calvinist tone," Simonson observes of these writings, "pointing to a world that nature does not symbolize, that a writer's consciousness does not assimilate, that his word can never record. At times this realm is terrifying." The death of Muir's father, in 1885, turned his mind to last things; but as early as 1878, when he began taking field trips to Alaska, his outlook had begun to darken. In Alaska he encountered a wilderness much more savage than beneficent California's. A famine in the winter of '78–79 had killed thousands of people, and when Muir visited coastal Alaska in '81 he saw whole villages with no one left alive, with decomposed corpses still in the huts and hundreds of bodies lying unburied. He witnessed the slaughter of walruses and seals for market and was profoundly disturbed, and his journals contain references to grinning skulls "looking out here and there" from the charnel-house-like huts, and to the ubiquitous "black water" that dashed against the treacherous sea ice, which the ship he traveled on, the *Corwin,* negotiated with care.

Alaska intrigued and even moved him, but it was a wilderness of driving gray sleet, insane winds, and seabirds screaming as if in agony, and the journals from the *Corwin* are somber and haunted. Earlier, while vagabonding in the West, Muir had sometimes felt an emotional insufficiency among the sunny summits: "In all God's mountain mansions," he wrote, "I find no human sympathy, and I hunger." The messy life of ordinary people down in the lowlands, which he disdained and eagerly escaped as a youth, called to him more and more as he got older. He had many friendships as an adult, and eventually he married well and found fulfillment as a father and a grandfather. In 1893 he returned to Dunbar, Scotland, his birthplace and the scene of early struggles with his father. With thoughts of this father in mind, from Dunbar he wrote home to a beloved daughter, Wanda, saying, "Ask Mother to give you lessons to commit to memory every day. Mostly the sayings of Christ in the Gospels. . . . Find the hymn of praise in *Paradise Lost*, 'These are thy glorious works, Parent of Good, Almighty,' and learn it."

Two years later, on the occasion of her fourteenth birthday, Muir wrote in his journal, "I dread pain and trouble in so sweet and good a life. If only death . . . could be abolished!" Simonson observes about this un-transcendental-sounding sentiment—the sentiment merely of a devoted father—"These are not the thoughts he enjoyed in the high Sierras . . . when death seemed like some sublime victory, some beautiful corroboration of nature's eternal laws. . . . Although he had experienced abounding and overflowing life, in which sickness, pain, and death seemed not to exist . . . Muir yet heard the bell that tolled him back to his [mortal] self."

There's the rub: for a mountaineer like Willi, or a fearless solo climber/explorer like Muir, death has been fairly vanquished, faced down on so many occasions that at last it's been brought into perspective. The transcendental mind-set, the religious immersion in holy nature, is another blow against the reaper, providing ecstasies so intense they seem to outweigh all risks, and providing also a metaphysics with a consoling message: to die is to merge with the All. But nature is disturbingly silent over "the great doctrines of the fall of man and the wonders of redeeming love," Simonson notes, and the climber who connects with others and who loves is right back in the tragic arena with the rest of us. He can have his heart broken. He can fail himself or, worse, fail the people he loves. Thoroughly steeped in Shakespeare as well as the Bible, Muir recognized the dread geography he began to walk as soon as he came down from his summits and entered the lowland life. It was the world of fathers and mothers and all those who open themselves to inconsolable loss, who risk moral destruction, à la King Lear, by way of attachments of the blood, who love well but sometimes not well enough. Lear, as it happened, "but little knew himself," and his ignorant and imperious rejection of Cordelia, his one true daughter of three, set in motion a series of catastrophes so awful as to be unbearable. For Lear, as Shakespeare describes his tragedy, the greatest love becomes the source of unendurable suffering. There's no real answer to this suffering, and no end to it except in Lear's own death, nor is the pre-Christian world that Shakespeare creates softened by the possibility of redemption.

Muir greatly needed that possibility. He was ever more aware of "human finitude and appalling contingency," according to Simonson, and his letters to his wife note the deaths of many friends and occasionally contain frank statements on the order of "As for the old freedom I used to enjoy in the wilderness, that, like youth and its enthusiasms, is . . . of the past." There's a note of self-pity in this, but in fact Muir's embrace of lowland life and connectedness bespeaks a compelling sea change, a growing beyond the nature Romanticism he discovered in his youth. The problem with the pantheistic paradise of the transcendentalists is its very excellence: blissed out in contact with charmed nature, man escapes his fallenness, his moral ambiguity, his penchant for violence and irrationality—everything inborn in him that makes for tragic outcomes. There's no sign of a self at war with God or man, but this is exactly what it means to be human much of the time: to be in conflict. To face impossible choices. To endure loss. Late in life, Muir entertained this darker vision in a serious way, and he understood it mainly in terms of the Calvinist Christianity of his youth, a faith that by its harshness communicated a certain honesty.

Like Muir, Willi chose to dwell more and more in the lowlands as he aged. As he often told his students and lecture audiences, he had tried living like a holy man once, but got bored after a couple months. He needed messy human contact, lots of it. He was Christian through and through, and when he talked about the awe-inspiring *mysterium tremendum* he showed an emotional understanding of the terror that for many people lies at the heart of faith. But his *mysterium* is less a vision of the void or of the unknowable Other than it is a way of exciting audiences, of suggesting the awesome majesty of the world, especially the mountainous part of it. Willi's Christianity, almost as learned and as thoughtful as Muir's, grew out of the vitalism of Bergson rather than a sense of man's inherent sinfulness, nor did Willi seem completely serious when he invoked an unbridgeable distance from the holy. The human spirit could get you a long, long way in Willi's theology—maybe not all the way to the big jackpot, the final beatitude, but close, and the point was never to stop trying. Human sinfulness, the "dark shadow emanating from Jerusalem," as Simonson calls it, was not salient for Willi. The half century that separates him from John Muir was arguably the most horrific in human history, but it was also a time when the idea of a tragic component in human nature fell out of favor, when political and psychological theories of our condition abounded.

Yet we need a tragic sense—most of us do, anyway. We need it because life deals with us harshly at times, and we want to survive those times if we can; not be driven mad by them or forced to amputate too much of our thinking and feeling capacity. Muir's great discovery was that life contained both the "emanating shadow" and the potential for transcendence, that it was wider than his father's biblicism but also darker than an excited view from a summit. Muir sought balance, and in his last years he mostly achieved it. "To soar with elevated thoughts changed not a whit," Simonson observes, "the retributive reminder that . . . pain . . . and death pervade the only life one really knows, and human love and divine grace afford its only hope."

For Willi, this dual understanding, a visionary capacity under-girded by a consciousness of sin, remained elusive. He might have grasped it intellectually, but his hopeful nature and the professional requirements of the roles he chose to play pushed him in another direction. His was to the end a unitary faith, generally well suited to the kind of life he advocated and tried to embody. It was a faith of mountaintops and splendid vistas, warmly consoling for all those moments when in fact there was little need of consolation. When things grew dark, however, as they finally did, he found himself cut off. The philosopher of belief was betrayed, not by the beliefs he had but by those he had left behind.

. . . .

TWENTY TWO

September 4: A beautiful day, one of the finest of the expedition, cannot be turned to advantage by the people in IV. They lie around recuperating from the Buttress, and meanwhile Roskelley down in Camp III gets ready to leave the mountain for good. Dr. States has to stay on in case of emergencies, but Roskelley's finished and now he's out of there, headed for Base Camp by himself. His decision to leave might appear hasty or even unseemly, but mountaineers who summit almost always want to get back to better food and richer air as soon as they can. Reichardt's also in a mood to descend: his wife back in the States is about to have a child, their first.

That there's no love lost between those still hoping for the summit and those who've already bagged it doesn't really matter. Roskelley, who only recently was prophesying disaster, claiming that the second party was too weak, writes differently in his book: "We felt that all the climbers would summit in the next three or four days if everything worked out well. Already the second team was in position and the Indians needed only to perfect their jumar technique to follow a day or two later." Roskelley wants them in good shape so that he can feel okay about leaving, and he does leave in the middle of the morning on the fourth, descending on ropes to Camp II, then to Camp I, then to Advanced Base—finding all the campsites in a shambles, empty and spooky, the tents collapsed. Ravens are pecking at the few remaining supplies, and everything's "wet and filthy." "Like a victim of war," Roskelley says, "I scavenged the dead camp."

Oddly, he writes, "I never felt so insignificant. . . . Dropping over a small cliff above Advanced Base, I [expected] to see a lively camp with several of the high-altitude porters, but . . . [b]efore me were the ghostly skeletons of three [lowered] tents." He adds, "The mountain was silent. . . . I decided to continue down and across the glacier for Base because [this] was too depressing." His great struggle on the Buttress, alone on scary unknown ground, didn't reduce him to feelings of insignificance, but these scenes without people— and the missing people include several he can hardly stand—plunge him into despair. At Base he at last finds the porters, and in human company again he begins to recover. Like his prophecy about Devi and like the words he spoke to Elliot Fisher, this solo descent of the mountain shows us Roskelley in a weird state of mind, full of strong feeling of an indeterminable kind—one element of it probably an unacknowledged compassion.

September 5: Willi heads for the Buttress again, on an overcast day. The problem, again, is the Indians: they need more jumar instruction, and their progress is deadly slow. The idea of an *Indo-American* expedition still has force for Willi, and he exercises great patience in the face of painful provocation: all he wants is to get up this stupid wall, be with his daughter in Camp IV, yet as the weather deteriorates and a wintry chill comes into the air, he can only poke along.

At the fourth pitch, Willi comes upon Captain Kumar, who has flipped upside down in his ascenders. This is the third time Kiran has managed to flip upside down. Wearing a heavy pack, and operating his jumars on iced ropes, which decreases their efficiency, Kiran is unable to right himself; thoroughly exhausted, he wants only to back down, but he's unable to make his jumars reverse.

"This is something not usually taught," Willi later told audiences, "when you learn about crevasse rescue [using jumars]. Coming out of a crevasse, there's no particular reason to want to go back down in, you see. . . . I came up on the nine-mil rope, and I was gonna show him how to reverse, but by this time he'd recovered, and he went on up. But it was an *hour and a half* he'd been hanging on the ropes there, and this really sucks it out of you."

This carnival, this eleventh-hour jumar seminar—exactly what Roskelley was warning against—would be funny but for the cold and the frayed ropes, and Willi has to manage Kiran sensitively, give him every chance to succeed, then pull the plug decisively. "Everything was in slow motion . . . we reached Sugar Delight Snowfield after four P.M., and I vetoed any further progress. Kiran was *really* keen to go on . . . he'd had a setback the year before, taken an eight-hundred-foot fall on Changabang, and he needed this to prove he still had his nerve. We had to coax him down."

They make it back to Camp III, deeply exhausted, late at night. The Indo-American idea has been honored, and now perhaps it can be allowed to die. That same day Devi and Andy rested at Camp IV: a second day of resting at an altitude, twenty-four thousand feet, where rest is hard to achieve, where the body does not readily replenish itself, although according to a radio transmission that night, Devi's been feeling stronger. "The first two days at Camp IV," Willi explained, "she had very bad dysentery and gastric upsets. Then she seemed to improve. She was taking Lomotil at all three meals, and she finally got it under control and seemed in pretty good form." Willi's been having the same kind of problem, bolting out of the tent at all hours to relieve himself. His toeless feet have been aching in the cold, and his thumbs are arthritically painful from manipulating ascenders. Still, he feels pretty good, all things considered. Strong enough to do whatever needs to be done, and the news about Devi is cheering. The morning of the fifth, although he doesn't know this, she told her tentmates that she would be resting for another day so that Willi would have time to catch up with them. By all means she wants this summit, but what she wants most is to get it with her father.

Lev doesn't need to wait, though, and on his own he sets out to reconnoiter the route above Camp IV. September 5 is not the temperate day that the fourth was, but he feels strong and more than up to the technical challenges. Climbing alone at such an altitude multiplies the risks, and he makes sure he can down-climb everything he up-climbs. "It was mixed ground," he recalled later, "with a little rockface. . . . I practiced going up and down [the face] to be sure I could reverse the moves, then climbed it and went beyond. There was a nice snow ridge up there, a knife edge. . . . I took a photo straddling it, looking down."

No reason Lev wasn't included on the Roskelley summit team, other than the frankly personal one: that he had made himself unpopular, been an irritant to Roskelley's plan for a long time, therefore they didn't want him. "They didn't want me going for the summit with them, that's all . . . they said that there wasn't enough food, enough space in the tent, that they needed a good night's sleep . . . I understood. I understood." Climbing well, Lev senses the summit within reach; he completes the technical sections, but then, "Snow began to flurry . . . there was a buzzing all around me, then lightning. I wasn't far from the top, but it felt sketchy to be going alone at that point, so I turned back. Going down I reversed the rock-step, got onto the mixed ground. . . . I was facing out as I climbed, and I tripped . . . a big, cartwheeling fall, lost my ice ax along the way. Somehow I did a cat arrest on all fours, and one of my crampon points caught on a rock." He had slid almost too far—out and over the Northwest Face. "If I hadn't stopped where I did I would've been gone. I crawled back up. I retrieved my ax. I was . . . real shook up."

He finds Camp IV despite a mist that's blown in, and on his way to the tent he passes the latrine they've been using. Something captures his attention: there's blood in the snow, somebody's bloody stools. "Before this I had stuck my head in the sand," Lev says, meaning he'd stayed out of the question of Devi's physical condition, ceding her authority over her own well-being, on the grounds that she was a competent mountaineer with a level head. Going back to the incident at Dibrugheta, there'd been enough contesting of the physical fitness of the women participants, it seemed to him, and Devi was not only competent to decide, she was climbing the mountain with her father and a lover. But the stark symbolism of the blood in the snow unnerves him. He enters the tent, and sometime in the next twenty-four hours, in a private moment, he tells Devi what he's seen and asks her to account for it. And she does, casually: "I'm okay, and anyway, Dad'll be up in a while. Don't worry—I'm okay."

The next day, the sixth, Lev rests from his summit try. Devi makes radio contact early with Camp III, learning that Willi plans to start up after breakfast. From the base of the mountain, all the way down in the meadows of the blissful Sanctuary—where the rainbow-hued display of July wildflowers has now succumbed to hard frosts—Roskelley looks up at the distant summit, noting snow plumes and clouds speeding by. He imagines that "someone had reached the top" by now, someone from the second party, and his worries center not on Andy or Devi but on the Indians: "Kiran scared me," he writes, "because he was irrational when it came to 'saving face.' I knew he was not technically proficient. . . . Now that she had overcome the difficulties of the Buttress, Devi worried me less." At around noon, Reichardt also arrives in the meadows, having decided to head out and try to make it back to his wife's side in time. He also imagines the others on top, or soon to be. "We briefly wished each other success," Roskelley writes briskly, "and he continued [down to the Rishi Gorge], loaded with all the Gumperts drink mix and chapatis . . . I could give him."

Two miles higher in the sky, Andy ventures out of the Camp IV tent. They're here to climb this thing, aren't they? Devi also comes out, but after only a short trek uphill she confesses that this will not be her day to climb anything. She's too weak. No pain, and as long as she doesn't exert herself she feels okay. Maybe another rest day will do it. They return to the tent together—Andy seems not to have considered going up without her, going anywhere without her.

On the radio that afternoon, Dr. States interrogates Devi. He wants to know all her symptoms. "I have no pain," she tells him, and she assures him that she's hiding nothing. To Andy, who some- time in recent days reached a momentous and joyful decision, Devi seems weary but basically all right, not medically compromised; he later told Roskelley, "Nothing suggested urgency, just her lassitude and diarrhea [seemed notable]." Still, talking things over with Lev, they decide that Devi should probably descend, get off the high Buttress; down at a lower elevation she'll be able to recover better. For the moment, they sit tight and await Willi's arrival.

Willi's having a good time meanwhile—a Willi sort of good time. That morning he hurried out of his tent to squat at the Camp III latrine, noting in his discomfort that the day looked fabulous, and that, despite all the tiring jumaring of the day before, he felt fit. "Kiran, I'm going up," he told the Indian officer, knowing that

Evans and the Indians were too exhausted to stir out of their tents. Kiran protested, claiming that Willi was trying to "ditch" them, to which Willi replied, "I'm going up to be with Devi, Kiran. . . . I want to be with Devi."

Having freed himself of the Indians, in as decent a fashion as possible, he sets out for the Buttress again. In his account written for the *AAJ*, he communicates joy at having only a tough little mountaineering challenge to handle: "The familiar ground flowed smoothly past under my jumars. . . . I was elated to see that to the midpoint it had taken [me] only two and three-quarters hours. . . . My pack was very heavy now, but I found the beauty and boldness of the route totally exhilarating." If only life were climbing mountains! What a relief not to have all that other stuff to worry about! "I was on to a Gibbs [ascender]," he told his audiences, "so I could rest at any point. . . . I picked up a tent and a food bag [at Sugar Delight], and despite the enormous load I never felt better. . . . You can't run or hasten on jumars, it's just a slow, smooth, totally-in-control process that fits a fifty-year-old, over-the-hill climber. It's consonant with your pace in life . . . I *like* jumaring, I *like* it."

Seven P.M., he finds himself near the top of the final pitch. "From twenty feet away I yodeled . . . it was a very difficult last pitch, we'd cut into the snow lip there, and I wanted 'em to throw me down a rope. But they never heard me in the tent. The acoustics are amazing over an edge like that . . . you had to make a final free move [unclipped from ascenders], kind of a dicey move . . . when I rolled over that lip, it was *sheer ecstasy* to have made it."

Everyone takes courage when Willie arrives—that's the effect he has. "There was a great eruption inside the tent," he recalled, "as Devi found her old dad once more with her. We spent a very close night in the one tent"—four people, Willi crammed into the vestibule—"it was too cold outside to [try to] pitch the second tent, a blizzard was blowing." The weather has taken a turn this evening: the day that looked fabulous only that morning, that Roskelley noted for the winds blowing off the summit, signals with an absolute clarity the end of the monsoon season, the turn toward Himalayan winter. "Before that evening," Lev recalled, "I was often out climbing in just a sweater and a windbreaker ... this was a *cold* storm, not a warm monsoonal one. It was the jet stream now, westerly, northwesterly, and cold, so cold."

They pass the night, Devi playing some tunes on her harmonica. Next morning, September 7, the snowstorm continues, still fierce and intensely cold. Once again, the mountain has changed its mood exactly when it wants, and with a dramatic flourish. Good spirits obtain, however, inside the jammed tent, everyone talking story, happily lying back: "It was a day full of liquids," Willi wrote, "and [full of] the easy talk which fills rest days at high altitude." In his public addresses, Willi went further and described the day as "a high point in our total climbing careers. . . . We all just lay in the sack and reminisced about other climbs we'd been on. I'd guided in the Tetons with Pete, and Pete and Devi and I had done the South Buttress of [Mount] Moran. . . . Andy was a very congenial host, and we just lay in the sack and [brewed tea] and drank *copious* drafts."

Devi, though weak, has gotten over her diarrhea. That's to the good, but in the afternoon she declares, "I hope you all go to the summit and leave me here," a simple statement that they all understand, a recognition of realities. The four, their bodies pressed together in a mass of down bags and parkas, head to foot and elbow to rib, have almost a single central nervous system when it comes to sensing how it is with her (or with any of them); should the weather break, then, the three men will try to rush the summit tomorrow morning, returning to camp in time to pick Devi up and descend the Buttress with her. That night, though, Devi begins to suffer. It was "a bad one for her," Willi wrote, "[h]er stomach generated gas in such quantities that she simply could not sleep and spent most of the night sitting up. . . . By morning she was extremely tired." In his speeches, he made a kind of bitter comedy of the circumstances, the four of them in the tiny tent, Devi belching sulfurously every twenty minutes or so: "Devi had *fabulous* intestines, the most active known to the species . . . she produced gas which went up or gas which went down, and this particular [time] it was all upward-directed, and it continued all night." She had gone to sleep in the center of the tent, the men huddled protectively around her. When she sits upright, she disturbs the others, and by morning they're all a bit ragged, and Lev opens his eyes on a terrible sight: her fair countenance blue-tinged and bloated. The crisis, whatever its origins, has not passed in the night.

Andy palpates her abdomen. The hernia's in place, but her stomach seems distended. As Willi later recalled, "She was still happy, still cheerful," but in the confines of the little tent the uncanny transformations of her face and body are upsetting to witness. Andy in recent days has asked Devi to marry him, and she's agreed, and they've told Willi about it, and he, more than pleased at the prospect, has given his blessing. So Devi now lies in the arms of her lifetime companion, near the summit of the mountain of the goddess after whom she's named, at the very turn of season that marks the return of Nanda Devi to the icy abode of her divine mate—the concordance could not be more complete, not that anyone cares or is even aware, and at this moment, the sense is not of some divinely sanctioned consummation but, sadly, the opposite. They'll have to take her down. She's too sick to go on, and their summit try has not come off. "It was clear that we had best wait no longer," Willi remembered, "and we aimed at twelve noon to finish our preparations to descend. We had no doubt that we would return as soon as the weather improved, and that in the next spell of good weather, we would all go to the summit together."

The wind's still howling—the blizzard does not relent. Hoping for a break in the storm, they pack without special haste; Devi assures them that she can handle the Buttress, she'll be okay descending in bad conditions, but they all know they'll be taking a grave risk. Lev later recalled that as the morning progressed, Devi's face grew more swollen, and just before their time of departure she took a turn for the worse. She's sitting up, trying to drink from a cup of cocoa. She asks Lev to take her pulse, and he replies, "I'll do it a little later, when I'm ready with this," meaning, when he's finished lacing up his boots. He glances her way, and her troubled gaze seems to relax at that moment.

Holding his own gaze, she says, "I'm going to die," then falls forward. Her eyes roll up in her head and she vomits what looks like coffee grounds.

Andy rushes to her. Willi, already dressed and outside the tent, hears his name being called and comes back in. "We're in bad trouble," Andy tells him, and Lev adds, "She just said she was going to die, Willi." As Willi himself later described the scene, a scene of defining heartbreak for him, "She lapsed into unconsciousness and was gone in under five minutes. [When] I came back inside, Andy and Peter were in distress. I saw what had happened and . . . started artificial respiration, with Peter [adding] CPR. It was . . . an utterly forlorn hope."

They continue trying to revive her. Willi implores her not to die: "Don't leave, Devi . . . please, please. Oh—don't go." But her lips turn cold under his own, and nothing avails, nothing. Lev recalls their anguish and a sense of "pandemonium . . . I sort of shrank in the corner, while Andy and Willi dealt with her. Both gave her mouth-to-mouth. We could not revive her." Even after more than twenty-five years, Andy does not speak easily of that hour: "Those events are nothing like twenty-five years old for me," he says, and would rather leave it at that. All three men seem to have been profoundly shocked. That Devi might die seems not to have been one of the options they considered. She'd been at twenty-four thousand feet for almost five days, ill with assorted intestinal complaints, possibly even including amoebic dysentery (which can cause internal bleeding), but almost up to the last moment she seemed cheerful and about to rouse herself. There was something inextinguishable about her. The unimaginable next step now begins to take form in Willi's mind; because the storm's still raging, they still need to save themselves, get out of there if they can. But, what do you do with the body of a daughter? The most precious, the most sacred in the world to you? What do you do?

Moaning, breathless with grief, he thinks through the steps. A process that in all decency should take days, the spirit of the dead and the spirit of the bereaved somehow finding resolution in the ritual necessities, is here whipped up to maniacal speed, furiously intensified as if it were an aspect of the storm howling outside. Do they leave her here in the tent? That seems insufficient and unendurably ugly. Do they carry her down the mountain, maybe with the hope of burying her, if they can manage the descent, in the meadows of the Sanctuary? She would rest then in a place whose beauty would echo her own. Willi isn't thinking completely straight at this moment, and probably no one can understand fully the thought processes growing out of such a frenzy of grief; at any rate, he rejects that idea, after discussing it briefly with Andy and Peter, and instead announces, "We will commit her to the mountain. As if in a burial at sea."

They secure her body in the sleeping bag, with the drawstring hood closed over her face. Then half drag her, half carry her out of the tent. The storm almost upends them as they carry her a short distance up the slope. They lay Devi in the snow above the most profound precipice on the mountain, the ghastly Northeast Face. Here they fall to their knees, sobbing, and link hands in a circle at the foot of Devi's corpse. Willi's prayer, reported in Leamer's book as well as in Roskelley's, and described by Willi himself in speeches, goes something like this:

"Thank you, Lord, for the world we live in . . . the kind of world that offers us both the beauties and the challenges of the mountains. Thank you for such beauty, posed against such risk. Thank you. Thank you."

Each man says his private farewell, then with what Roskelley describes as "a horrible shove," they launch Devi's remains into the swirling storm. According to Lev, "It was just an immense precipice, ten thousand feet down. And . . . we dropped her." Willi told audiences, "We'd decided not to evacuate the body, because I've always been of the opinion that as we have drawn strength from the mountains when alive, we should continue to do so when we are dead. . . . As Devi's body disappeared from view, I essayed a final yodel, which so often she had answered when alive. . . . We [had] committed her body to the snows."

. . . .

TWENTY-THREE

They must descend, for survival's sake, but even more because the tent is now a place of horror. Willi takes a few precious items of Devi's, puts them in her Lowe pack and straps this on top of his own pack—an ill-advised load of dangerous proportions. The descent is almost fatal to Lev, who finds himself midway down swinging loose on an unanchored rope. "It was desperate," he said, "only my prusik [a safety knot] saved me. . . . I pendulumed twenty feet or more, over and over, trying to get my boot up onto a ledge, which was iced. I hadn't put my crampons on. . . . I shat my pants. . . . at last I got it, so squeezed in my harness that I could hardly breathe."

Willi descends second, then third after Andy moves ahead of him on the ropes. He's going on automatic. Any one of a thousand possible missteps might bring him the kind of peace that his instincts won't allow him. The traverse between the bottom of the snow gully and Sugar Delight Snowfield almost decides matters for him: he has to edge out along an eight-inch ledge, his body, with the huge double pack strapped on, pushed farther and farther away from the bulging wall. When he slips off, the looping sideways rope stops his fall, but the double pack and his body weight begin to strangle him in his harness. "There was only one choice he could make to survive," Roskelley writes. "He had to get rid of his pack and, with it, Devi's keepsakes."

Leamer places this incident farther down the wall, below Sugar Delight: "Willi was going last now. . . . The two packs were very heavy. . . . The harness that he was sitting in . . . was squeezing the very life out of him. [He] looked fifteen feet below where Andy and Pete stood on a ledge looking up. 'Help me, Andy,' " he begs, but there's nothing Andy or Peter can do.

"In a few minutes he would be dead," Leamer writes. "His bowels let loose. . . . Willi pulled himself up. . . . [He] couldn't carry the two packs, or even one pack. He strapped [them] to a piton and jumared slowly down."

Even this small solace is to be denied him: possession of these few personal objects, final symbols of his dead daughter. The mountain has effaced her or, to look at it another way, has required that every shred of her be left in Nanda Devi's ferocious grasp. To their surprise, the camp at the bottom of the Buttress has been abandoned; the tents are down, everybody's gone. Where's Dr. States, where are the Indians, can everyone have taken leave with a party of climbers still above, contending with the summit in a storm? It's hard to understand. They radio down and hear that Dr. States escorted Evans to Advanced Base, and Kiran escorted Nirmal, who had taken sick. (John Evans remembers this differently: Nirmal was experiencing chest pains, a worrisome symptom at altitude, therefore Evans and States escorted him down, Kiran also descending.) According to Lev, "At the bottom of the Buttress . . . there were tents but there was nothing in them. It was our big staging camp, and they'd cleaned out the tents. The explanations they offered never satisfied me. . . . Willi'd had to abandon his pack, so he had no sleeping bag. Andy and I zipped ours together [saying,] 'Come in here, Willi, come here,' trying to coax him in."

Willi cannot at first be coaxed. He spends most of the night wearing some of Lev's down clothing plus his own, incommunicative and dazed. "He was just so grim," Lev remembers. "So anguished. We'd had hours of struggle getting down the Buttress. . . . Lying in my bag, at last at some kind of rest, there was a sharp jabbing pain in my calf. I thought, 'This is it—thrombophlebitis.'* I reached down to my calf and felt this small, incredibly hard object inside my pants leg. It was a frozen turd, from my desperate moment on the Buttress."

According to Lev, "The next morning Willi's hair was white. It

---

*At high altitudes, human blood thickens as more red blood cells are produced, the goal being an increase in oxygen-carrying capacity. Blood clots are a danger to climbers and other visitors to altitude. Clots can form in the legs or other parts of the body and travel to the heart or lungs. The results are often fatal.

Nirmal Singh's symptoms suggested a possibility of thrombophlebitis (a fibrinous clot in a vein), one reason it was thought important to get him down the mountain quickly. He soon recovered.

To understand Devi's death from a medical perspective, Andy Harvard over a period of years consulted Charles Houston, Drummond Rennie, Peter Hackett, and other physicians with a research interest in high-altitude medicine. Devi's sudden death, in the absence of symptoms of cerebral or pulmonary edema, suggested, according to some experts, a possible clot in the mesenteric artery, which provides blood to the membrane surrounding the intestines. A blockage of this artery can produce immediate loss of consciousness in a formerly lucid subject.

An expert in emergency medicine, Mark Smith, M.D., a medical school professor and chair of the Department of Emergency Medicine, Washington Hospital Center, Washington, D.C., suggests other possibilities. A sudden death with no intermediate period of confusion indeed indicates a vascular cause, but not necessarily a mesenteric thrombosis. "My experience with people who say they are going to die and then do die," Smith explains, "is that they are having an aortic dissection or an acute myocardial infarction [heart attack]." Devi may have had gastrointestinal bleeding over several days, possibly from a duodenal ulcer or chronic ulcerative colitis, making her progressively anemic and therefore increasingly weak. Anemia compounded by altitude may have given her "little oxygen to transport in her blood," according to Smith, leading to "a fatal cardiac arrhythmia [resulting in] ventricular fibrillation."

had not been white before. And his beard—his head and beard were white."

After a day of rest they continue down. Willi does what he has to in a mountaineering sense, attaching many rappels, keeping up with and sometimes getting ahead of Pete and Andy. In the article he wrote for the *AAJ*, Willi fleshed out the account of the prayer he'd recited over Devi's body; this prayer appears to have been just what he wanted to say, the best thing he could think of saying, not something wholly inadequate that ever after tortured him. "[We] each chanted a broken farewell," he wrote in the *Journal*. "My final prayer was one of thanksgiving for a world filled with the sublimity of the high places . . . for the surpassing miracle that we should be so formed as to respond with ecstasy to such beauty . . . for the constant element of danger without which the mountain experience would not exercise such a grip. . . . We then laid the body to rest . . .on the breast of the Bliss-Giving Goddess Nanda."

One of Willi's hands, exposed when he lost a glove, is mildly frostbitten. His feet are also slightly frostbitten. According to Roskelley, "He shuffled along on the sides of his feet, then hobbled where the going was better." He makes it down to Base Camp on September 13, but before that, on the evening of the eleventh, he radios Roskelley and, after informing him of Devi's death, instructs him to keep the news from the porters. He isn't concerned for their feelings, but for the possibility that news might leak out to the wider world before he's had a chance to inform his wife and before he can compose the news in a way to communicate what he wants the world to think of this event. John Evans recalls, "Willi was already worried about rumors getting out . . . his plan was to get Roskelley to take a message to the end of the road [at Lata] and send it out in confidence. Meanwhile, Lou Reichardt didn't know anything about Devi's death . . . when he got to a phone, he called my wife to report 'a great expedition,' and then that night she saw it on Walter Cronkite: Devi Unsoeld's death."

Willi doesn't really entrust the news management to Roskelley. He handles it himself, sending a cable to his family and another to the head of the Indian Mountaineering Federation, the government body supervising the expedition. He plans for a press conference, and he asks the team for "our cooperation in handling the press when we reached New Delhi," according to Roskelley. The requirements of grief are one thing, the requirements of public relations are another. No one who saw Willi in those days, who understood anything of his anguish and distress, presumed to find his behavior in any way inappropriate, and in fact, John Evans and others were impressed with his demeanor. "He handled everything," Evans says, "never asked to have any burden taken off his shoulders. He was a great showman, with presence, and he refused to ask for help."

Maybe the experience is only endurable this way, and Willi cannot slip the harness for even a moment. He can't go on but he must go on, and the task of organizing the retreat from the mountain, ordering the garbage cleaned up and getting the porters to pack out the gear, is a relief, something real and therefore blessedly manageable. He's still the Old Guide, and he learned on Everest '63 and in the Peace Corps and at Outward Bound the importance of shaping events. On the trek to Lata, where the team arrives on September 17, he wears his suffering with dignity, and according to Leamer, he continues the effort begun almost with the moment of Devi's death to fit this appalling tragedy into his larger structure of belief. "If we can accept reality as it is," he philosophizes at one point, "then we have to accept death. We wouldn't appeal the laws of gravity, would we, even though we know that gravity can kill you."

Andy walks along with Willi, and he remembers this period as "a strange walk out, and a special time as well." Willi keeps pausing to look back at the mountain of the Bliss-Giving Goddess, each view of the peak from the Rishi Gorge perhaps the last he'll ever have. Then he takes a photograph. Like Roskelley, like States, like Ad Carter, he's amassed a lot of slides—he can't be thinking of a slide show anymore, but still he collects images.* Andy takes comfort in their friendship and tries to look out for the bereaved father. But his own catastrophe is only partly salved by philosophical reflection; what happened to Devi and to their hopes is too searing, too large in a human sense, to succumb to conscious manipulation of even an enlightened kind. "The others left," he recalled years later, "but basically I couldn't leave India. For a couple months I was in Chandigarh with Kiran and his family . . . he'd become a good friend, he understood what I needed. Then I went to Kashmir and Ladakh. . . . I rarely spoke English during that whole period, mostly stayed in the mountains. It got to be winter . . . I returned to Delhi because my [plane] ticket was running out, but back in Delhi I found that I still couldn't leave, and I went on to Kathmandu. Al Read was trying to get a river-rafting business going there. I worked with him that winter. . . . I didn't return till well into the new year."

Roskelley's book, written right after his return, did not find a publisher for many years.† When it finally appeared in the late eighties, the account of events after Devi's death was temperate and

---

*Willi gave his first slide show about the expedition less than a month after his return from India, to the Seattle Mountaineers.

†*Nanda Devi: The Tragic Expedition* remains one of the most compelling adventure narratives published by an American writer. Roskelley's intense focus as a climber finds a *(cont.)*

kindly; a father himself, Roskelley showed an appreciation of Willi's agony and suggested that Devi's death had continued to haunt him, too. But on the trek out, according to other team members, Roskelley is in fact highly intemperate. He confronts Willi over the philosophical effort to subsume the tragedy into a larger body of belief; he's been at war all along with Willi's search for "meaning," with the social engineering of bringing women along just because they're women. As if unable to stop himself, he keeps rubbing Willi's nose in the fact of what happened. Someone wonderful died because errors of judgment were made, and not to recognize that or want to dwell on it is a compounding of the error. Always the Buffalo Demon, Roskelley goes way off the charts sometimes, as for example when, on the road trip out from the mountain, he blows his stack at Willi's slow return from a dinner break. "It was a backcountry gas station," Andy recalls, "where you could also get chapatis. We all wandered back to the truck, Willi coming a little later, and John started yelling about everybody getting back to the truck, getting back right now! Then he really lit into Willi . . . said he was dangerously slow, slow on the mountain, slow all the time, and look what had happened."

The most memorable outburst, according to several witnesses, occurred during the same part of the trip. Lev later wrote a public

---

complement in his writing style, which is forceful and clear, and which leaves ambiguities trampled in its wake. There is above all other things a strong point of view.

Roskelley submitted the manuscript to Simon & Schuster and to Knopf. They declined to publish, in an era when mountaineering books had often a very small audience. He next showed the manuscript to The Mountaineers, the leading American publisher of mountain narratives and guidebooks. Roskelley was puzzled by their rejection of his book, and he made sense of it this way: "They made their decisions in a committee. . . . I'd stepped on the toes of some of the people on it, and they didn't like what I had to say about Unsoeld. So they turned it down. . . . I put it away for six years, then I showed it to Stackpole, and they published it in '87," ten years after it was written.

letter, addressed to Roskelley, that described it; the occasion of the letter, which Lev personally handed to Roskelley at Snowbird, Utah, in '88, was the publication of Roskelley's book, which Lev found grossly inaccurate. "But it all ended in tragedy [Lev writes]. We have to really sympathize with you [John] when during a break driving out from the mountain you declared, again in the presence of several expedition members, how unfair it was that because Devi died all the world's attention was on her, and that your great Him-alayan climb would be eclipsed. This no doubt, was the reason why the U.S. Embassy in New Delhi was not inviting the expedition to an official dinner. Bitterly disappointed, you evidently felt betrayed by your country, or perhaps by some of the other expedition mem-bers. By now, our hearts were really going out to you, John Ros-kelley, especially Willi's."

Roskelley was physically sick now: he recalls riding on top of a lorry and "I just couldn't keep my eyes open. I mean the lids wouldn't stay up, the muscles wouldn't hold them up," a sign of meningitis. But his outbursts and his grudge against Willi are not just a sick man's pique. He's always had a hard time putting a stopper in it, that's just his character, to blurt things out no matter what. He might try being more sensitive, ask himself why he needs to be so brutal, but his attacks are almost never without some ra-tional basis. His argument with Willi's philosophizing is a legitimate one. Perhaps Roskelley recoils at the too swift reconciliation with Devi's death, the rapid invocation of mountain sublimities. We are here face-to-face with an actual transcendental processing of trag-edy, and there's something almost creepy about it. If Willi were only a little off his rocker, driven mad with grief and seeking solace in talk of the wonders of nature, that would be one thing; but he seems to have all his wits about him and to be very little changed by this unspeakable misfortune. The real surprise is that Roskelley does not make a complete scandal at the press conference in Delhi. There, an audience of respectful Indian journalists asks questions about Devi's death, and by prior agreement only Willi and Dr. States offer answers. Willi speaks of Devi's "enormous love for the high Himalaya." He asserts that she "died fulfilling her dreams," and that "[Devi] now lies in an eternal part of her namesake." In response to a question about regrets, Willi denies having any: "To do so would be [to deny] reality."

John Evans recalls "a very civilized event . . . they didn't hammer him with hard questions. These were reporters, after all, but there wasn't a dry eye in the place." The transcendental tone takes everyone to a higher realm, meanwhile exerting a kind of social control. The more merciless questions are ruled out as distasteful. Even so, one can imagine an only slightly more intemperate Roskelley, eyelids drooping and voice cracking, standing up suddenly at the back of the hall, breaking the mood of mournful sympathy with a few pointed inquiries. "But why did Devi have to die?" he might want to know. "Why didn't you get her off the mountain when I told you to, Willi? And what in God's name did you mean when you said, 'What's a father to do?' *I'll* tell you what he's supposed to do: he's supposed to save his child, not let her get in over her head and end up dead. And not name her after some star-crossed peak on the other side of the world, either, so that she grows up obsessed with climbing it. Is this your precious 'spiritual values of the wilderness'? This awful waste? Now please: tell me more about how you don't have any regrets."

TWENTY-FOUR

The porters did not write any books, unfortunately. Their responses are lost, although we know that they were enamored of Devi in a nearly worshipful way. Evans, arriving three weeks behind the rest of the team, kept hearing about her as he hurried to catch up: "The local people were taken with her. . . . I heard about her at the hotel in Joshimath, and then in Lata. This beautiful blonde, able to speak good Hindi . . . her name fascinated them, of course."

The Garhwalis saw the expedition in their own way. Devi's progress toward the top of the mountain could not but remind them of the holy pilgrimages, of the myth of the goddess enacted in those pilgrimages, and her death resonated in the poetry of their ancient faith. That the young woman called Nanda Devi had died near the summit of the goddess mountain was sad but also wondrous. They were heartbroken at the news, and they were not surprised. The important thing was that she had chosen to remain: her identification with the mountain, her personification of the goddess, achieved thus a kind of completion—a consummation, after all.

Ad Carter, in his article in the *AAJ*, offered a tribute to Devi that included an interview with Vasudha Rajgopalan, a scholar of world religions at Harvard. On the subject of possible Garhwali interpretations of Devi's death, Rajgopalan said, "Every fresh incident which hints of the supernatural is interpreted in light of . . . the goddess. . . . [I]n each place she has a distinct personality and is a vital power, a real being who participates in the lives of her people. Thus, the people around the Nanda Devi area would look upon every major incident in the area as an expression of Nanda's favour or displeasure."

He added: "It is extremely probable that the 'death' of Nanda Devi Unsoeld . . . is interpreted in two ways. . . . The first [interpretation] would probably be that the goddess, loving the young girl, took her to her 'kingdom,' or unto herself, to be her own, to protect her from the world. The second . . . would be that the goddess Nanda Devi, seeing a young girl named after her, a mortal who was young and charming, was filled with apprehension [and] wanted to include the mortal as her devotee or enlist her as a friend."

Carter spoke to a number of people about the expedition, including some of the porters, and he offers a third interpretation: "[W]hen in 1948 Willi Unsoeld announced that he would name his daughter after the most beautiful mountain he had ever seen, the goddess Nanda . . . caused herself to be reborn as his daughter. She lived for some years as a human, not really knowing her divine qualities. She was instrumental in organizing the expedition which brought her 'home.' One of the Indian members . . . has written, 'Devi lives; she has not died. She was the goddess personified.' "

Arriving in Lata, the team visits the porters in their homes, then follows them up to the temple of the goddess. Here a crowd of village men has already gathered, and the porters present Willi to a village elder, who unlocks a number of doors leading to the inner sanctum of the shrine. Willi and the elder enter alone. A few minutes later, the other team members are allowed to enter, and Roskelley is among those paying their respects. Later he describes what he sees in this way:

"Candles cast an eerie light on a distorted mannequin . . . a woman's image with stringy hair, a large mouth, and wide eyes. It was dressed gaudily in ornate cloth and brass ornaments. Cloth, bowls, brass figures, and spears adorned the room. Several large knives were leaning against the walls. . . . [W]e bowed and prayed for Devi and the Goddess Nanda, then were escorted outside. Willi remained [inside], briefly. He came out [with] tears in his eyes."

The porters produce a goat. They set it in front of the grieving father. While one man holds the goat on a lead, another sprinkles water in its ear to get it to shake its head—an animal offered for sacrifice must seem to give assent, according to local custom. A single stroke of a heavy sword severs the goat head, and a copious spill of blood splashes on the courtyard stones. The priest daubs some of the men's foreheads, and then, as Roskelley reports with evident relief, "the rite was over."

Willi's still going on automatic. Back in the United States he has his family to face, and a new school year is getting under way at Evergreen, with manifold responsibilities and pressures. Again he has no opportunity to slip the harness, which is either a blessing or the opposite. When he worked as a national officer with Outward Bound, he helped shape, and also absorbed, a philosophy of toughing it out no matter what, an approach more or less indistinguishable from his natural response to life. "He had more heart than a herd of turtles," says William Turnage, a head of the Wilderness Society and one of Willi's close friends in his last ten years. "He was absolutely the real McCoy in terms of having and evidencing a philosophy. . . . I think it had to do with studying Bergson when young," Bergson being an example of an almost demented consistency, a philosophical approach taken to all of life's issues. "He simply wasn't going to let himself fall apart on the descent from the mountain or afterward . . . he was very disciplined in his funny way, very on-target and indomitable with objectives. Probably got this from mountaineering."

Turnage got to know Willi through their unusual feet. Both had to special-order hiking boots from custom bootmakers, and on an afternoon in the late sixties they met in the Peter Limmer and Sons fitting room, when Willi was there to pick up a new pair of the toeless boots he wore everywhere. Willi was then the most distinguished living American mountaineer, and Turnage was a graduate student at Yale who knew him by reputation—on the spot he invited Willi to address the mountaineering club at Yale, and Willi accepted. Turnage became Ansel Adams's business manager a few years later, and he still serves as trustee of the Ansel Adams Publishing Rights Trust. His friendship with Willi, interesting in its own right, suggests the quality of Willi's friendships in general; their range and number is staggering, Willi being someone "able to fill a room with charm," according to Turnage, but also entirely present one-on-one. Lynn Hammond, Willi's colleague at Evergreen, discovered the extraordinary number of people who believed they had a special relationship with him only after his death. "I got to know him a year and a half after Devi died," she says, "and even under those sad circumstances he was one of the most powerfully charismatic people I ever met. There were women at Evergreen with crushes on him, but as far as I know, these were never consummated. . . . Did he charm, flirt, and court adulation? Yes, he did, but not for conquest, for mundane goals like getting his courses approved. Did he use his seductiveness to screw or hurt people? I never saw that—and I was looking for it.

"I still haven't dealt with all the consequences of his dying,"

Hammond told me twenty-one years after Willi's death. "A lot of people who knew him felt cut off at midstream, and there was a hurtful lack of closure. In '99 there was a twenty-year memorial service at Evergreen, and for me this indicated the way in which he was still alive, that he was like a father figure to many people, and they still haven't accepted his loss. In hindsight, the special closeness each of us seemed to enjoy didn't seem quite true . . . that's one of the problems of his legacy, that in his absence it doesn't seem possible, and you start feeling there must have been something fraudulent about it."

Turnage was fifteen years Willi's junior, although their relationship was one of coevals. "Willi's life was all about working with younger people," Turnage says, but Willi was capable of making friends with almost anyone, and he brought to his relations a *feeling* of equality. "The young ones tended to guru-ize him, and he was comfortable with that, if that was all it was going to be." Turnage spent time climbing with Willi in the North Cascades, and their connection over the years was full of frank exchanges and acts of thoughtfulness. The "best job I ever had," Turnage says, was as executive director of the Wilderness Society, which came to him because Willi recommended him and lobbied hard for him. (Willi, for his part, was named to the Society's governing council on the recommendation of a former student, an environmentalist with the Alaska Coalition.) Turnage also encouraged his younger brother, Robert, to study with Willi when the young man's situation seemed unpromising in the extreme. Robert had shown a powerful allergy to organized education, but Willi took him into his home, got him admitted to Evergreen, and mentored him in a suitably hands-off way—Robert finished his course work and went on to take graduate degrees at Yale and elsewhere.

Willi was a high-order educator, in fact, devoted and committed in a style often seen in the seventies, when hierarchy seemed like an outmoded idea. He made himself available to students and colleagues in a way that bespoke a great generosity. "He didn't stop at forty hours," Hammond says, "and the experiential part, the crevasse rescue exercises and taking people out for kayak rolls, was on top of the bookwork. He gave his weekends away, too . . . many more hours than most." Evergreen is a college in the Washington State system, but in the seventies it attracted most of its students from elsewhere. This was in part a testimony to Willi's national reputation, which was importantly furthered by his lecturing. "[My] [a]ttendance at numerous national conferences," he wrote in a self-evaluation in '73, has "enabled me to bring Evergreen's name into greater national prominence. . . . My [appearance] on a number of national television shows has resulted in . . . inquiries from prospective students and faculty." When he began at Evergreen, academic year '70–71, his salary was $17,000. His lecture fees, often arranged by his wife, added amply to his yearly total, with his rates ranging between about $250 and $500 per. In January of '78, for example, she responded to a request for an appearance at the Inter-Mountain Alpine Club Banquet: "[Willi] has been charging $250 or $300 plus travel for 'banquet-type speeches.' He already has a full schedule for first three months of this year and usually schedules his talks four to eight months in advance."

In November of '77, he appeared at U.C. San Diego's John Muir College, speaking on "how to teach people about the wilderness." The college invited him back the following spring, and in '78 he also appeared at Western Washington State College, giving an address on "Wilderness and Consciousness," and at Oregon State, where he presented his Nanda Devi slide show. For $500 plus expenses he spoke in Westport, Connecticut, and he returned to Philadelphia to appear at the "Westtown" event, where he'd spoken several times before. After a talk to the L.A. chapter of the Sierra Club ($500 fee) he received a note from Mary Ferguson, a club officer, which suggests why he was always being invited back: "[E]veryone here is still raving. We have had letters and phone calls to the office, all extolling the virtues of Willi, Devi, and the mountains. Even the cynics were moved, as one of them confessed to me. . . . I am . . . deeply indebted to [you] for this emotionally enervating weekend. [You] gave unsparingly . . . and must have slept for at least three days when [you] got home."

For $575.59 he spoke on "Wilderness and the Spirit" to trainees of the National Park Service, Grand Canyon, November '75. Throughout the seventies he appeared before organizations as varied as the National Conference on Outdoor Education, the National Conference of Christians and Jews, the Unitarian Fellowship of Olympia, and the Knife and Fork Club of Grants Pass, Oregon. He appeared in Kaiserslautern, West Germany, at a U.S. Army Dependents' School, and on a second overseas trip in Heidelberg, lecturing on outdoor ed. There can be no doubt that he was a gifted, inspiring lecturer in the tradition of the Chautauqua circuit of the late nineteenth and early twentieth centuries, nor is there any doubt—nor need there be any embarrassment—about his financial motive for maintaining such a schedule. He had a wife and three surviving children to support, and ideas he wanted to promote. He also loved the contact. "I like people," he told an interviewer for the *Southern Sierran,* a Sierra Club newsletter, or as Lynn Hammond puts it, "This is a guy from the seminary . . . at heart, a mesmerizing preacher."

The point is there were good reasons, many of them, not to slip the harness. Willi fit his daughter's death into his presentation and thereby remained a spellbinding lecturer much in demand, while becoming an example of his own philosophy, someone so weathered in the mountains and steeped in their wisdom that even tragedy could not break him. He underwent a trial far exceeding anything required of Muir or Emerson or Thoreau: his love of mountains led him to bring his own child into the temple of the peaks, where she then perished. If the "spiritual value" of such an outcome was insufficient to outweigh the heartbreak, the squalid sadness, then he had been a fool. But if there was an upside to the exchange—if it served an educational function, if it could be made the occasion of group insight—then maybe not.

The slide show he gave, on many occasions, is the work of a professional, powerful in its emotional effects, entertaining every step of the way. Even Will Rogers might have been baffled by this material: the story of a climb full of obstacles and conflicts, unsettling in its own right, which was also the story of the death of the narrator's daughter, a death in which he was deeply implicated. Many of those who knew Willi well were dismayed that he would talk about Devi at all, let alone within a month of returning from the Garhwal. They remain puzzled and distressed a quarter of a century later. A more typical response, though, is suggested by Mary Ferguson's comments ("everyone here . . . still raving"), and as a professional Willi would only have continued to trot out the show if he sensed it was going over. Aided by the many slides he'd taken, he led listeners through the whole experience, from Devi sitting in Ad Carter's living room and cheerily tossing out the idea of a climb, to the arguments over fixed ropes, the struggle over women's participation, the qualities of Garhwali porters as compared to Sherpas, the hike up the Rishi Gorge, and so on. His voice in the taped versions, many of which survive, is the same old Willi voice, comical and spoofy, but also a little tense, with a holding-forth quality, a bid for formality. He calls the Himalaya "the Him-*al*-ya," accent on the second syllable, the technically correct way, and his jollities sometimes seem forced. But he has great confidence, and he soon warms to this wonderful yarn he has to tell, with opportunities for mimicking the Indian members and for talking about Tilman and Shipton, the great Nanda Devi pioneers. He presents Devi as a force of nature, carrying heavier loads than anybody except maybe Reichardt, wrestling Roskelley to the ground, stoic in the face of her medical problems, which he says weren't all that bad. And then she dies. He re-creates the scene inside the tent, going so far as to duplicate her rumbling belches *("Awwwrrrroooouuuurr"),* and when he comes to the terrible moment of actually losing her (Devi pitching forward, not responding to CPR), his voice goes lower, he has to pause to get control—and the audience, which has been laughing and gasping at the rollicking high points, falls silent.

At the Alpine Club annual meeting, December '76, he asked rhetorically, "So how does one handle the death of a daughter?" And then he replied: "You don't—it handles you. It rubs your nose in the reality of your mortality. . . . We live so fragilely—which is the essence of [life's] beauty."

He announced again that he had "no regrets," but added that "[this] leaves the nonphilosophical part of you unappeased. In my wrestling with this [matter] . . . I've proceeded with two [questions]. The first [is], 'What if we had descended earlier—what if I'd ordered her down with all my shreds of paternal authority—what if we'd done it just a little differently?' And the second, 'Why Devi? Why not me, who was old and decrepit and supposed to die . . . why did it have to happen?'

"[But] those two questions," he immediately answered, "I label illicit. You simply don't ask them—you don't allow them. You shut 'em off at the source, [because] that way madness lies. In the final analysis, all I can hark back to . . . is the sheer visceral enjoyment of the world ... the deep-down joy of being sculpted by the terrain ... [the] closeness with the ice, brotherhood with the rock. This is the kind of living which strikes joy into ... the very basis of the heart.

"I offer you that joy," he concluded. "Joy which gives one the courage to go on, the confidence to know that what*ever* lies beyond that tragic break in our awareness, [it] can only be better than ... that which we have already experienced."

At this same annual meeting, Roskelley spoke and showed his slides, after Ad Carter first spoke and showed *his* slides. Roskelley was again being on his good behavior, referring only briefly to Ad's abandonment of the expedition, and mentioning, but not making a big deal out of, Devi's illnesses. Perhaps in gratitude, Willi praises Roskelley's climb of the Buttress to high heaven. The Alpine Club meeting that year was organized by a famous Western rock-climber, someone who admired Willi but who found himself outside the lecture room, pacing the corridors in agitation as Willi went on with his Nanda Devi speech. Something seemed off: "Unreal was the feeling ... a not taking of responsibility. It was, 'We went up, she wanted to climb, then this happened,' but that wasn't enough, you know." Then he noticed a number of other club members—people he knew as thoughtful, experienced mountaineers—also driven out into the halls, also looking perplexed. "There was something oblivious and disconnected ... something unfathomable [in what Willi said], and it disturbed them."

Other friends of Willi's who happened to catch his show more than once noted that the emotional high points—even the pauses to collect himself—came at the same places, as he presented a performance that generally went very well. It was like the many, many lectures he gave after Everest '63: "I estimate this is the three hundred fifty-seventh talk I've given about the ascent," he would joke in the sixties, telling audiences that he'd had a tape cassette implanted in his chest. But Willi was a professional lecturer, he earned income this way, and it would be unfair to expect him *not* to fall into routine as he went along. He had planned on making a slide show from the start, before he ever went out to India, and he was only following through. "He was very disciplined in his way," says Turnage, and his daughter's death wasn't enough to deter him.

That's admirable, in one sense. But in another, it's slightly horrifying. We don't have to be self-righteous about it, judging him as if we knew better, to find his behavior odd and to want to know the reasons for it. According to Turnage, "Devi's death had an overwhelming impact on Willi . . . the experience broke him, and afterward the bonhomie, the optimism, the positivism, [were] a ritual, I thought." There was an outer response, for public consumption, but the inner response, as far as Turnage was privy to it, was different: "Devi was killed by the thing he most loved . . . in retrospect, he knew he should've gotten her off the mountain, he knew it absolutely. He understood that people thought his [public performances] strange [but] he needed to carry through so as not to break down."

When we say that Devi's death was *tragic,* we mean that it was sad, untimely, perhaps inevitable—an awful thing to happen to such a young person. But Devi's death also has the trappings of a darker, deeper category of experience, tragedy in the ancient sense; and this is the sort of human episode that Willi, with his transcendentalism, his Bergsonian vitalism, was trying to address. In an ordinary life, those beliefs might have been enough, but Willi's life and Devi's death were not ordinary. The challenge he faced—to use a word that itself seems inadequate—was to try to comprehend a catastrophe that brings to mind Lear and Oedipus, that threw his entire life into question, almost to the point where that life seemed but the prelude to such a disturbing drama. So many lines of "fate" had converged at once—Willi's becoming a mountaineer, glimpsing Nanda Devi in his youth, and predicting a namesake daughter; Devi born with his bold, warmhearted spirit, fulfilling the myth of the goddess in so complete a way; Nanda Devi and its place in mountaineering history, and the weird desecration of the peak by American cold warriors, which seemed to demand propitiation—that an eerie *too-muchness* surrounds the experience. Indeed, Peter Lev's overriding memory of the expedition is of "feeling like I was trapped in a predetermined story, like it was a play . . . everyone forced to play roles that they later felt ashamed of." Roskelley, like the Buffalo Demon, but also at times like the Fool in *Lear,* has a personality that made him blurt things out at the wrong time, but again like the Fool his blurtings were often mysterious, troubling, prophetic.

Willi was always modest about his attainments as a philosopher; in comments to interviewers, he would claim expertise only in the area of ethics, since he'd written his thesis on the moral problems of mysticism, and he was famous for posing ethical conundrums for his students. What did he think, then, of the cruel destiny that had put him high on the slopes of a Himalayan peak, only to trap him in a classic Hegelian tragedy (tragedy about the conflict between competing ethical claims)? On the one hand, he wanted to support Devi in her dream, get her to the top for a whole host of excellent reasons, but on the other, he wanted to get her back alive. When he said "What's a father to do?" to Roskelley, he wasn't confessing weakness, nor in all likelihood was he just trying to get the guy off his back—he wanted to know, exactly, *What is a father to do? What's he supposed to do?* With hindsight most people would say that he made the wrong decision, but at the time his strong support of his daughter's autonomy, and his belief in the higher value of embracing risk, carried the day.

Willi's story is also tragic in the better-known sense—the Greek sense. A larger-than-life figure, not so different from the high personages in Aeschylus, he falls into disaster through the workings of fate abetted by his own mistakes. After Nanda Devi, he becomes a physical cripple, as Oedipus was crippled, going through the motions of a busy life in a way that invited the pity of many of those who loved him. "The tragic hero," according to the scholar M. H. Abrams, "moves us to pity because, since he is not an evil man, his misfortune is greater than he deserves; but he moves us also to fear, because we recognize similar possibilities of error in our own . . . fallible selves." Where Willi differs, crucially, from the tragic figures in Aeschylus or Sophocles is in his response to his tragedy. He has a dreadful reversal of fortune, but he never has a profound recognition, or, to be more exact, the two years of life that remained to him seem to have been devoted to an active *refusal* to recognize what had happened. Publicly, at least, he carried forward a campaign of denying his and Devi's tragedy as tragedy, beginning with the statement to the press in Lata ("no regrets") and continuing with his much repeated statement about some questions being "illicit." He claimed that "that way madness lies," but the truth is that that way, and only that way, lay a possible way out.

Here we see some limits of the transcendental approach. Every emotion plays out in a higher, finer register, and the awfulness of real tragedy provokes a sort of embarrassed squirming. It's as if to admit the darkness would be to lose membership in a new company of the elect. Those who take inspiration from the sublimities have a hard time dealing with cruel, mocking blows of Providence—not that anyone has an easy time. Willi had a right to hide away, to don sackcloth and ashes, but almost from the moment of Devi's death he was making public gestures: the "burial at sea," the clasping of hands in the snow, prayers of thanks. In the Book of Job, the upright man whom God and Satan decide to torment refuses to deny heaven, but as his sufferings mount up and deepen—death of his children, loss of all he owns, onset of loathsome disease—he finally cracks and begins to curse fate, condemning the monstrous God who would treat him this way. The path that Job follows as he declines is harrowing, and at last he has nothing left and his formerly pious speeches become a spew of despair ("You would toss me into a cesspool, and my own stench would make me vomit. . . . Why are you so enraged . . . [i]s it right for you to be [so] vicious?"). Job declares, "My soul is weary of my life [and] I will give free course to my complaint; I will speak in the bitterness of my soul," and though he finds no immediate relief with these honest words, he has turned a corner.

John Muir needed something more than blissful nature worship at life's end. Willi may also have needed more, but he had cast himself in a role that severely limited his possible responses: not the Old Guide anymore, more a sort of New-Tempered Wise Man, someone forged in the fires of misfortune and now back with a familiar message. He remained an ideologue of outdoor education, and he continued to locate spiritual value in the active encounter with wilderness. He was still eager to take people out there, especially young people whom he identified as being in need of a bracing dose of genuine risk. As he told Bill Turnage, "If I were to change my philosophy because it was my own daughter [who died], it would make the whole thing worthless, and it isn't worthless." Talking to the interviewer for the *Southern Sierran*, he explained why he wasn't raging at heaven, why he couldn't rage: "The bottom line . . . is my belief in the basic ultimate reality. . . . Plain language can't really touch this belief although there is the conviction that at its core . . . is 'Good,' good that conveys a feeling of joy. . . . [With] this overriding conviction, I've been able to weather all types of crisis. The loss of toes to frostbite were just nine drops in a bucket. Even the ultimate challenge . . . the death of my daughter—if you can handle something so shattering . . . you know you . . . have something to work on." And he concluded proudly, "[I]t didn't destroy my equanimity . . . there's no conceivable occurrence that could, as it's all part of the 'whole' that we're wrapped up in . . . [which] is to be accepted."

TWENTY-FIVE

March 4, 1979: On the last day of his life, Willi's on a stormy mountain he loves (Rainier), with the kind of people (eager young outdoor-folk) he effortlessly inspires. He's doing the sort of thing that he was born for, dealing with a real blizzard and avalanche slopes and crevasses—the whole nine yards, the lovely mountain hyperreality.

Their group, Willi plus twenty-one students from Evergreen, has been on the mountain for a week. As they were just getting started, February 25, they ran into Yvon Chouinard, the California rock- and ice-climber, in the ranger station parking lot. Chouinard said he didn't like the look of the mountain—too much avalanche potential. He was turning back. But Willi and his group have come to Rainier precisely to deal with real problems, to experience winter mountaineering in the raw. They will continue on, with due caution.

The group numbered twenty-nine at first. All were students except Willi and a woman named Nancy Goforth, an accomplished mountaineer. From the ranger station at Paradise, at 5,400 feet, climbers usually ascend to an all-season hut on a ridge at about ten thousand feet, called Camp Muir. In summer the climb to Camp Muir usually takes no more than a few hours, but the weather in the next few days is so miserable, and so many of Willi's students need basic snow-camping experience, that the group doesn't arrive till February 28. At Muir several of the students decide to go back down, and Nancy Goforth also leaves the mountain.

"The first part, meeting Chouinard on the way down because of avalanche danger," says Frank Kaplan, one of the students, "was okay, handled okay, because we made good snow caves and correctly waited out the first batch of bad weather. Then we got some good weather, and we continued up. Willi had tried to get other experienced climbers to come, but they all backed out, and then Nancy went down, so there he was with the bunch of us. Some of us had some experience, but others were pretty clueless about climbing in those full-winter conditions."

Clueless, but not helpless. Outdoor-education types, they've prepared for their ascent by assembling basic, but reasonably adequate, equipment; everyone has shelter, food, gloves, hat, crampons, ice ax. Several have sewed insulated overboots, for $5 per pair in materials, on a borrowed sewing machine. Their clothes are mostly woolen, no longer the fabric of outdoor choice even in '79; the ropes they're using are Gold Line brand, also not quite the best for the time but again, adequate, and they've put together makeshift sleds for gear-hauling up to Camp Muir.

The climb of Rainier, planned to coincide with a solar eclipse (February 26), was one of several outings in the program that winter. Participation was optional. Lynn Hammond was leading a Canyonlands desert trip at about the same time, and there were other choices as well; those who elected to go to Rainier did so because they liked the idea of being on a real mountain in late-winter conditions—to the extent they were able to imagine such conditions.

Seven of the students had no climbing experience. Another eight had a modest amount, and the remaining half dozen served Willi as rope leaders and assistants, making up a cadre of fairly competent people he could depend on. The whole enterprise had come together in that shuffling, organic way he liked, beginning in actual desire (the students themselves having requested Rainier) and continuing at every step with debate over the feasibility of the effort, with just enough gathering of gear, just enough training, to lift it out of the category of the fanciful.

It was Willi's first true climb, his first adventure after Nanda Devi. In March and June of the previous year he'd had hip-replacement surgeries. "He was mentally the same guy but physically not even close," Bill Turnage says, "but the surgeries turned things around. They led him to want to try out those newfangled hips, get into a for-real mountain situation again." Turnage thought this a bad idea. He considered going up on Rainier, with many inexperienced students, akin to madness: "We had a heated exchange when Willi passed through D.C. for a meeting. . . . He revealed that he was going up in a couple of months, and I told him he had no business taking himself or any students up there," because the surgeries were so recent and, though successful, not miraculously so. Furthermore, Rainier is a formidable mountain. It's the fifth highest in the lower forty-eight and sees a great deal of snowfall most years. This often stupendous snowfall feeds fourteen intermarrying glaciers, which together comprise the greatest expanse of unstable ice outside of Alaska.

Willi also faced strenuous opposition from some colleagues at Evergreen. The philosophy of growth through risk struck them as dangerous—dangerous because philosophically incoherent and morally dubious. From the point of view of the student, it might be reasonable to say that risks are a part of life, and that more students die every year in car accidents or from alcohol poisoning after a party than in all the rock climbs and kayak trips undertaken. But from the point of view of the instructor, to say that personal revelation arises from encounters with danger is to assert an unprovable proposition: What does "revelation" mean, anyhow, and how do we measure "personal growth," and what about the ones who get scared, fall apart, and end up feeling worse? Young people trying to find themselves, coming under the sway of charismatic outdoor heroes, who instruct them in the unique value of risking their necks: surely this is a questionable premise for higher education.

Willi listened to his opponents, but he was not persuaded. *Not persuaded at all.* One explanation may be that he had too much invested in the program, that he'd gone down that road too far, and another may be that he was desperate to prove that he was whole again. "[The climb] was all tied up with his virility," Bill Turnage says, a plausible enough explanation; another may be that Willi was depressed, looking for a way out. Three years before he'd already been talking about death, a swift clean death in the mountains, as he prepared for Nanda Devi. Since those days, nothing much had happened to deepen his belief in the "basic ultimate reality" of life's joyousness, no matter what he told his interviewers. He had Devi often on his mind, and a number of people have reported conversations in his last years when he spoke of her as if she were still alive or emoted unexpectedly at mention of her or expressed shame at how he'd used her memory. He was sad because Devi would "come no more, never, never, never, never, never," as Lear says when Cordelia dies, but he also was troubled by all the questions he wouldn't allow himself to ask. The evidence for this disturbance in his thinking is both nowhere—denied by his busy schedule, his undiminished energy—and everywhere. One way of looking at what he did in his last days is to see it as a brave coming to terms with terrible torments, leading to a final assertion of the Unsoeld spirit; and another is to see him in the grip of a strange compulsion, with a fatal outcome the result.

"Should that group have been up there at all? I think you can make a good argument for no," Frank Kaplan says, "because of the inexperience. But people that age are susceptible to romantic appeals . . . plus, Willi had taken many people on adventures in the past. Nothing as risky as this, though." Phil Pearl, another of the outdoor-ed students, declined to go to Rainier because "I saw it as nuts. . . . I'd been up there in winter before, on the northwest side, and I knew enough about the mountain not to go. No one was even a fully competent mountaineer except for Willi . . . they were a group of beginners, basically, and I wasn't going to be part of that."

Another student in the program, who did choose to go, later worked for Outward Bound and became a psychotherapist. He'd also been on Rainier before, but "being there in March was real different. I was nineteen at the time . . . in awe of Willi, who seemed to me by far the most remarkable person I'd ever known. He *still* seems the most remarkable person I've ever known. After the death of his daughter, he said 'No!' to any regrets, and I've decided to say no to any regrets I might have had about Rainier.

"I'd been climbing for about three years at that point," he told me, "and I was used to harsh weather conditions. But I didn't see this as a narcissistic exercise [on Willi's part] . . . [rather] I saw it as something generous, a unique opportunity he was giving us to experience Rainier. I knew people died in such circumstances, and I accepted that. What happened on the mountain has never seemed really horrific to me."

The second night out, still short of Camp Muir, Willi shares a snow cave with Janie Diepenbrock, a transfer student from a school in Wyoming. Diepenbrock has a sparkling spirit, and Willi shows a marked fondness for her, praising her to Nancy Goforth, who also shares their cave. Diepenbrock, about Devi's age when she died, came to Evergreen to study with Lynn Hammond, who had been a teacher of her brother's. Not a lost soul or a dependent personality—not at all—she had planned to go to Utah that winter with Hammond, but in the end she couldn't resist the full *seriousness* of a winter ascent of Rainier. Her connection to Willi, warm and immediate, seems to have formed under a favorable sign— higher up the mountain they choose to share a tent, and Willi arranges for her to climb with him, in the second position on his rope.

At Muir, the weather suddenly breaks: blue sky shows, the storm lows out. In their shambling way, the party of inexperience has already accomplished something substantial—just by putting one foot in front of the other, taking it easy but not giving in, they've climbed a long way up this mountain. Their nervousness abates somewhat. Maybe they even belong up here. Despite the massive seasonal accumulation of snow, evident in every direction, the avalanche danger seems manageable, and it will be less if the clear weather holds. On March 1, a rest day, clear weather continues, and in the afternoon Willi and a small party head out onto the Cowlitz Glacier, which spreads in a snowy bowl to the north of Muir. On the other side of the glacier, on a ridge parallel to Camp Muir's, is Cathedral Gap, the most commonly used pass on the way up to the summit. About a quarter mile west of Cathedral Gap is a second pass, Cadaver Gap, which offers an alternative: steeper, more avalanche prone, but giving access to a shorter route to the top.

In the crisp conditions, Willi and his coterie traverse above crevasses and head for the challenging slope below Cadaver Gap. Here they begin a trial ascent in the shadow of an immense, ziggurat-shaped rock called The Beehive, postholing in the fresh snow. No problems, and they make it up to the U-shaped gap with plenty of daylight left. Willi hollers with the sheer pleasure of being out here again: out in his meaningful mountain whiteness, his beloved high landscape, blue sky above and a windy summit near. As he's promised his students, Rainier in winter is a challenge of Himalayan proportions, not in terms of altitude but because of the dangers and the raw grandeur of it, the rockfalls, icefalls, the huge snowcap. It may be only fourteen-four at the top, but to get up there you have to have the crucial encounter, that moment when you recognize how pathetically small you are, that you've ventured upon grounds of planet earth not meant for puny man. And in that act of trespass—driven on by your unaccountable will—you feel the *spirit* of the place infusing you, if you're paying any attention at all.

In a radio call next morning, Willi reports to Gary Olson, the ranger at Paradise, that the group will be going up by way of Cadaver Gap, after all. The avalanche danger doesn't look so bad— he reports to Olson that it's "very low." The group readies itself, then it ascends, successfully, later in the morning. One of Willi's assistants places wands in the snow, to mark the route for their descent, although the superb conditions make it hard to imagine having to feel their way back down in a whiteout. Beyond Cadaver Gap, the route heads north and west directly for the summit, up a gradually steepening headwall that feeds the Ingraham Glacier. It's a lot of snow-slogging, basically, and as the weaker members of the group begin to tire, Willi declares a halt, and they pitch camp just short of twelve thousand feet, near an outcrop called Gibraltar Rock. But Willi himself isn't tired—with a coterie he again climbs higher, to about thirteen thousand feet, supposedly to check out the route they'll be following tomorrow, but mostly to exult in the sweet harsh beauty.

All mountain expeditions are the same, in a few respects; all mountains are similar, in a general way, and may be made to deliver similar feelings to those who climb them. For this reason it makes a certain amount of sense for Willi to tell his charges that they're in line for a "Himalayan" experience, a real high-mountain encounter, and it's also why as he climbs these snow-slopes on his artificial hips the progress he makes evokes the progress he made on Nilkanta, on Makalu, even on Everest. It may only be Rainier, but they've had to make a high camp just like on the other mountains, because they have to stay warm and eat something, and because tomorrow they'll be going for a summit maybe not so challenging as the others, but definitely within the class of summits it's best not to take for granted. And if they do make it to the top, all of them—and what a lovely triumph *that* will be for the idea of group spirit—they'll have done so in the face of fear and altitude and diarrhea and rope-management problems, all the usual impedimenta, and they'll be partaking, in a small way, of the same transfiguring exultation that world-class climbers feel. But for these inexperienced young people, that feeling may not be "small" at all. And here is another reason why Willi, on his new hips or on his old, on toeless feet or on no feet if it eventually comes to that, will always want to lead parties up: because the cosmos shows its ineffable compassion in this way, too, in the way that it scales its blessings even for those of small attainment.

It's why he's always loved to guide, and leading people on a familiar route for the ten thousandth time has always been a joy to him. But another reason why this climb looks like a good idea, why it seems the *right* thing to do, rather than a harebrained thing, is because it fulfills the old dream once again, rings the same old bells; as on those other climbs, even on star-crossed Nanda Devi, the effort presents an opportunity for forging something strong and good with people, for taking the disparate and imperfect materials of flawed humanity and making something fine. And in ways of

which Willi himself may not be aware, the climb is also a chance
to get it right, to take all the old elements and stir them together
just once more—people of differing ability, women as well as men,
a forward party of stronger summit-types—to better effect. There's
even a daughter figure, someone he's keeping close to him this time,
only a few feet behind him on his rope. On March 3, at around 3:00
A.M., he wakes them all, and the team organizes itself for its bold
attempt. The weather is fine. They start out about two hours later,
but almost immediately the weather falls apart. Clouds descend,
strong winds come up and snow starts coming down, hard. "The
real mistake," Frank Kaplan recalled, "was that from our high
camp we made this attempt, this false attempt on the summit. The
weather got very bad very quickly . . . my gut feeling is that it was
a doomed gesture, completely futile, because the weather was just
too threatening. We lost time, too."

Some of the students reach a height of 12,800 feet. At this elevation, the angle of the climbing on the Ingraham headwall is fairly
steep, and upward progress is a question of cramponing carefully
in wind-compacted snow. But here Willi turns them back. They're
in a real storm now, a blizzard, and many are just too challenged.
They descend in a whiteout, and for the rest of the day they huddle
at their high camp, where accumulating snow tears the fabric of
some of the tents. According to a report later filed by Park Service
investigators, some of the tents collapsed to the point where students had to pass the night of March 3 in snow caves, and on the
morning of the fourth many of them are cold and unnerved. "The
thing about being in that situation," Kaplan observed, "is that you
were there with *Willi* . . . being with Willi meant that you were able
to do it, or at least you felt you were. It wasn't so much that he
was going to save you personally but that his presence provided
this great *encouragement* . . . he had a quality that people re-

sponded to, that invigorated them, and they wanted to participate in whatever he was doing."

On Nanda Devi, Pete, Andy, and Devi also responded to this magic encouragement. As Lev observed, "It was always good to see Willi." The students on Rainier, many of them cold and only now, perhaps, realizing what they've signed on for, are saved from despair by his great heart, by Willi's yodeling, harmonica-playing, cannot-be-daunted mountaineer's soul. In the face of hell itself he would probably smile and narrow his eyes and say, "Yes, but," and end up arguing the devil out of his due. March 3 passes with Willi telling stories, bucking them up with the evidence of his refusal to freak out, and then on the morning of the fourth, a Sunday, as the blizzard continues, he allows as how they'd better get down. Three feet of new snow has already fallen. Though it feels very cold, with winds up to sixty miles per hour, the ambient air has in fact gotten warmer, and Willi thinks of the avalanche danger as he tells his group that they'll be descending by Cathedral Gap, not the steeper Cadaver Gap, because the former is safer. At around 10:00 A.M. they set out.

Willi leads on the rope. Following him are Janie Diepenbrock, a student named Peter Miller, and Frank Kaplan. According to Jeff Casebolt, a student on another rope, "There was a total whiteout with no more than twenty or thirty feet of visibility. You couldn't hear, you couldn't see, you were lost in your own world." Willi knows that the Ingraham Glacier, which they'll have to descend partway, is full of crevasses, some of which may be hidden by fresh snow. He changes his mind about the route. Cadaver Gap, with its greater avalanche danger, is closer; they already know how to get to it, and they also know how to descend it, following the wands they'd stuck in the snow two days before. Several students are near-hypothermic as the teams gather at the top of Cadaver Gap. The virtue of going down this way, rather than by Cathedral, four hundred yards farther along the glacier, is that they have a straight shot at Camp Muir from the bottom of the slope, and at Muir the all-weather hut awaits.

Willi leads out, and in moments he's invisible even to the people on his own rope. The steepness of the drop from Cadaver Gap is suggested by Jeff Casebolt's description: "When my turn came [to descend], I had to plant my ice ax and turn completely around, facing into the mountain, to get over the crown . . . down-climbing on my crampons." The three-foot wands placed two days before have vanished. This means there's been a great snowfall, but it also means, contrary to Willi's expectations, that the brutal, scouring winds have not stripped the slope bare, that it holds all that mass still in potential. He continues on anyhow. On Nanda Devi he whistled past the graveyard of the terrible glacier snout, unfazed, and here he simply does what he's put himself in a position to have to do, since turning back is not an option. He only needs to be lucky one more time. On Masherbrum he led his weaker teammates down from a high camp, counting rope lengths in a similar whiteout, and here he chooses a like strategy by re-creating in his mind their ascent two days ago, straight up this steep little face; he can't see the wands, but he *knows* where they are, and he aims for them as he descends. To either side of the face are ribs of rock, offering a modicum of protection from slides. But he stays in the middle, not sheltering beside the one that's to his right, which he could easily reach; climbing down along the rocks might take longer.

Maybe it's better not to think at all. Boldness will do—it has before. At the top of Cadaver Gap, one of the students asked about avalanches, and he told her that some people think about them, and other people don't; not that he *hasn't* thought about them, but once in the lion's den the time is upon you, and you must walk your path. He takes a step down on his crampons, then another. The wind catches him and threatens to blow him off his feet; the memory his body gives his mind is maybe a happy one, of the West Ridge, Hornbein and him and the other young madmen, being blown around in their tents like scraps of paper. He takes another steep step down. Tents turned into kites, men turned weightless: not a bad feeling, after all. And they survived that time, and great things came of that time, as great things may always come if the spirit engages. He enters the whirlwind, sky and slope of the same blinding blankness, and when the face first loosens with a casual, unimportant-feeling slipping away he has an instant of that other sensation, that weightlessness. Then the bottom falls out; the mountain becomes a vast, fatal river, one that he finds himself afloat upon. He drops away. He doesn't think anymore. He is swiftly and finally borne away.

EPILOGUE

....

To Frank Kaplan, coming last on Willi's rope, the fatal events of
the early afternoon of March 4, 1979, were indecipherable: he
could barely make out Peter Miller ahead of him, and then the slope
began to move under all of them, and he was taken. "I remember
being very *uneasy* on the snow slope just below Cadaver Gap. . . .
I saw a few chunks of snow flowing past me and then I was flowing,
too, slowly and smoothly at first, then faster." He tries to swim.
He flounders and tries to get his backpack off; anticipating trouble,
he's undone the pack strap across his chest, but his hip belt is still
attached and won't release. The avalanche, a slab fracture fully as
wide as Cadaver Gap, is three feet deep at the point of shear; it
runs a distance of over five hundred feet, down to where the slope
angle at last begins to lessen. As it slows, the snow starts to set up,
like half-cured cement, and Kaplan frees himself of his pack at last
and thrashes his way to air and life.

All this happens in the equivalent of complete silence; that is, in
the jet-engine roar of the storm, which hides all screams and all
sounds of the avalanche itself. Ahead of him, Kaplan sees, in the
frozen tumble of avalanche debris, a single object that doesn't fit:

a human arm protruding from the snow. He begins to dig with his hands, then with a shovel from his pack, and succeeds in a few minutes in uncovering Peter Miller's face. The encasing snow is almost ice-hard already, and wind-drift from the storm keeps blowing over Miller's face, and he passes in and out of consciousness. After about fifteen minutes, people from a second rope team appear out of the storm. Kaplan screams for them to hurry, to help him dig Miller out and to follow the rope from Miller's body. In another ten minutes, Miller is out of his snowy tomb, but Janie Diepenbrock, when located and dug out, after about another quarter hour, is cyanotic—blue in the face from lack of oxygen—and all attempts at reviving her fail.

Willi, buried more deeply than Janie, also found lying facedown, with his backpack adding to the compression of the hardening snow, is likewise cyanotic. He had failed to release his belts, as he led down a threatening avalanche slope, and the pack finally has to be cut off him. The other rope teams arrive, and after more than an hour of failed attempts to revive the two victims, in a scene growing ever more desperately chaotic—the storm, if anything, is intensifying, and people are abandoning their packs and clothing, inviting a much larger tragedy—a few of the climbers lead off, in an absolute whiteout, and stumble on Camp Muir.

Two people dead—only two, after all. In comments published later, friends of Willi's and of the program he led at Evergreen praised the courage and resourcefulness of the students, finding a vindication of the program in their ability, at the end, to save their own skins. But before we find in this sad scene of loss another triumph of the spirit, we need to recognize how close that larger tragedy was. Jeff Casebolt, who made a career later with Outward Bound, remembers it as "one of those situations where you do stupid things, where people are getting terribly cold, dropping gear, succumbing. Some of us with some [medical] training tried to decide whether to work more on the bodies or give up, and meanwhile people were going hypothermic. . . . We were unroped. . . . I myself lost a glove, and later I lectured my own students that this is how disasters start, with small acts of inattention.

"The storm was unbelievably intense," Casebolt adds. "We roped up again, then headed in the direction we thought might get us to Muir. We couldn't find any wands . . . if you went too far right you'd get to the Nisqually Glacier, and too far left you'd get on the Cowlitz Glacier," which is heavily crevassed. Casebolt, twenty-one, and Bruce Osterman, twenty, navigate mainly by the angle of the slope, stopping now and then to reassess. They can't see, and according to one investigative report it takes them two and a half hours to travel a distance of five hundred yards. "Bruce and I stopped, and as we were talking there was a lull in the wind. . . . Suddenly we could see a piece of frozen rope in front of us—a length of frozen clothesline. We followed it and my God, there we were, fifty feet away from Camp Muir."

Their pluck—and the levelheadedness of Ian Yolles, another student, and Frank Kaplan's smart behavior in the avalanche—deserve praise. But whether this was Willi's indomitable spirit already taking up residence in their hearts, or whether they were simply acting like competent outdoor types in a bad situation, it seems impossible to say. Outdoor-education majors tend to be in reasonably good shape, and they tend to have thought through danger scenarios in advance: this, after all, is part of learning to be useful in the outdoors, and Frank Kaplan's unbuckling of his straps is but one example of it. Ian Yolles, when he fell off the shear fracture just below Cadaver Gap, immediately led his rope team over to the rocks to the side of the slope, which Willi had failed to do; by then, the avalanche had carried the others away, but his instincts were surely correct, and he led his team the rest of the way down along the rocks, which was wise.

That length of frozen rope—only a few feet of clothesline—was the bit of luck that saved their lives. They were strong enough, barely, to take advantage of it when it came to them. Fortunate outcomes in desperate situations often turn on something small, just as tragic outcomes often depend on one loose rock, one piton that fails, a single moment of distraction. In a similar way, the tragedy of the Nanda Devi expedition of '76 would seem to depend on a single unhappy fact: that Devi Unsoeld did not make her summit, that she, a fascinating and promising young woman, died rather than lived, that she vanished too soon from our world. So close was the expedition to going down as a triumph—an interesting trip, despite all its irritations, and an advance in mountaineering—that Lou Reichardt reported it as such on his trek out, not having yet heard of Devi's fate.

Part of the problem lies in the terminology of victory, triumph, and challenge that thoughtful mountaineers such as Willi or Reichardt have always deplored, preferring to talk, in Willi's case, of inward experiences, of the gathering of spiritual wisdom. Probably all metaphors for climbing are inadequate. A human activity as complicated as the '76 expedition—with its local religious dimension, its elements of political and social history—has to be spoken of, if speaking of it is to be useful at all, in all the words it takes to describe all its parts. Willi was sympathetic with this sort of exhaustive effort: his life was one long monologue, with passages of rich dialogue, about the mountain experience writ large, and his honest reports of his spiritual openings remain moving. They add to the unstoppable process whereby more and more of human attention is brought to more and more things, so that tight-lipped reports on the order of Mallory's "Because it is there" no longer suffice. Willi's own answer had to do with his mystical search, which he likened to the classic Christian awakenings, and his popularity as an educator proves that he was onto something: that other hearts were also prone to these sensations.

When he spoke of his experiences, especially about the vision he had on Makalu, in '54, he was always *conditional,* refusing to make absolute claims for them. *Something* important had happened to him up high, and it colored the rest of his life, but he stopped far short of saying that his thrilling outdoor visions were truly *equivalent* to the Christian revelations. There was a quality of the not-quite-grasped in the experience, something slippery about it; part of why his accounts influenced so many other people is because he refused to go too far, to assume or assert too much. In a speech given in '74, as part of a Spiritual Life Symposium at Evergreen, he talked about this evanescent quality. "The sacred is strange," he said, "you can't quite get a handle on it. Those ultralogicians, the Hindus, say, 'If you can get a handle on it, you've just lost it.' " And he asks his audience, with all seriousness, "Now where does that leave us?" meaning, how do you build on something ephemeral?

In the video that survives of this address, Willi looks good; it's still two years before Nanda Devi, before the final acts of what his friend Bill Turnage has called "a rich and untidy life with a *really* untidy ending." His hair is combed, his beard trimmed; as a concession, perhaps, to the governor of Washington, who shares the stage with him, he's dressed casually but not flamboyantly, and his stories are amusing but not too salty. He begins by mocking the whole idea of spiritual values programs—"The Buddha was tempted to stay in paradise," he says, "but came back for forty-five years of spiritual life symposiums." He explains that he, Willi, is really a pragmatist: "You don't go into a situation with hang-ups that'll stand in the way . . . anything that'll work, that's me." But then he wonders why he feels so reluctant, so out of sync, today: "I'm [just] not into this [symposium]. . . . I distrust mass movements—I tend to be a nonorganization man."

Having cleared his throat, so to speak—and he *does* look a little reluctant, maybe even a little depressed—he shoulders his pack and just gets on with it, warming to his subject and making a lot of sense. "You know what value is, spiritual value . . . it's *what we're after*," he says. "It's *what matters*. The good and the true and the beautiful . . . the spice of our lives." He explains that value used to be located in heaven or God, but that "I want to disagree with that . . . today we find a different locus of value . . . in *nature*. *That's* where true value is sited. The processes and organic growingness of the natural sphere—the only blight upon which is man."

He quickly corrects himself: he isn't really antiman, in fact he's a humanist, and "my locus of value is where man is. My *summum bonum* is how we treat each other . . . not what we know, [and] not our warm visceral surges," either. But the realm of man eventually grows tiresome. "[W]e are a stiff-necked breed, and . . . it gets to be a drag. You get beaten down just having people pass through, filling you with their ideas . . . their *really groovy notions* . . . you just get more and more tired till you . . . slam the door."

There's a way out, though. "This brings me to the whole function of spiritual values. For me it's an alternation, a regeneration . . . I want every weapon in the arsenal [to make life with people livable]. And if one of those weapons happens to be a total change of pace, where you shift gears to such a [degree] that the cosmos dissolves about you, then so much the better." And he concludes, "So the function of spiritual values is . . . to mobilize one's flagging energies. To energize the belief [that] there's meaning . . . a spring to resuscitate the faith of man."

This is a philosophy that's hard to argue with. It says that we need to take breaks—call them vacations, if you will—and that wild nature is the best place for them if we, like Willi, are the kind of people who take inspiration there. "The whole enterprise is somehow phony," he adds, "but absolutely crucial," and again, it's hard not to nod assent. There isn't much talk about ecstasy anymore. Maybe the memories of his illuminations have faded; maybe he's decided that there *is* no way to build on them. He betrays a kind of exhaustion, almost a nausea, with the ordinary human realm, for which we may plausibly read the lecture circuit and the committees he sits on and the thousands of eager people who find him so inspiring, who believe he stands at the portals of transfiguration. This belief in him is something he's encouraged them to have, but now he's worn down by the responsibility. He needs a break himself—an interlude in which to feel once again the cosmos dissolving around him. And he recommends this experience for everyone else, too. His generous nature, his encouraging spirit, are much in evidence, for he assumes that everyone's as strong as he is, that we can all stand the confrontations with fate and loss that sometimes come to people having adventures.

The great mystery is how this sage leader, this mountain man, with his carefully worded advice and his fund of common sense, becomes a party to the tragedies of '76 and '79. We have to conclude that he really did dissolve in some way when he got up high again, because the man who occupies the stage so compellingly in '74 is hard to conceive of as Roskelley's antagonist, driven to distraction by a younger man's brashness. As a self-confessed pragmatist and skilled manipulator of groups, he might be expected to have tied Roskelley up in knots, but the Buffalo Demon's provocations seem to have slightly unhinged Willi and his faction, leading them to make a series of marginally unwise decisions. Devi acted on her own, of course, choosing to go higher on the mountain, but her friends and father abetted her in that decision; they showed their belief in her, even their love for her, in doing so, but the outcome came to haunt all of them. Pete Lev was deeply saddened upon returning from Asia and had problems dealing with "anger at Ros-kelley, at myself, at the powers that had put all of us in this script," as he describes it. Andy Harvard mourned Devi naturally and pro-foundly, remaining as long as he could in the mountain zone that she had loved; he charted his own course there, grieving for the most immediate and powerful of reasons: because his loss was that large, because he needed to to go on.

Willi was a victim of his own way of grieving. There should be no doubt about the darkness that descended for him or the guilt he felt, despite his public claims of being transcendentally at peace. His quietistic, "Eastern" way of understanding the loss of his daughter, seeing it as but another turn of the wheel of life, may have consoled him as he carried on afterward with that great fortitude that had made him a hero, but he was not shriven of his guilt or placed thereby on the road to feeling healed. He may not have wanted to heal. Lear with Cordelia in his arms does not heal, he dies. His loss and his responsibility for it are literally fatal. The two and a half years between Willi's return and his death on Rainier likewise have an aspect of suspended doom, as he proceeds in the usual frenzied way to perform, teach, counsel, and provide for his family. But once his new hips are in place, he can go where he needs to go. The winter climb of Rainier, with a group of inexperienced young peo-ple, is both "like" a typical Willi adventure, helter-skelter and bold, and "like" nothing ever seen before in his life—a falling away from his honorable history as a dependable guide. Strong forces led him to undertake such a doomed task. The outcome depended on lucky breaks, as well as terribly unlucky ones; but his being there, with so many people, shows a change not predictable from his prior history of courage and judgment.

Before darkness rolled over him that last afternoon, he had days and days of feasting his eyes on ice, rock, snowcap, and storm: all the glorious elements that for him made a realm of incomparable meaning. He was going strong at the end. Every step was a risk, but a welcome one. He would have told wonderful stories about it later, in lecture hall and around campfire, teasing out the significance in every moment. Whatever else it was, it was an adventure, and he had lived for that.

ACKNOWLEDGMENTS

....

As soon as I began investigating Willi Unsoeld's story, I discovered
that a number of people did not wish it to be told. I was perplexed.
Willi was open; he was welcoming; whatever else his life was about,
it was not about a reluctance to communicate. I decided to proceed,
despite the discomfort that my project caused in some quarters.

Right after discovering that I had opponents, I found that I also
had good friends. This was Willi's doing. He had lived in such a
way as to attract many remarkable people. There was a richness
and power to his personality that evoked a complex response, and
often a great deal of love, in a number of thoughtful people. In the
way that chopping your own firewood warms you twice, I felt that
Willi had benefited from these remarkable companions throughout
his life but that he had also laid up a rich store for a student of
that life.

In no particular order of importance, these generous friends of
Willi's included William Turnage, James Lester, Gil Roberts, Lynn
Hammond, Peter Lev, Nick Clinch, and Andrew Harvard. Robert
Turnage, John Evans, Al Read, Allen Steck, and Keith Hillsbury
likewise put Willi in perspective for me as a mountaineer and a

man. Norman Dyhrenfurth, Himalayan climber and filmmaker, was encouraging and forthcoming with historical materials, making possible the re-creation of the Everest '63 expedition in this book. Beryl Unsoeld, Willi's older sister, was charming and astute, and made me feel when I was in her presence that I was in contact with some of the authentic Unsoeld magic.

Some of the best American writers on mountaineering—among them Steve Roper, Galen Rowell, Nick Clinch, and Andy Harvard— instructed me by the grace and truth of their written works. Michael Chessler added perspective, and John Roskelley and Jim States answered my expedition questions fully, giving me the benefit of their strong points of view. Laurence Leamer, Willi's biographer, set a high standard with his prodigious researches twenty years ago, and William S. Sax, author of the superb ethnography *Mountain Goddess*, taught me whatever I know about Garhwali religious practices. This book took shape only after countless exchanges with Robert Spertus and Ward Little, my own climbing partners, and improved immeasurably after close readings by them and by Nick Clinch, Peter Lev, and Michael Vitiello.

Fran Loft, American Alpine Club librarian, dealt wisely with my countless questions and requests for research materials. At the Evergreen State College, Randy Stilson, archivist and research librarian, showed me how to deepen and widen my inquiry.

George Witte, my editor, saw worth in this unusual project and contributed value to it greater and more lasting than the author had any right to hope for. My agents, Michael Carlisle and Neal Bascomb, thrashed the project into some kind of commercial shape; from the beginning they shared my belief that this was a story that warranted telling.